C4 361984 00 C9

D0121451

'Mungo is, in my opinion, one of the best cameramen I've worked with. He is always in the middle of the action and tells the story perfectly.'
Simon Cowell (X Factor *and* American Idol)

'I have worked with Mungo on many TV shows. He is just a great guy to work with. Amazing at his job, professional and hard working. He never complains, always has a smile on his face and the team he works with adore him. You could not find a better combination: a lovely bloke who is great at his job (and is jolly handsome!!!).'
Davina McCall (*TV Presenter*)

'I worked with Mungo on a Channel 4 Series titled *Escape to the Legion*, and to say that the cameramen had a tough job would be an understatement! He was up at all hours of the day and night, often is 40 degrees heat in the mid-Sahara, running over sand dunes balancing huge cameras on his shoulders, pouring with sweat and, unlike most of my other fellow Legionnaires, Mungo always seemed to have his well-known huge smile plastered across his face! Everyone I know loves working with this man.'
Bear Grylls (*Adventurer and TV Presenter*)

'I've had the pleasure of spending a very uncomfortable night burrowing through hedges dressed in army camouflage and night vision goggles with Mungo on *Lads Army*, have had his lens trained on me whilst we travelled the country listening to all kinds of stories and songs on the *X Factor* and *Pop Idol* and have listened to his tales over many a beer upon his return from shoots in all four corners of the world.

Having become a close friend over the last few years I don't think he'd mind me saying that he is a real one off – to the point of being weird, or maybe just mildly eccentric. He's the only person I know that relaxes after a strenuous six week audition tour by climbing Snowdonia or chills out on a Sunday by cycling twenty-six miles around London in the rain, before heading off to church and making it to the pub before last orders! I hope his sense of adventure and the experiences he's enjoyed during his time as a cameraman travel as well to the page as they do in conversation.'
Kate Thornton (*TV Presenter*)

MUNGO
THE CAMERAMAN

*Adventure, Celebrity and Extreme Travel
as Seen from Behind the Lens*

PAUL MUNGEAM

CM Publishing

CM Publishing
'The Hoppers'
Goblands Farm
Cemetery Lane
Hadlow TN11 0LT

Copyright © 2007 Paul Mungeam

First printing July 2007
Second printing August 2007

All rights reserved. No part of this publication may be reproduced, stored in a retrieval system, or transmitted in any form or by any means, electronic, mechanical, photocopying or otherwise, without the prior written consent of the publisher. Short extracts may be used for review purposes.

ISBN: 978–0–9555650–0–7 (Hardback)

NEWCASTLE UPON TYNE CITY LIBRARIES	
C4361984	
Bertrams	27.11.07
910.41	£18.99

Editor: Sandy Waldron
Cover by Scamp Design (www.scampdesign.co.uk)
Cover picture: Chadden Hunter
Typeset by CRB Associates, Reepham, Norfolk
Printed in Malta

To my great friend and mentor Simon Niblett.

You generously invested in me,
created a channel for my enthusiasm and
gave me the opportunity to live my dreams!

Thanks, Si.

Contents

Acknowledgements

Firstly, I would like to thank all the many individuals and crews who have shared with me in the experiences that make up this book. I'm sure you'll understand that there was simply not enough room to mention you all by name, but you know who you are! Thanks for your camaraderie – and for putting up with me.

I would also like to thank all the production companies and broadcasters who, over the years, have chosen to employ me as one of their cameramen.

A big thank-you to Sandy for agreeing to edit my first real effort at writing. Your sensitivity and well-honed skill has retained the simple, conversational manner in which I wished the book to read.

Finally the biggest thank-you to my Dad. You are a constant rock in my life and have been the one who has enabled me to write this book. Your unconditional love and genuine belief in me gives me strength, and your hard work and unceasing encouragement has helped me achieve this goal. Thank you, Pop!

CPR/CAR
MCh ?)
late bil — Short

FCE R gyr

Introduction

I write, sitting in a tent at 14,000 feet on a mountain in Northern Ethiopia. It's 8 a.m. my time and 6 a.m. in London.

The sky is blue, the sun is warm and the view from where I sit is of three valleys stretching for hundreds of miles below me. In a word it's 'majestic'!

When I stop to think of where I am and why I am out here – filming Gelada baboons for National Geographic – I feel truly blessed. The Simien Mountains are spectacular and to be filming a wildlife documentary for National Geographic is close to the pinnacle of a cameraman's career.

People always say to me, 'It's alright for you, Mungo, as no matter what you do, you always land on your feet!' And they're right! Although I contest that it's not because I'm special or uniquely talented, but simply because I have adopted a basic philosophy by which to lead my life: I will always take hold, and make the most, of any opportunities that arise for me.

Walt Disney once said, 'If you can dream it, you can do it!'

Living with such an attitude has, over the last ten years, taken me to over fifty countries, only four of which I have paid to go to myself – the remaining forty-six I have been paid to go!

I could be back in London waking up to another day of cold weather, as it's late October. My job could entail commuting to an office where I would stay for eight hours staring at a computer screen, confined by four walls within which I would see little daylight. I would be required to wear a suit and clock in and out to show my superior that I am in attendance. Instead, right now, I sit in a tent on top of a mountain, clothed in walking boots, combat trousers and a fleece. I have no boss as such, just a director who, if he were any more laid back, would fall over! The only things that are bothering me this morning are the flies that continually buzz around me, occasionally landing on my face, forcing me to react with a reluctant swipe.

Our world is an amazing place, and through taking hold of those opportunities offered to me, I have been extremely privileged to have seen a large amount of it. It is from that experience that I write. I am acutely aware that there are many in my profession who have seen more, and there are those who have lived the life to a far greater depth than I – by this fact I am humbled and so I strive not to give the impression that I have 'done it all'. I aim simply to share my experiences and tell some stories that I hope will be of interest.

One of my constant frustrations in camera-work is that no matter how good a camera operator you are, you can never fully portray what is in front of you. In my work I am limited to the width of a lens, or the two-dimensional aspect of the picture. Within these limitations we cameramen do our best, but I can't help but wish that somehow I could share the full experiences, sights, sounds, smells and other senses that are overflowing when you stand where I have stood. I would love to show my family just what I have been through. I long for my friends to experience the world's education that I have acquired. I would love the viewer to really take on just what we are exposing them to through our pictures. Yet I am resigned to the fact that the only way to truly do this is to physically take them there! Obviously this is not always possible, so I stick to what capabilities I have and remember that it's better than not sharing my experiences at all.

One of the most frequent questions I am asked about my work is, 'Out of all the countries you have visited, which is your favourite?' Such a question is almost impossible to answer, as all the countries have bestowed on me such a varying encyclopaedia of experiences, some good and some bad. Though, at a push, I have to say that Cambodia stands out by a mile. I have covered most of South-East Asia over the years shooting travel documentaries. To me this part of the world offers unparalleled warmth of people group, breathtaking scenery, fascinating history and exquisite food selection. It may well be that Cambodia remains one of my favourites, as it was one of the first countries that I covered in the travel documentary genre. I remember attacking the assignment with such an excitement and enthusiasm during those early years, which now, looking back, seems to have been born from my youth and the feeling that I would be unlikely to cross those shores again. Sadly, with age and experience, that excitement and enthusiasm have somewhat diminished and I have grown hardened to the amazing situations that I still regularly find myself in. Nowadays it is unusual for me to go to a place that is like nothing I have seen before: some would say that is sad, and to a degree I agree. Though, because it's a major facet of my vocation, it's just a fact of my working life. However, when I do go to a place that is like nothing I have seen before, you can imagine just how precious it is. When I arrived in my current location, the Simien Mountains of Ethiopia, I experienced just that! Seeing the views from the vast escarpments overlooking the lowlands of Northern Ethiopia I was struck dumb with disbelief at what I was seeing – so far, unequalled sights.

It is at these times that I am forced to re-evaluate my position in life, to pinch myself and soak up all that I am privileged to see. Most will never get to see such magnificent examples of the richness that our world offers us and for that opportunity I am truly grateful. As well as seeing the beauty of the world, I equally value the opportunity to observe, first hand, the pain and tragedy that so many encounter in this life. I say this not to gloat over my fortune and others' misfortune, nor to count it as purely a lesson to be learnt of all that I have been given and must be grateful for, but, far more than that, to be aware of my responsibility as a member of the human race and to be accountable for my gift of a secure, comfortable, educated and privileged life.

This may sound somewhat worthy, but when you meet, face to face, those who have literally nothing of material worth and who are forced to live each day at a time because of their lack of certainty in terms of their health and their country's insecurity, ignorance can no longer be counted bliss – it has been obliterated!

Sadly, it is all too easy to slip back into the western world's way of thinking when you return home and, after a brief mourning for what you have seen, it is far too easy to forget those whom you have left behind in their torment. Ignorance has been obliterated, but numbness and de-sensitisation remain! Only the conscious jogging of your memory can stir up the emotions and memories of the less fortunate, and then it takes strength of mind not to fall prey to the desire to blank them out due to your own sense of personal guilt. There lies the challenge!

As I arrive on location to a shoot, I am introduced to the Talent (presenters/actors) or to the Contributors (Joe Public): 'This is Mungo, the Cameraman.' Yes, basically I am a technician and ultimately that is what I am paid for – to record informative and pretty pictures. Yet, all of us hold secrets and experiences that no one else will ever know, or understand, unless they were present. I, for one, am so aware of all that I have seen, felt emotionally, physically touched, tasted and smelt . . . I feel so much more than simply a technician!

This is my humble offering. Enjoy!

Paul Mungeam (*Mungo*)
April 2007

1

Arms Fair Fiasco

I felt as though I was in a Bond movie, but this was for real!

It was a balmy night and, suited and booted, I approached the formidable building before me. My hands were sweating as I carried the bag of equipment towards the group of security guards who surrounded the electronic frame that could expose my purpose. Desperately trying to compose myself as if all was normal, I slipped the bag to the side of the frame and walked through the metal detector. The momentarily distracted guards didn't bat an eyelid. With a tangible, yet short-lived sense of relief I joined the back of the function's reception line.

Mark was three places in front of me, wired up with a radio mic with the capability of recording the compromising conversation that we were hunting for. As we slowly proceeded down the line, I subtly unzipped the bag and reached in to press the record button on the hidden camera. Time seemed to slow down as I found myself thinking of these 'stupid' positions that I get myself into. This was like being at a formal wedding reception, queuing to be greeted by the bride's and groom's parents. This time, though, it was no wedding: we were undercover-filming, now waiting to shake the hand of the Greek Foreign Minister at the Reception Party for the International Arms Fair in Athens.

Our plant, Mark, was one person away from meeting the Foreign Minister. What would he say? Was the hidden camera recording? Would the sound be going to tape? These are the usual pressure-driven thoughts of a cameraman at that crucial point of no return. It was too late. Mark was moving forward to take the extended hand of welcome. I craned my neck trying to hear what he would say ... He took the Foreign Minister's hand, opened his mouth and said, 'Hello, Sir, it's very nice to meet you. May I say that I love your yoghurt!'

Mark Thomas is the UK's well-known comedian turned activist. In his award-winning series *The Mark Thomas Comedy Product* he uses his razor-sharp wit to challenge, expose and often make a mockery of previously unchallenged injustices and abuses of power. Whether confronted with police sent to arrest him or an embarrassed company executive who rapidly turns into an irate monster, you can always count on him to throw in a one-liner to disarm an increasingly tense situation.

Our mission ('should we choose to accept it?') was to catch the International Arms Fair delegates, on film, admitting to what they are actually doing – making a very good living out of manufacturing tools of death and destruction. What we eventually came home with was material that blew away all our expectations!

The International Arms Fair boasted delegates from all over the world. Some were simply salesmen and women for various weapon-making manufacturers, but many were top industry professionals and there were also a number of Foreign Ministers present (including that of the UK).

As we moved through the plush entrance hall and into the party arena we were confronted by a scene of around two hundred guests, sipping champagne and nibbling on canapés. The party was set around a grand, beautifully lit exterior swimming pool. Every detail was executed with the most exquisite taste and style. Mark and I entered the party, accepted a glass of champagne from a waiter and acted as if we belonged. Although we had infiltrated safely, we could not relax. We had every right to be nervous, as although we were officially invited to the International Arms Fair and the Reception Party, we were there under a false guise. As far as the organisers were aware, we were operating as a Public Relations Company for the Arms Industry – servicing the dealers with professional advice for their awkward public relations exercises. For example, how does one respond to probing questions on live television or radio about hardware such as anti-personnel landmines – whose special selling point is that they no longer just blow their victims up when stepped on, thus maiming them, but instead they now jump four feet up into the air and tear their victims' torsos apart, thus causing instant death! Any ideas?

Our PR company was fictional and our identities were also false. This was no small stunt!

As the crowd mingled and Mark tried out his well-researched and well-rehearsed spiel on some of the less-threatening delegates, I slid off with my camera hidden in a bag to film an establishing shot to set the scene: Mark Thomas, the stand-up comedian, conversing with some of the world's leading Arms' dealers! Looking around, the only place that would give me the vantage point I needed for the shot was up on a terrace that overlooked the party in the pool area. This was fine, but how would I get up there? I walked around trying to look relaxed with a glass of champagne in one hand and the hidden camera bag in the other. Moving around among the guests, I sidled towards a patio on the left-hand side of the pool area. Here there were only a few guests milling around, probably having a quiet word in each other's ear about a shipment of Kalashnikovs, I thought! From this position, further towards the main building I could see a staircase, which was roped off. I edged towards the staircase and found just what I was looking for ... The staircase appeared to lead straight up to the terrace and my desired vantage point. The Reception Party was obviously under heavy guard – these people were in seriously powerful positions and no one (due to the nature of their business) trusted the man or woman standing next them. Most of the higher-ranking delegates had their own personal protection teams – security personnel who would stand a short distance behind their client with their hands crossed in front of them, feet shoulder width apart and donning the giveaway 'covert' earpiece spiralling down from their ear to the gap between their crisply ironed shirt and smartly pressed suit jacket.

Now was the time to move before thinking too much about

what I was about to do. Without hesitating, I slipped one leg over the rope, and then the other. Not wanting to stop and by doing so appear suspicious, I kept my head down and kept climbing the stairs two at a time. If all went according to plan, I figured that I would be up on the terrace, recording the shot, and back down in the party within four or five minutes.

I was steadily making my way up the curvy staircase, praying that it would deliver me to the exact point that I needed to be on the terrace. But there was a problem. As I turned the corner, the stairs arrived at a landing, which offered me two options: either an entrance to the exact spot I was aiming for or a doorway with a guard posted at it! Seeing me arrive in front of him, the guard on the door was startled. I figured that he was a low-level guard, probably one of the least experienced since he was tucked away in a low-risk and low-profile area. Low rank though he might be, he still posed a major threat to my purpose, as he was obviously meant to be keeping the likes of myself out of that area. Thinking on my feet, before he could say anything I took the initiative and spoke first, 'Could you tell me where the toilets are, please?' His eyes showed a hint of life as I had obviously woken him from his standing slumber. He smiled strenuously, nodding and pointing away from himself towards the terrace opposite. I nervously smiled back and turned quickly to take my leave towards the terrace. That was a close call, I thought, as I arrived on the terrace and quickly found my spot . . . Luck was on my side as it was exactly the spot that I was looking for. Resting the camera in some flowers on a low, narrow wall, I tilted the lens down and filmed for close to three minutes – Mark making his way around the eclectic group of important guests, who were totally unaware that they were talking to a comedian and being filmed for British television. When I'd completed the shot, I breathed a sigh of relief. That wasn't too difficult, I thought, only a small amount of breaking the rules and I've got the 'Money Shot'!

All done, I slid the camera back into the bag and headed back down the way I came. The guard 'sleepily' nodded to acknowledge me as I smiled at him while briskly returning down the staircase. He must have seen the relief on my face, but you and I know that it was nothing to do with drinking too much Bollinger! When I reached the last few steps of the staircase, my heart stopped pounding and my nerves returned to normal. The rest of the night was going to be plain sailing. I would rejoin Mark, sip some more champagne and enjoy the party ... My job for the night was in the can.

However, having just stepped back over the rope at the foot of the stairs, I noticed that in the short time I had been upstairs the patio area had filled up with people, including some very serious-looking gentlemen with their even more serious-looking bodyguards. Among the newly formed crowd was the Greek Foreign Minister himself, who was sitting in exactly the area that I needed to pass through in order to return to Mark. No problem, I thought. I'm an invited guest, I've got nothing to hide: I simply visited the alternative toilets and now I'm passing through on my way to rejoin the main party. I took a deep breath and confidently walked straight towards the Foreign Minister's table. All seemed normal ... that was until I reached the table when, to everyone's horror, there was a series of enormous ground-shaking explosions! I cowed as the rampaging barrage of explosions filled the sky and shock sucked up the air. We were all instantly blinded with light as bright as that generated by fierce lightning strikes. Their training taking over, the guards had already sprung into action. They had reached for their firearms, slung in shoulder holsters beneath their suit jackets, and were rushing towards their client to offer them protection. It was a few split seconds of pandemonium, until everyone slowly began to realise what had happened. It was an unannounced, extremely big firework display! Perhaps not the best party-planning idea for an Arms Fair function!

People quickly composed themselves, desperately trying not to appear flustered by the embarrassment of the panic. Emotionally exhausted, although dreadfully relieved, I staggered back to the pool area. There I found Mark, acquired another glass of champagne and finally breathed a huge sigh of relief. Mark just grinned at me, knowingly. That was it; I'd had more than enough excitement for one night!

That first night had set the tone for the remainder of our visit. Over the next five days we lived on a knife's edge, having to be careful of what we said and did when in the public eye or within earshot of absolutely anyone. Whatever we did, we couldn't give away the fact that we were spoof delegates, acting as 'PR consultants for the Arms industry' – making a hard-hitting, truth-telling comedy show at their expense! We were sharing our hotel with the other delegates at the Arms Fair, so everywhere we went we remained strictly in character. Our production meetings were secretly held in one of our bedrooms and, as we planned our next moves, our voices were kept hushed. At the time, it all seemed just a bit naughty and mischievous, yet in retrospect we were playing a very serious game!

When I had received the call from the facilities company that provided the crews and kit for *The Mark Thomas Comedy Product*, I remember wondering why they were being so secretive about sharing the details of what the job was. All they had said was, 'There's a job next week in Athens, but I can't tell you exactly what it is until Friday. Oh, and you'll be leaving early on Saturday!' By keeping the details from me until the last minute, I now see that they were reducing the chance of me backing out of the shoot . . . due to its high-risk factor. I do remember stopping to think why the usual main cameraman on the show wasn't doing this trip himself. The reason being that the risk was just too high and with a wife and kid there was too much at stake. As for me, I was young, single and had no dependants, which made me (in harsh terms) dispensable! It also helped that I am a self-confessed adrenalin junkie – which interestingly helped me to get a number of future jobs, the ones the more level-headed of my colleagues shied away from.

On the day before our departure, when I had been told that I was going to the International Arms Fair, in my mind's eye I had imagined a market scene from an Indiana Jones movie – a rough Arabic bazaar, set in the back streets of Cairo, full of dodgy-looking men wearing turbans and carrying swords. The reality couldn't have been further from that dramatic scene – although what we found was, in a strange way, far more unnerving! The Fair we attended was held in the International Conference Centre situated on the waterfront in Athens. Far from the dramatic scene you might see in a movie, it was just a normal, run-of-the-mill, sterile corporate conference. The stalls were the usual twelve-by-twelve-foot, metal-framed boxes, manned by suited, booted and overweight salesmen. In these booths, the company's goods were on display accompanied by glossy colour brochures presenting the full range of the products. The products on sale encompassed every deadly contraption imaginable: from automatic firearms to antipersonnel landmines to Challenger tanks to huge riot water cannons and, unbelievably, you could even purchase missiles! You name it ... it was there. It was this clinical, businesslike environment that made one so sick. By all appearances they could well have been selling something as mundane as office stationery, but what they were actually selling were tools of death and mass destruction!

We were not there to make a 'comedy show': we were there to show the British public exactly what goes on inside these sorts of 'events'. With our fabricated PR company we had officially applied to attend the Arms Fair. Quite surprisingly, our application had been accepted, with seemingly no security checks to see who we were and what our (false) company did. In fact, there was no resistance whatsoever. So off we went to Greece.

Mark (Presenter turned PR Consultant), Chris (Producer turned PR Consultant) and myself (Cameraman playing PR Company Technician) arrived at the conference centre and got to work on setting up our stand. Both Mark and Chris had done an enormous amount of research, enabling them to discuss 'The Arms Industry' convincingly with fellow delegates and give the impression that they had been involved for a number of years. The first people we met were busy setting up our neighbouring stalls. The older gentleman to our right was proudly selling lethal anti-personnel landmines, which as I described earlier had been 'improved' so that they no longer just maim their victims, but blow their bodies to smithereens.

We planned to catch our victims on camera by setting up a mini 'mock' studio within our stand. Here Mark would play out a simulated TV interview. Sitting the guest down, he would fire deliberately awkward questions at them. Once they had attempted to answer, he would then advise them on how they could deliver more confident answers and improve their body language, etc. I stood behind the camera openly filming this whole scenario, supposedly to show them how they came across to the viewers. What they were blissfully unaware of was that the questions Mark asked were well researched true stories! Added to that their answers weren't being recorded to videotape purely for their benefit, but this whole event would be broadcast on national television back in the UK. They were being duped into confessing that these particular events actually happened – and they had no idea at all!

Throughout the days ahead Mark and Chris would invite particular, targeted individuals into the (mock) studio for a demonstration of what our (fabricated) PR company could offer their business. Before long we managed to land two enormous fish!

We would hear on the grapevine which 'VIPs' would be passing through our area at what time, and that is when we set our trap. On time, as tipped, a general from the army of an Asian country was passing through. Being a stand-up comedian, Mark is supremely confident when it comes to a verbal stand-off and, as soon as he caught sight of the General, he barged his way through the surrounding entourage and within seconds was shaking hands with him. Amidst a hail of rapid-fire words, Mark explained the concept behind the PR consultancy that we were offering and in no time had convinced the General that he should take a few minutes to sit in the 'mock' interview simulation.

Mark is so quick with his verbal barrage and cheeky smile that such dignitaries (whose aim is to 'publicly' please everyone) just can't refuse. Before we knew it, the General was seated right where we wanted him and the camera was rolling.

With no hesitation, Mark hit the General with a question about a horrific atrocity involving his army in which hundreds of innocent people were killed. This event was rumoured to have taken place, but had never been admitted to – it had been carefully swept under the carpet by his government. Convinced that we were on his side and were trying to advise him on how to deal with such Press questions, the General went ahead and confessed that the atrocity had indeed taken place! He asked Mark how he could best cover for it or move the questions onto other subjects. This was the gold for which we had come. Having advised our guest on methods for turning unwelcome questions around, Mark, in his unique comedic way, awarded the General with a plastic toy diver! The General left feeling better equipped to tackle the media, while we (the media) rubbed our hands together with glee!

Whenever we recorded great footage, it was my job to copy the rushes (shot footage) to another tape, which I would then 'Amtrak' back to London that night. The reason for this was that if we were caught, I could hand the 'original' tape over to the authorities, secretly knowing that there was a copy safely back in London. This was a wise precaution, but meant many hours more work for me, sitting transferring tapes, hour after hour, back in my hotel room. When the day had ended for everyone else, I was often up into the early hours of the morning transferring tapes.

Each morning, we would meet at 7 a.m. in the hotel restaurant for breakfast. Over breakfast, Mark would check that the copied tapes had left safely and that all the team were happy. We were – in fact on this particular breakfast meeting we were in tears! Mark and I were first to arrive in the restaurant, along with four or five other delegates of various nationalities. As we queued at the breakfast buffet, Mark and I chatted about our night's sleep etc., constantly on our guard not to slip out any mention of the 'tapes' or 'television'. Back at our table I was tucking into my omelette and Mark was pouring a coffee when, from the other side of the restaurant, there came a loud, strained, cutlery-shaking fart! Before we could stop ourselves we both erupted into guffaws of uncontrollable laughter! The German delegate that had let it slip carried on with his eggs, blankly, as if nothing had happened. The trouble was that we had both 'gone'. My head was thrown back and my shoulders were shaking violently as tears rolled down my cheeks. Mark was doubled over and the coffee had gone everywhere as he shook and wheezed with delight! It was only when we realised that no one else had even tittered that it dawned on us that our overreaction may have blown our cover. Fortunately for us, we seemed to get away with it. Maybe they just put it down to the strange British sense of humour!

In the periods when there wasn't an interview simulation going on at our stand, I would go for walks around the conference centre. Sometimes I would walk simply to stretch my legs, but other times I would have a hidden agenda. With a camera rolled up in a magazine and placed under my arm, I would follow Mark as he wandered around the other stalls. He constantly wore a radio-operated microphone, which allowed me to stand twenty feet away, pretending to be interested in something completely different, while pointing the camera under my arm at Mark conversing with another delegate, all the while recording the picture and sound. This was a risky business as sometimes Mark would choose to stop at a stand where the only way for me to get a clean shot of him would mean standing next to two guards armed with semi-automatic machine guns. The few seconds it took to film these short conversations would feel like hours. It was always well worth the risk, though, when you came back with footage of Mark attempting to buy a case of anti-personnel landmines from a very serious-looking man. The reason that he gave for needing to buy them (not that you needed to give a reason!) was that he had 'a terrible problem with moles in his lawn'! Another time, when he quizzed a German salesman about how far the jet of a huge riot water cannon on top of a huge red truck would carry, he asked, 'If I took it home, would it be able to shoot right over my house?' The salesman proudly nodded and said that wouldn't be a problem. 'That's perfect!' Mark responded. 'You see ... I've got this terrible problem with pigeons on my roof at home!' The salesman stared at Mark blankly, in disbelief of what he was hearing. Then to add insult to injury, Mark got his credit card out and tried to buy one! Comedy proved to be a great vehicle for high-lighting the absurdity of what this Arms Fair was really all about – a money-making machine, with no real regard for what use these lethal implements would be put to!

It was nearing the end of our week when we recorded another interview simulation gem. This time Mark wooed a high-ranking East African military figure into opening his mouth on UK national television. This man admitted to the gross abuse of women by his army, stating on camera that this was an accepted, normal practice, even though it was not necessarily right. He clearly needed some further tutoring on what and what not to say when being interviewed! So Mark decided to take this opportunity one step further. He suggested that the military official went back to his country's London-based embassy and proposed that our (bogus) PR company taught all the embassy staff and officials the PR skills that he had just learnt. To our surprise he seemed to like the idea! We all smiled, as Mark awarded this enormous black statesman-like man a little red toy car as a prize for his new interviewing skills and then he left to make more serious deals!

As we had two serious confessions on tape and many other snippets of humour, Mark thought it wise that we should leave the Arms Fair a day early, to avoid any last-minute hiccups jeopardising our safe exit. It didn't take a lot to convince Chris and me that this was a great idea! The following morning we were on the plane flying back to London.

Looking back over the week in Athens, we became aware that the intense environment we had lived in had had a profound effect on us. Whether it was the constant paranoia of possibly getting caught, I don't know, but the tension was clearly shown by the release of cooped-up nervous energy expelled by overhearing a simple fart! Personally, the whole week had left me physically and emotionally exhausted. I remember saying to my friends at home that I felt as if I had lost a few years from my life.

Not until the flight home did Mark share with me that the production company's lawyers had said that if we were caught, we could have been prosecuted for spying against Greece! That was no small crime, and the consequences would have been severe. No wonder the facilities company had kept the details of the job quiet until the last minute! Had I known the weight of the situation, would I have still gone? Almost certainly – yes! But I wouldn't have told my parents until I was home safely.

Based on the two confessions we filmed, *The Mark Thomas Comedy Product* was presented with an award by Amnesty International. The Government of the African country whose high-ranking military official we had advised, went on to hire our false company to undertake the PR training of their UK-based staff. Mark only went ahead with the first few lessons, but the footage was later included in his hit show on Channel 4.

2

'He Lives My Dreams!'

It was behind the scenes while filming a wedding that I met two people who would dramatically change the course of my life! It was a beautiful summer's day in a picturesque county in the South-West of England. The location was an old country church, which would have looked quite at home in a Jane Austen novel. The wedding reception was being held right next to the church in a large country house, which had been converted from an aristocrat's hunting lodge into a magnificent, upmarket country hotel.

Andrew Gemmell and I were there early to set up to film the wedding day. Inside the church building we positioned microphones strategically around the sanctuary, running audio cables and making final adjustments to the audio-mixing desk. Once all was in place for the sound recording of the wedding ceremony, we set about shooting GVs (General Views) to establish the stunning setting of the location.

It was close to lunchtime by the time we were nearing the end of our preparations. While I was fetching the last pieces of camera equipment from Andrew's car, which was parked at the front of the hotel, I heard the growl of a car pulling into the driveway. Turning to look, I saw a well-used Epsom-green Land Rover Defender lurching off the road, the tyres crunching as they rolled through the gravel. The car held my attention not because it was an unusual sight in such a setting, but because it had been my dream vehicle ever since my 'Action Man' toy figure had driven one when I was a small boy. As I had grown older, I had come to respect fast cars for their elegance, speed and agility, but the Land Rover Defender was, to me, the epitome of power, toughness and adventure ... nothing else came close!

I continued to watch it as it drew to a halt next to where I was standing. The doors opened and two people hopped out. From the driver's door came Simon, six foot two, mid-length scruffy blonde hair and a thin, but incredibly athletic frame – a rugged good-looking man. From the passenger's side appeared Sally, who was the personification of the cute, outdoors girl, with a sporty yet feminine physique, long brown hair and a bronzed smiley face which spoke of fun!

They had no idea who I was, just as I didn't know who they were. However, at that precise moment Sally spotted Andrew who was heading out to welcome them. Sally received two kisses from Andrew ('Very continental,' I thought – where I live, the girls only get one cheek!), and then Simon and Andrew greeted each other with a firm handshake. As they turned their attention towards me, Andrew as always was the model of courtesy, 'Paul, I would like you to meet Simon and Sally.' Personally I would have preferred to have been introduced as 'Mungo', but we exchanged smiles and handshakes. Andrew then explained to me that Simon was a top professional cameraman, from whom he rented office space in Plantation Wharf, Battersea. As well as being his wife, Sally worked with him as his sound recordist. As always in life, first impressions are so important, and I remember both Simon and Sally showing incredible warmth and sincerity in their greeting. That day I experienced what most new acquaintances feel with the Nibletts: I was very impressed by them both, for not only were they as people close to perfect aesthetically, but they were also incredibly nice (sickening!). As we left the vehicles and walked towards the church building, Andrew explained that they had joined us to help rig a mini-cam set-up, which was at that time way above our level of technical ability.

Not too long after their arrival it was time to break for lunch. Andrew suggested that Simon, Sally and I went to the local pub while he stayed behind to make some finishing touches before the start of the wedding ceremony. The local country pub was equally as idyllic as the wedding venue. Sitting on stalls around the small wooden table, we chatted and tucked into a hearty pub lunch. It wasn't long before our conversation turned to the subject of adventure sports, in particular surfing.

I was still fearsomely passionate about the sport as it was only a few years since I had returned from three years living on the northern beaches of Sydney. During my stay there I had had the privilege of lodging with a wonderful family called the Hardwicks. 'Wick', an ex-professional surfer, was married to Terri and they had six kids (at the time all under the age of fourteen years!). Having come second in the first ever Coke Classic, an international surfing competition held at the infamous Bells Beach in Victoria, he was literally the king of the surf at the ten or so world-class surfing beaches located along the peninsula where we lived. Not only did he own a surf shop where I worked part time while studying Fine Art in the city, but he also taught me to surf. I'll never forget him telling me that he wasn't sure whether it was a good idea to teach me to surf as it would almost certainly change my life and possibly consume it! Obviously I rebuked his doubt and threw myself into the challenge headfirst (literally on many a wipe-out!). In retrospect, he was right: surfing did affect my life and I was hooked. Over the next three years I proceeded to surf for as many hours in each day as the strength in my arms would allow.

I recall Sally Niblett saying to me that she loved the way I lit up when the subject of surfing came up. The remainder of the chat was about sport, kit and the Land Rover, and we also exchanged a number of stories of human daring. These two, and their friends, sounded like just the sort of people that I wanted to be hanging out with, as our interests were so similar. Sadly, with our plates now empty, in the distance wedding bells were chiming . . . we had work to do!

A few weeks later on a beautiful, crisp autumnal morning, I straddled my mountain bike and cycled to Plantation Wharf in Battersea. My destination was The Last Word office where I was going to collect a cheque from Andrew for the wedding shoot. On my arrival, at the rear doors of the house/office, I met Simon and Sally again. Dressed in The North Face fleeces and with walking boots on their feet, generally looking very 'outdoorsy', they were loading an impressive amount of flight cases into the Land Rover. They told me that they were off to shoot a Volvo commercial. How cool, I thought – loading intriguing-looking kit into the boot of cars and heading off to an exciting film shoot – these guys are living the ultimate exciting life! Looking back it was funny that I didn't have a clue what the kit was or what a film shoot actually entailed, but what I did know was that, without any doubt, I wanted to do the same. This man, Simon Niblett, was living my dreams!

As I was waiting for Andrew to write the cheque, Simon came back in from the car to offer me the proposal of a lifetime: 'Mungo, recently I've been thinking about employing a full-time camera assistant and I wondered if it is something you would be interested in?' At this point in time, having left my last 'transitional' job as a youth worker, other than working the odd weekend for The Last Word shooting weddings, I had been unemployed for three months. Even having only had the tiniest glimpse of what this 'Television World' was all about, something within me sparked! My instinct told me that this was my golden opportunity.

'Yes, definitely!' I replied without hesitating.

'I can only afford to pay you £250 per week . . .' – let me tell you, informing an unemployed 24-year-old that you are prepared to pay him £250 per week for being cool, wasn't dissimilar to handing him a winning lottery ticket! – 'but, if you're up for it, you can look after the camera kits and come out on shoots with me wherever possible.'

'Perfect!' I said, hardly believing my luck. 'When do you want me to start?' I was thinking in two or three weeks perhaps!

'How about you come in on Monday and I'll run you through the kit . . . ?'

Quite soon then, I thought, considering it was Friday!

'That'll give you a day to get your head around everything, as Sal and I are going to Uganda on Tuesday for a three-week shoot.'

What! I knew about as much about television broadcast camera kit as the average grandmother! Simon's company Eurocam had around six full broadcast kits, worth somewhere in the region of half a million pounds. I was going to have to get my head around it all in one day and, to cap it all, he was going to leave me in charge for three weeks? After *one* day???

'Susie will be around . . . ,' Simon continued. Susie was Simon's office manager and Eurocam's only other employee. Well, that was a relief! At least Susie would be able to run the place and point me in the right direction . . . '. . . until Thursday, then she'll be away for two weeks on holiday.'

Nodding my head as if this was a very sensible and perfectly normal proposition, I was thinking, 'Hang on a minute! This must be a wind-up? Has this man got *any* idea of what's just come out of his mouth?'

'No worries, I'm up for it!' I replied. Hang on a minute! Did I have *any* idea of what had just come out of *my* mouth?

'Great! I'll see you on Monday, then, mate. Say, ten o'clock?'

'Great! See you then,' I said automatically. My mouth was on autopilot and my brain was beginning to smoulder as it tried desperately to compute all the information in the deal we had just struck. But that was it. It was too late anyway for

Simon had already swept out the door to join Sally, who was waiting in the car outside.

I couldn't believe what had just happened. In a matter of minutes, I had agreed to take on a phenomenal amount of responsibility for something that I knew absolutely nothing about. Simon was either extremely confident in my ability to learn quickly, or he was totally and utterly out of his mind! (Having got to know Si well over the last twelve years, I conclude that it was probably a bit of both.) The huge engine roared with delight as 'Landy' growled its way out of the driveway.

Standing with my cheque in my hand, I looked at Andrew, somewhat bewildered. He, enthusiastically as ever, congratulated me and seemed genuinely excited at the prospect of having me around. I was thrilled, although I'm pretty sure I was more over the moon about the prospect of getting £250 per week than witnessing the birth of my future career!

The Eurocam office was located in a modern development built on the banks of the River Thames in Battersea, South-West London. It was the type of development that had multiple private houses built on top of modern studio office spaces. These had proved very popular for small businesses, enabling them to keep their work close to home. In the late 1990s it seemed as though the whole of South-West London was exploding with such 'apartments' and in the early years of the new millennium the trend has only increased.

The block where the Nibletts' house and the Eurocam office were situated was called Cinnamon Row. It was in a long row of houses/offices sandwiched between walkways and driveways with allocated private parking spaces. There was also a private underground car park that extended beneath the entire complex. Having secure car parking in that part of London was a big selling point giving the properties extra value.

On entering the building through the front 'Private' walkway you were greeted by a normal suburban-looking front door. On entering through the 'Office' driveway you were met by two large glass-fronted doors. Eurocam was based on the rear office side and it was that rear entrance that was most commonly used.

As you entered the office through the two large glass doors you stepped into a long and narrow open-plan space that stretched from one side of the building to the other. Immediately on your left was a metal spiral staircase that led up to the first floor where you found a small cosy office. This is where Susie and Simon had their desks – the nerve centre of Eurocam. A door from that office led out onto a small patio that in turn connected the house to the office. This patio was a suntrap and, over the next few years, during the summer months many a lunchtime was spent sitting there, drinking a bottle of beer with Si as Sally knocked up one of her legendary sandwiches – it was awesome!

Back down below on the ground floor, as you walked up through the open plan area on your immediate right, opposite the spiral staircase, there was a tiny little office, not much bigger than a walk-in wardrobe. For a year or so Mark Stewart (son of racing driver Jackie Stewart) squeezed his desk into that space and began Mark Stewart Productions. Carrying on into the building, the second door on the right was Andrew's office, from which he ran The Last Word. Complete with edit suite and sofa bed, Andrew would spend hours upon hours, and often the entire night, editing high-society weddings or other events that he had filmed over the previous weekend. Gradually, over a number of years, both he and Mark have built their small businesses into very successful companies, boasting some impressive broadcast commissions.

Parallel to The Last Word office was Eurocam's kit room. This was about the same size as Andrew's office (the size of a double bedroom) and was literally crammed from wall to wall with flight cases, cameras, tripods, lenses and tools, etc. This was to be my domain for the next two years and I liked to call it the 'Engine Room of Eurocam'. Further down the corridor there was a small kitchen on the left and then a door that separated Simon and Sally's house from the offices.

Looking back, the office space was fairly small and over-crowded, though we all got on incredibly well and, due to the fact that we were all in the video/television industry, it served as a kind of co-operative, each small business helping the other out. For the majority of the time it was also a very happy environment, with Mark and I constantly exchanging a barrage of playful banter from one end of the building to the other. He sat in his wardrobe and I in my kit room. The exchanges would often fly to and fro as poor Andrew, sandwiched in the middle, was trying to talk to high-flying clients on his phone. It wouldn't take long before he slammed his door shut in an effort to try and shelter them from our banter!

Before I left the office on that Friday morning, I climbed the spiral staircase to the 'Eurocam nerve centre' to meet Susie. As you arrived at the top of the stairs you saw an enormous circular window on the right and then two wooden dining tables placed back to back. Simon's desk was on the right with

Susie's opposite. On both desks sat good-sized computers and matching phones, the difference between them being that Si's desk was in 'organised' (as he would insist!) chaos and Susie's was busy, but properly ordered and in relative calm. On the left of the door (leading to the patio) was a large wooden wardrobe that was brimming with files and numerous editions of *Production* (a TV industry publication) and *National Geographic* magazines. In front of the wardrobe was a rope hammock chair, attached to a ceiling rafter with a sturdy rope and tied by an impressive-looking knot.

Susie Winn is an instantly friendly, jovial character. She has a petit frame with mid-length dark hair. As I arrived in the office, she was sitting at her desk speaking on the phone. While I was standing by the staircase, waiting for her to finish her call, I was sure that I heard a strange, high-pitched whimper. 'Strange,' I thought. I threw a subtle glance at Susie's face, looking for any sign of blushing or embarrassment . . . but she was totally unaware and remained engrossed in her conversation. Then I noticed a movement by her feet, below the desk. As I looked more intently I could just make out the silhouetted shape of what distinctly looked like a dog. It was a dog!

All through my childhood my family had a steady succession of pets – everything from hamsters, rabbits, goldfish, five or six cats to a dog – not all at once, I hasten to add! Our dog, 'Smudge', was easily my favourite member of this small zoo. He was an Old English Sheepdog (more commonly known as the 'Dulux Dog'), whom we had had since he was a puppy. Named after the pink smudge on his nose, he was a small bundle of fur who over a year or so grew into an enormous bundle of fun. He was so big that my three sisters and I could ride on his back all at the same time! Having a big dog at such a young age meant that I grew up with an adoration of them.

As I stood, fairly relaxed, waiting for Susie to finish her call, the timid-looking dog sat at her feet looking somewhat vulnerable. Seeing this as a great opportunity to appear at ease, I crouched down onto my haunches, smiled and called the mutt to me, 'Come on!' In a flash this timid-looking dog had turned into a bounding, doting black Labrador puppy (a black version of the 'Andrex Puppy')! Before I knew it, she was jumping all over me, which was great fun ... but then the inevitable happened – every man's nightmare, she kept sinking her nose into my crotch! I playfully pushed her away, but she was relentless in her mission to sniff me out! After a few minutes it was not so amusing, but still she continued. Out of the corner of her eye Susie must have noticed the commotion and with a simple sharp command, 'Tipple, come here!', Susie's 'sniffer' finally removed her face from my groin and disappeared under the desk to sit back down at her master's feet. As I brushed myself off and stood up again, I noticed that Tipple was now relaxed and it was me who was looking timid and somewhat vulnerable! Too late ... Susie had finished her call.

In the course of chatting to 'Sooze', as I took to calling her, I couldn't help but notice that, although she seemed glad to have me on board, there was an underlying sense of 'another one of Si's spontaneous ideas'! However, this didn't last long and we soon developed a great working relationship, with her at the helm and me downstairs in the engine room.

The following Monday morning I got up early to prepare myself for my first day at work. Due to the speed of the chat

Si and I had had on the Friday, I really didn't know what to expect. I arrived at the office on the dot of ten, to be let in by Andrew. Simon and Susie were upstairs. When Si heard that I had arrived, he came bounding down the stairs to greet me. As usual his welcome was accompanied by a warm smile. 'Hi, Mungo, how are you doing? Right, first things first,' he said, 'let's get a cuppa.' We walked along the corridor to the small kitchen area, where I stood in the doorway as he made the tea (as far as I can remember, that's the first and last time he ever made me tea!). With huge mugs of tea in hand, we went into the Kit Room and the memory exercise began.

My first impression had been that the 'kit' we had originally talked about me looking after was what you could see when you stood in the doorway, but oh no – how wrong could I have been! Si systematically began to open draws, bags and boxes that I didn't know even existed. The sheer amount of kit and the intricacy of the smaller pieces soon became quite overwhelming. For example, not only were there numerous lenses with very technical-sounding names, but there was also the Matte Box,[1] with various adjusting rings and filters, the French Flag sunshade, etc., etc. Of course, now, ten years later, it all sounds normal to me, but on that first day I was literally dumbfounded and somewhat terrified by the sheer amount of items to remember and all the detailed information I was being given about each one. I thought to myself, 'How am I ever going to remember what a "Zoom Demand" is or a "Sennheiser 416"?' As Si continued to plough through more and more equipment, I stood beside him frantically scribbling notes. For all the 'fly by

[1] Item fitted onto the front of the lens, to shade the element from the sun and also hold two glass-effect filters.

the wire' traits found in Simon Niblett, there is a surprising amount of order and systems to his work. Yes, there was a phenomenal amount of kit, but it was all to be found in the right place. So long as you knew where that place was, you had control.

The Kit Room was laid out in order on large metal shelves (as found in a warehouse). On the top shelf was housed the larger equipment, such as empty flight cases, camera bags and foam to pack the delicate items with. On the middle shelf could be found the camera bodies, lenses and battery kits, etc. On the bottom shelf lived the heavy lights, lighting stands and various tripods. Bridging the two side walls was a workbench, which was heavily laden with hundreds of tools, of all varieties, shapes and sizes.

As time went on, the list of kit grew longer and longer. I'm still not sure how we managed it, but by 6 p.m. we seemed to have pretty much covered everything. I was mentally overloaded and Si had yet to pack for Uganda. So, with the presentation of keys, my first day came to an end.

My first duty on day two was to drive Simon and Sally to Heathrow. Finally the time had come for me to grab the reins of 'Landy' (Si's Land Rover). I have always been very confident behind the wheel of any car and over the years I have driven dozens of cars of all makes and models. However, when driving Landy I was in my element. I felt like the king of the road, as we snaked our way around the back streets to find the A40 that would lead us to the airport.

When I joined Eurocam, it was a flourishing business. Four or five of the six broadcast kits that the company owned were on permanent hire contracts with Sky Television. This meant that Eurocam was earning a good income without really having to do much, just occasionally service the kits as they inevitably went down under the strain of constant use. The remaining kits were used by a long list of freelance cameramen, including, of course, Simon himself. Due to various Aussie acquaintances of the Nibletts, Eurocam was regularly frequented by Australian cameramen, most of whom came to the UK to gain wider experience in camera operating. Coming from a sport-mad country, many of the Aussies found their first jobs shooting sport – hence the Sky TV connection. I grew close to many of the guys who came through the office, as it was me who would physically put their kits together or attempt to trouble-shoot their queries. The crews that I met were never short of banter and they appeared to warm to my best efforts.

Occasionally I would get the kit wrong, but as Si once said to me, 'It's OK to make mistakes, but never make the same mistake twice!' I have always been someone who wants to please others, so it was the thought of disappointing Si, or someone else that I respected, that gave me enough drive to succeed in learning from my mistakes. I was also motivated by a daunting fact that Si had shared with me: he told me that the secret of his success was that in over fifteen years of filming, he'd never made a serious mistake! That may sound like a very high standard to set, but in the close-knit, competitive and businesslike world of TV, if you make a big mistake, word gets around quickly and you will simply not be employed again. Not wanting to make a mistake meant that every day was a high-pressure situation; yet through it I learnt that, as your experience grows, your ability to shoulder responsibility grows too.

So Simon and Sally were filming in Uganda and Susie had disappeared somewhere hot on holiday. I had been at Eurocam for four days and for the next two weeks I was at the helm! Not much pressure? Not too much room for mistakes! The situation I found myself in was intense enough without the added complication of rupturing the ligaments in my left ankle while playing football the following Saturday. To my horror my leg was put in plaster up to my knee for the next eight weeks! This meant that I had to hobble around on crutches while sorting the kit out and crawling upstairs to answer the phone . . . What had I done? Refusing to let the side down, I decided that I would still be able to drive the Landy with a few adjustments and some added care – after all the kits had to be delivered and the show must go on.

During the second delivery trip I managed to steer into the side of a car sat beside me at some traffic lights (to my shame nothing to do with my disability!). Fortunately, the driver was so distraught that Landy had gouged a hole in the side of his car that mercifully he didn't notice me hopping out of the car to exchange insurance details with my leg in plaster! It goes without saying that I learnt from that mistake and never drove with a leg in plaster again.

Throughout these first two weeks, other than the car accident, things went very smoothly and being someone who learns by doing, opposed to reading it from a book, I learnt an incredible amount. There were a few moments when I rang the 'emergency number' of a friend of Si's who had agreed to be on call to advise me but, given the circumstances, that was inevitable. On top of learning about all the kit and the way things work in the 'crew' game, I also had my first taste of how much money I could make, should I ever reach the dizzy heights of a broadcast cameraman. I took a phone call from a production manager asking if Simon would shoot at a daily rate of £250. I almost fell off my chair backwards, as I was earning that in a week! It's sobering to look back at my naivety as nowadays I'm earning way more than that as a daily rate, but at the time it seemed a lifetime away. Without a doubt this was the career for me!

I spent the next sixteen months working for Eurocam. I occasionally went out and assisted on shoots and, when able, would take a camera into Battersea Park to play with and learn how it worked. When office bound, I looked after all the camera equipment, prepared and packed kits to go out on shoots, washed the cars and made thousands of cups of tea. I was the 'Kit Monkey' but I revelled in it!

We all have our inspirations, our role models, those who steer our development, leading us to what we eventually become or do. Simon not only steered me on to my career path, but effectively became the big brother that I never had. Many years on, I have practically become part of the Niblett family, even being godparent to one of their four kids, little Bo.

Some years later Si's brother, Ben (whom I had met while shooting on the Formula One Grand Prix circuit), invited me to join the Niblett family in celebrating his birthday with a meal hosted by Simon and Sally. Sitting at the dinner table I explained to Si's mum and dad how I owed my entire career to Simon. He was the one who had given me the golden opportunity which led to my successful career as a cameraman. Overhearing what I had said, Si interrupted by saying that actually he could have given a number of people that opportunity, but credit was due to me for making the most of it!

At the time of the meal I had been filming as cameraman for at least six years and had some great credits under my belt, such as *Lonely Planet*, *Streetmate*, *Blue Peter*, etc. You can come across an open door, but it's up to you to walk through it successfully.

People trying to get into the media often say, 'It's not what you know, but who you know.' While I tend to agree, it's not impossible to work your way in not knowing anybody, but it will likely take longer and require more effort!

I remember while at school in Tonbridge lining up outside a classroom where we were to receive our 'Career's Advice'. I thought to myself that I had *no* idea what I wanted to do with my life. I went in and said to the grey-looking careers advisor that I wanted to be a stuntman! Apparently the boy before me had stated that he wanted to be a cowboy! Being asked to choose your career path when you are fourteen years old is a joke! Looking back I think the grey man reluctantly suggested that I should be a commercial artist or join the army! That wasn't a particularly imaginative suggestion for a kid who was only good at art and sport!

One of my favourite questions to ask new acquaintances is, 'If you could do anything in life, what would you do?' I love hearing people's mixed responses: some sell themselves short, while others dream of reaching dizzy heights. My point behind asking the question is that today's world offers us numerous opportunities to reach our goals and so we should follow our wildest dreams – who knows what could happen!

3

Celebrity Tinsel Town

The world of television is said to be glamorous. It is said to be the workplace where you rub shoulders with the rich and famous, where you can make a lot of money and are invited to flash parties. Well, as someone who has worked in the TV industry for the last ten years – I completely agree!

Granted, there are times when you wonder what on earth you are doing with your life. But isn't that the norm in any 'job'? The truth is, working in television can give you opportunities to do things others just don't get to do, and allows you to meet the people that most dream of one day meeting.

I've heard it said that there is a definite 'type' of media person. Being on the inside, I find that hard to discern. However, it is clear to me that some people simply wouldn't fit in! In any field of work, to be a freelancer takes guts. Not knowing when your next pay cheque will arrive takes time to get used to, so if you want to be in it – you've got to be confident enough to take risks! Ultimately, television is a creative industry full of creative people ... who are always a little bit different.

I have worked with numerous 'famous' people, too many names to recount. Some are more memorable than others. Some are more straightforward and pleasant than others. Yet, in every case without exception, my job has taught me that all 'famous people' are normal people, just like you and me – the difference being that they are in front of the camera and I'm behind it.

Having said that, I have also observed that there's a marked difference between those individuals who want to be famous (just for fame's sake!) and those who have become famous for what they have achieved.

The difference between working with a pop star and a rugby player is stark! (At this point I stop as I see that professional footballers create a grey area here – despite predominantly being sportsmen ... most of them act like pop stars!) Of course, it's mostly to do with personality, etc., but generally speaking a pop star desires to be famous, whereas a rugby player just wants to play rugby! It is where one's ambition lies that draws the line. The pop star is driven to be rich and famous, and the rugby player is delighted that he can make a living by playing his sport!

Early one evening, Johnny Wilkinson came to my flat. Simon (Niblett) was directing a documentary on Johnny and in the process they had become mates. Johnny was always banging on to Si about how he wanted to learn the guitar, and

Si always said that he must meet Phil and Mungo. Phil and I shared a flat in Wandsworth and we were constantly jamming on the guitars together. We weren't quite Simon and Garfunkel (more like Bert and Ernie!), though we played well enough to entertain our friends over a beer with a few party pieces. It was a Tuesday night and Phil and I were jamming in the kitchen when the doorbell rang. Answering the door we found Si, who came up the stairs with Johnny Wilkinson in tow. After saying our hellos the jam session resumed and we all sat around like hippies (minus the aran jumpers, I hasten to add!). After we had played for an hour or so, we just chatted and soon got on to the subject of our musical influences, upon which I offered to lend Johnny some of my CDs to listen to. He ended up borrowing about eight of my favourite albums and promised to send them back as soon as possible . . . five years on, there's still no sign of them! However, as he played a major part in bringing back the Rugby World Cup that year, I've found it in my heart to forgive him. Johnny is a great, yet very normal guy. The only difference between him and us is that he's an incredibly good rugby player. To me, the greatest testament to his normality is the way he seems to resent his fame.

Compare Johnny Wilkinson to the wannabee pop star, who will beg, steal or borrow for a chance to be on stage, being adored by the masses. Obviously there are the purist musicians who play for the sake of playing, but from my experience most pop stars are driven by the desire for money, adoration and fame.

I worked on *Pop Idol* series one and two, and *X Factor* series one, two and three. Could the contrast be clearer between people like Johnny Wilkinson and the 100,000 auditionees, who are desperate for the million-dollar record contract, despite the majority having little or no talent at all?

X Factor and *Pop Idol*

Our call time is 9 a.m. at Simon Cowell's house in Kensington. Three silver crew vans pull up to the gates of the large house on the dot of 9 a.m. We temporarily park on the single yellow line and two by two we get out, takeaway coffees in hand, and say our hellos. We loiter next to the vans parked on the opulent, yet surprisingly homely street, waiting to make sure that at least one of the production team has turned up before ringing the doorbell on the video entry system.

Making up the crews there are all the usual faces: Diddley (Sean), Shirley (Mark), Sarge (Rob), Vinnie (Vince), Burlsey (Simon) and Lloyd (Lloyd!). It's early and the sun is shining upon West London, which is looking how it should ... fantastic!

Within a few minutes a cab pulls up and two researchers hop out. The *X Factor* schedule is gruelling and, while we crews tend to dip in and out of the working week, the production staff take the full blow of the long hours required to make a TV show of this magnitude. The researchers look tired, yet as always they greet us with a warm smile and sincere handshakes. They ring the doorbell and make sure that we are not about to disturb the household, while we open up the back of the VW Transporters and begin to prepare our camera and sound kits.

As Simon's housekeeper is welcoming the researchers, we hear a buzz, then a low hum as the gates of the driveway are electronically opened. We are invited to pull our vans in, offering us the safety of the driveway and thus allowing us to avoid the omnipresent, circling, ticket-toting traffic wardens.

It's a well-known fact that Simon Cowell has a passion for flash, fast cars. His driveway confirms this, boasting three top-of-the-range models. There is a Mini Cooper Works, a Sports Mercedes and a spectacularly regal Bentley – all three cars are in black … of course! Over the five years that I have worked on shows with Simon, as well as the current show-room selection he has owned a Ferrari Spider, a Rolls Royce Phantom and, my favourite of them all, an Aston Martin DB7. Looking at the makes and models found on the driveway, it is clear that the owner himself has a love of driving and, as far as I know, he rarely employs a full-time driver.

Leading up to the front door of the house is a grand exterior staircase, the like of which, in London, normally leads up to an old Victorian house that has been converted into several apartments. Yet, make no mistake, these particular stairs and this enormous front door lead you into a house that has remained exactly intact for the purpose for which it was built – a magnificent private home. Entering through the great door you arrive in a large hallway, which on first impression you think very grand, though on second thoughts you realise that although it is immaculate and everything is perfectly in place, it remains very warm and homely. The rest of the house is obviously professionally designed by the best in the business. The décor is minimalist and resembles that of a first-class hotel interior – the logic of which would tell you that as the owner spends a lot of his time in such hotels, the chosen environment would make him feel at home!

Leaving the camera assistants to unload the camera kits, the remainder of us have a quick scout around the house to work out what's going to be filmed and in which rooms, etc. We first look at the 'set' as it stands – which chairs and sofas are suitable for the interviews, etc. Then we assess the light available to us, before we add any additional lighting of our own. Generally the light sources are fixed interior ceiling lights, lamps or, of course, the natural light pouring in from the windows. On location as cameramen we have to judge how much extra light is required to create the look that we are aiming for, at the same time calculating the 'colour temperature' of the light (artificial light is generally known as 'Tungsten' – an orange light – whereas natural sunlight – 'Daylight' – is a blue light). We can either isolate one of these light sources, thus creating a controlled set, or mix the two colour temperatures, thus creating varying looks and depths to the picture. We also, automatically, look to see how many power points there are in certain areas of the room, making sure that we can have enough outlets of electricity to source power for the chosen lighting rig and for powering the TV monitors, etc. As you'd imagine in a house like this, which has been so well thought out, it's relatively easy!

As we start work, rigging the kit and lighting the designated rooms, we're kindly offered tea and coffee by the housekeeper. I often think to myself that we film crews are actually just glorified tradesmen, and that is confirmed when you see the reaction to an offer of tea, coffee and biscuits! From this point on it's like watching ants at work. Everybody knows what he or she has to do and, without being told, each member of the crew gets on with the task ahead. Nowadays the scene of

crews setting up a location for filming is an everyday occurrence, but I distinctly remember in the early days when I
was camera-assisting being amazed at how quickly and
methodically the team works together, in an almost perfect
synergy. I remember times when I felt awkward and sometimes embarrassed because I didn't know what to do next,
worried that I might set up a light that might not be needed, or
I might plug a cable into the wrong socket. When 'wrapping'
(packing up) a kit, it is common that some of the production
team will ask if they can help – which is very kind and most
appreciated – but it is almost always easier to leave it to those
who know what they are doing, saving us having to retie
cables and repack lights, etc. On a large shoot, as this was to
be, the location soon becomes a hive of activity with various
bodies passing each other on the stairs, one carrying two lights
on stands while the other runs out a four-way extension cable
from one room to the next. To the onlooker it would most
definitely look like a chaotic jumble; nevertheless, within an
hour or two the house will be fully rigged, cables taped down,
and the cameras and sound mixers set up ready to begin
filming.

Having worked with Simon on *Pop Idol* and now on
X Factor we are used to his famous bad trait ... being late to
start filming. It always happens. While some think it's a power
play to show us who's boss, I believe that it's because he's a
highly successful businessman who simply has a hundred and
one other things to be doing, on top of filming.

This particular day is no exception to the rule. We all stand
around waiting, checking the kit, waiting, re-checking the kit
and drinking another cup of tea, waiting ... You get the picture.

We are pleasantly surprised, however, as this morning's wait is only three-quarters of an hour or so. We figure that it helps our cause, as Simon obviously knows that the sooner we start, the sooner we will all disappear from his house.

This day's filming is covering the decision-making for which contestants will remain in *X Factor* following the Boot Camp. After this shoot, the same day, we will have to take the remaining contestants back to their homes, to film them telling their families and friends the good news! This is fine, although we already know Simon's decision, which means that Matt (my sound recordist) and I will be taking our contestant home – who happens to live in Manchester! Once we have finished the filming in London, we will then have to drive all the way to Manchester and continue filming there into the evening. It is going to be a very long day!

I have always been pro Simon Cowell. Not because I want to suck up to the business powerhouse that he undoubtedly is, but rather because I simply admire his frankness and honesty. People think that his comments on TV are rude and offensive, though if you unpack the situation that he finds himself in, he's simply saving himself a lot of work and the hopefuls a lot of disappointment. Thousands of people wish to display their talents (or lack of talent in most cases) before Simon, praying that he will wave his golden wand of destiny and offer them a multi-million-pound record deal. If he kindly said, 'Well, you're not bad' (when they were frankly terrible!), then those individuals would remain in their dream worlds of pursuing a career within which they don't stand a chance – all the while persistently badgering record producers, who like Simon have a plethora of 'supremely talented' acts to work with! He genuinely is being cruel to be kind. It just so happens that it also makes fantastically entertaining television – adding another string to his bow!

On a personal level I have had little 'one on one' conversation with Simon, just the odd chat. I remember discussing cars with him while standing side by side at a urinal in the Excel building during the London *Pop Idol* auditions. On another occasion, cars were the point of interest again, as I polished his Mini, preparing to film it as a competition prize, while he sat on his exterior front steps and smoked a cigarette. One on one, he is a very warm man. It's frightening to think how 'fame' can distort our view of perfectly nice human beings. Sometimes we crews tend to feel as though we blend into the wallpaper, leading us to believe that the contributors we film don't even realise we are there, let alone know who we are. That was generally my experience with Simon Cowell until this day at his house.

Having rigged and lit the set in the living room, I am waiting for the contestant to come in for the interview. I am standing in front of the open fire, leaning on the stone mantelpiece and Simon is sitting on the sofa a few feet away from me. Having finished his conversation with one of his record company staff, he relaxes back in the sofa and turns to me and says, 'How are you, Mungo?' I am surprised because, one, he remembered my name (albeit Mungo isn't that difficult to remember!) and, two, he seems genuinely sincere in his question . . . and he is!

'I'm very well, thanks, mate,' I reply. 'I'm tired, as I've just got back from a shoot in Ethiopia and it's all been pretty much non-stop.'

'Yes – it must be hard work for you guys. You've lost weight, haven't you?' he asks.

'Not you as well,' I say. 'Only yesterday I received a card from my mum asking me to "eat properly and look after myself", as I was looking "gaunt and unkempt!"'

He smiles knowingly. They always say 'Mums know best' and now Simon Cowell has confirmed my fears – she's right! Still, it proves to me that he does know who I am and, even more than that, he takes into consideration how hard we work and is concerned about how we are doing. We then chat about where we are going to spend Christmas, etc., until finally the contestant enters the room and Simon is asked to leave so that we can film the 'Honest Interview' without him being present. It is a short moment in time, but it allows a rare glimpse – for most of us – into the normal man that is Simon Cowell.

So, it is decision day for the contestants to find out who is going to remain in the competition following the X *Factor* Boot Camp. We are rigged and ready to roll. By eleven the cameras are rolling and the production machine is in full swing. In the morning my camera position is just outside the living-room doors with the presenter Kate Thornton. I am to film Kate saying good luck to each contestant as they enter the room where they will meet Simon and his two beautiful female assistants. Simon will offer the contestant a seat and then, in his famously emotionless tone, he will reveal each individual's fate. They will either proceed into the finals and so be in the running for a million-pound record contract, or they will be out of the competition altogether! As they exit the room, Kate meets them again and we film their reaction – either jubilant or totally gutted! To be honest, it is the usual drill for us. We had filmed thousands (literally) of people coming out of doors over the last few months, during the auditions over the summer.

I am on automatic pilot for a while, partly because I have just returned from filming a wildlife documentary in Ethiopia, which means that I have no idea of who is who, or what has been going on in the Boot Camps. Still, it is great to be working with my mates again, as it is always guaranteed to be a laugh. And laugh we do . . .

Early that afternoon, various bits of filming are taking place, dotted around the house: contestant interviews, cut-aways and sound bites, as well as ITV2 who are filming on the balcony overlooking the garden. It is typically busy with everyone getting on with his or her particular job. I have just filmed one contestant walking from the living room through the dining room to ITV2 on the balcony, when I notice a small crowd of the production team peering out of the front window. I put the camera down and go to investigate what the commotion is all about. The window looks out over the driveway where all the cars are parked. All seems normal, except for the camera assistant who is skulking around the front end of the Bentley, which is now parked in the gateway. 'What's going on?' I enquire curiously. 'Ollie has moved Simon's Bentley and the automatic wrought-iron gates are opening and closing themselves onto the two front wings!' Oh my goodness, it's true. The Bentley, worth somewhere in the region of £150,000, is sitting like a duck, being continuously beaten on its sides by the two huge gates! Everyone inside is standing sniggering at Ollie's misfortune; one or two are even grabbing their mobile phones to take photos of the spectacle! But this isn't good enough – Ollie is one of our crew . . . one of the boys. If anyone was going to take the Mickey out of him . . . it should be us! And not hidden behind a glass window, but face to face! In a flash we are out the front door and asking innocently what is going on. The gates have been stopped by turning the override switch and poor Ollie is understandably in despair. After making a few quick jibes at him we then take it all a bit more seriously and decide to help.

By this time, two or three of the other crews are also out, walking around inspecting the damage, all the while mischievously chortling under their breath. This really is a *faux-pas* of legendary proportions.

The first thing we decide is that we should move the car out of harm's way, just in case the evil gates re-awaken from their sleep.

We stand around in a group.

'We should definitely move it,' someone says from the back.

'Yeah, you're right,' agrees someone else.

We all look at Sarge. Sarge is the old boy of the group, having been a cameraman for more years than all of us and so is by far the most experienced. You could always count on Sarge to look out for you ... or so we thought!

'Bugger that!' he exclaims. 'There's no way in hell you're getting me in there, to move that!' Hands stuck firmly in his pockets he walks off back into the house.

Sarge is known as a legend among the camera fraternity, mostly for being a loveable, grumpy old sod, who has a tendency to go absolutely mental after a few beers ... and on occasions even without a sniff of beer! There is a long list of fun crimes that can be associated with his name – probably the most famous of which is when he decided to strip off and jump onto the dining table during a fellow cameraman's fortieth birthday celebration. The venue was a classy Thai restaurant in Manchester and there must have been at least twenty of us, including the executive producers of the show. Sarge danced and gyrated like a pole dancer, singing, 'It's getting hot in here, it's getting hot, hot, hot!' as he proceeded to strip right down to his underpants and literally dived chest first down the centre of the table! Plates, cutlery and glasses of wine went crashing onto the floor and onto our laps as we all sat in disbelief. Thankfully, while the rest of us were trying to take a life-saving breath of oxygen due to laughing so much, Vinnie had the sense of mind to capture the entire performance on his videophone. The next morning, back on location, Sarge, the vastly experienced cameraman, husband and father of three, was very sheepish … to say the least! As I said, he's a Legend.

We all stand looking at the bruised Bentley and then at each other. It is obvious that no one is going to volunteer, so eventually I step forward and say, 'I'll do it – it can't be that different from a normal car!' Before I have a chance to change my mind, someone has thrown me the keys. I reluctantly walk over to the hulking machine, open the door and sit in the driver's seat. The seats envelop me like a big leather armchair. I sit there, desperately wanting to exude confidence to the boys, who are still standing in a group, silently watching me. I fumble around the steering wheel and dashboard looking for the ignition in which to insert the key. I find it, but it won't turn. I look around for any clues as Ollie sticks his head in the window and says, 'You start it by pushing that button.' On the central column of the dark, highly polished wooden consul there is a button that says 'Engine Start'. When I press it there is a deep growl as the impressive engine acknowledges its awakening and then it settles into a barely audible purr. I hold my breath as I move the gearshift into 'D' for drive and slowly take my foot off the brake. To my relief, the giant car submits humbly to my control and behaves as I ask it to. I slide the car gently backwards into the driveway out of harm's way. As I come to a halt, open the door and get out, I am desperately trying to wear an expression that says 'What's the big deal?' to my nervous audience, yet the truth behind the mask is a feeling of utter relief!

Poor Ollie was not to know that the electric gates would come alive of their own accord, Simon didn't bat an eyelid when told, and the Production Company picked up the bill for the repair to the Bentley's paintwork. And they all lived happily ever after!

Nearing the end of *X Factor* series one, I had asked Simon Cowell how he felt it had gone. He had replied, 'I genuinely believe that this series is target finding and that in the next series we will hit jackpot and find real talent!' How right he was. *X Factor One* was a hit, but *X Factor Two* proved to be a huge success and many people have commented on how much better the talent was in the second series compared to the first.

One stage of the *X Factor* auditions' tour was held at the Birmingham NEC. Having auditioned there before with *Pop Idol* and *X Factor*, it was pretty much the same old routine . . . the same designated areas, same rooms and, not surprisingly, a lot of the same faces that had come to re-audition!

Built in the late 1980s the once-great NEC is now somewhat shabby and in desperate need of a facelift. As a conference centre and concert venue the bare bones of the facilities are second to none, but when you have spent fourteen hours inside its belly, you can't wait to breathe fresh air and see daylight again! The saving grace for our time spent there is that the Brummies are always incredibly cheerful and 'up for it'!

The schedule for our shooting day was generally:

07.30   Breakfast
08.00   Depart hotel
08.30   Arrive at NEC and rig lights and prepare cameras, etc.
09.00   Turn over (start to film!) Film Session 1, then Session 2
13.00   Grab some lunch (normally catering is provided by the venue)
13.45   Continue filming Session 3 and Session 4
18.30   Finish filming
19.00   Return to hotel
19.30   Meet in bar
20.00   Go to restaurant for meal
23.30   Return to hotel for a nightcap (drink!)
00.00   Bed.

In order to keep the promise that *everyone* who applies will get an audition, when you are dealing with 100,000 applicants, it would be impossible for the celebrity judges to audition everyone personally. So, for about three days prior to the 'Judges' Days', it is down to the wider team to sort out the wheat from the chaff. To do this there are four separate audition rooms. In these cleared-out conference rooms sit a TV producer or record company representative who will be the judge as to whether the act is good enough or bad enough to go through. Many people in the past turned their noses up at this process, but it is simply the only way possible to see such a vast amount of people. Some people complain about the fact that the person next to them got through when they are obviously better (?). At this point you must bear in mind that we are making a TV programme and we are looking to entertain the viewers as well as ultimately find someone with the X-Factor! The 'funny' acts are always a highlight for those who watch the early shows.

These long days of shooting are an effort, yet when intermingled with the smiley faces and great sense of humour of the *X Factor* team, along with the odd game of football arranged by the younger lads in production, they are bearable and actually quite a good laugh.

It's funny how sometimes individuals at the auditions stand out from the crowd and sometimes the best simply slip by almost unnoticed. I remember how on *Pop Idol* series one, Steph (Producer/Director) and I were filming outside the audition halls in Manchester. We had been working our way up and down the queues of people, asking for some who would sing for the camera. When doing this, it's ridiculous how many go all shy and coy, until reminded by the director that they are auditioning for a television show and, in order to win the competition, they would have to be performing in front of millions, on camera, every week! That rousing speech normally succeeded in making them smell the coffee.

After recording a few random performances, some good, many bad, we came across a young guy and his sister. On this occasion it didn't take much effort to get them to sing, and the duet that they sang stays with me to this day ... it was truly brilliant. Once the song was over we then continued to film a quick chat between them, and even though they were going to audition individually, it was obvious that this was a strong story to follow through to the judges. Before too long they were inside and waiting to see the judges. I remember keeping an eye on them while filming the thousands of others in the waiting area, just to make sure we had them well covered. Not long before the guy was going into the Judges' room, all six crews had rotated – there were four in the Judges' room and two outside, one roaming with a PD (Producer Director) and one with Ant and Dec. At this juncture I was back in with the judges (Simon Cowell, Pete Waterman, Nicky Chapman and Neil Fox). A few auditions took place before the one I was waiting for and then finally my horse was in the starting box. Steph came in to see the judges before the audition to say that the next guy to come in had a speech impediment, but whatever happens, they must hear him sing!

This sensitivity warning was not that unusual by this stage of the auditions, since as there were some mentally or physically challenged people taking part, the judges were alerted to prevent any initial surprise. The judges acknowledged Steph's warning and called the guy in. It was Pete Waterman's turn to greet the auditionee and I for one was on a knife's edge. Gareth Gates walked into the room and nervously found his standing position marked on the floor with a star. I will never forget the gentleness with which Pete greeted him. He asked Gareth his name and his age and what he was going to sing. Nerves had got the better of Gareth and, when he tried to answer, he almost literally couldn't say a word. At this there was a tangible intensity in the room;

everyone was gripped by the situation being played out in front of them. Who was this kid who could hardly speak? Realistically speaking, what was he doing here at a television show audition? But then came Pete's final words, 'Don't worry, kid, why don't you just sing for us...? In your own time, a verse and a chorus.'

Needing no more prompting Gareth began to sing 'Everybody's looking for that something...' ('Flying Without Wings' by Westlife). Within a few lines of the song, everyone in the room sat agog at what they were hearing. I noticed that all three girls in the room were welling up with tears; the guys in the room could not take their eyes off Gareth, and the hairs on the back of my neck were standing on end. We were witnessing something very special, the kid who can't speak but sings like an angel! Without interrupting Gareth they let him sing and, while giving the obvious congratulatory feedback, I saw Simon Cowell jot down on a piece of paper, 'That's our Pop Idol' and slide it across the desk to Nicky Chapman.

Of course, it's easy to look back on the first series knowing the result and smirk, thinking Simon got it wrong! Yes, Gareth ended up coming second to Will Young, yet having witnessed that audition first hand one can't deny that Gareth was something out of the ordinary. It also has to be said that to come second in a competition with many thousands of people involved is hardly bad! It's a shame to think how the media ended up treating Gareth. 'Should he have been so foolish?' the public ask. 'Should he have been more responsibly looked after?' I ask.

Take a nervous eighteen-year-old from a very normal background up North and throw him into the mix of the music industry and the media. He's not likely to keep his feet on the ground for long! With the enticement of instant fame and celebrity status, on top of the mounting money (which I understand Gareth did well in, through various sponsorship deals), how was it possible for him to stand unaffected? I hate to think how I would have reacted. Still, when I marry Kylie I shall let you know!

Will Young was a worthy winner. He is very talented and bright, and overall he's a great guy. For me, Will went pretty much unnoticed throughout the auditions. He always seemed a little separate from the group, often found sitting in corners of the studio writing his diary. The turning point in Will's competition was while on the live show in the Green Room with Ant and Dec.

Throughout the studio section of the show I was filming 'Live' in the Green Room alongside my good mate, fellow cameraman Roo (Richard Farish). Roo's job on that occasion was to follow the act from the main studio, walking backwards and filming them until they entered the Green Room. He would then spin around and reposition himself, and I would pick them up on the long end of my lens and continue to film them as they sat down between Ant and Dec. As they sat, I would slowly lower my left knee to the floor – by kneeling I could keep the camera in a more comfortable position – on my shoulder – and the lens at their eye level, which is more comfortable for the viewer to watch. By this time Roo was on a single shot of the act and I would remain on a wide shot (with all three). We would then hold these positions until they had finished their chat and the Studio Director had cut back into the main studio. These moves we had rehearsed time and time again during the day, so we had everything pretty well covered. From those rehearsals we had learnt little things that would make our lives easier on the night, such as pre-laying our cable in certain positions to avoid getting tangled in it or tripping over it, and we had opted to wear shorts as with the heat of the lights and the weight of the cameras we would be sweating within the first five minutes. The one thing that hadn't crossed my mind was to check what was on the floor.

We were broadcasting 'Live' to the nation! We were on about the third act of the night. All had been going according to plan and all in the Green Room, including Roo and I, were having a great time. By now we were in the flow; our well-rehearsed routine was ticking like clockwork. Roo was in the motion of walking backwards with another act and I was poised ready to pick up my shot in a matter of seconds. Roo spun around and I took over. Smoothly following the act around, I slowly spun around with them holding my shot.

They arrived at the stools with Ant and Dec, who were in full flow, as I steadily sank my knee to the floor ... I almost went blind for a split second as something sharp sank itself into my knee ... yet, I couldn't move or stop filming: we were on live television and my shot was on air! I took a deep breath and desperately tried to focus all my energy on concentrating on my shot.

However, whatever I had knelt on had deeply embedded itself into my knee and no matter how much I tried to distract myself, the pain was too much to bear. My forehead began to drop beads of sweat and my body started to shake. Of course, this meant that the camera on my shoulder began to wobble and so my shot was also starting to move ... 'Camera Four, hold your shot steady...' I heard through my headphones from the Studio Director. Ant and Dec were in mid conversation and they were obviously going to keep going for a while longer, as I desperately tried to hold myself together. With intermittent huffs and puffs, and the odd violent shake of the camera, I was in pieces! 'Camera Four ... keep that camera steady!!!' – the voice was getting more and more aggressive, and still I had to keep going.

By the time Ant had passed over to Dec and they had wrapped up the interview, the last thing on earth I could think about was what I was filming. All that filled my consciousness was removing whatever had speared itself into my kneecap! The voice in my ear continued in expletives: 'Mungo ... for *@£*&* sake!' I don't know who was more relieved to cut back to the main studio, the director or me! But as I almost collapsed onto the floor, putting my camera down beside me, I lifted my knee to find blood trickling down my shin and a drawing pin fully embedded into my knee!

Note to self: Check floor for painful obstacles.

The more recent *X Factor* series have brought in Sharon Osbourne and Louis Walsh, both of whom I get on very well with. Both manage to hold their own against Mr Cowell and occasionally have even outshone him – for example, when Sharon tipped a glass of water over Simon's head and on a later occasion Louis threw water over a feisty contestant! Whenever we film in Sharon's or Louis' houses they are always fantastic, generous hosts.

To date the list of winners chosen from the cream of national talent are: Will Young, Michelle McManners, Steve Bernstein,

Shayne Ward and, most recently, Leona Lewis. It's funny how the public pass judgement on these lucky individuals when they first break out into the music industry, wearing their reality TV crowns. Each one has to prove themselves to the great British public before being deemed worthy of an ongoing career, and some have more success than others. I've overhead conversations when people have commented that Shayne Ward never amounted to anything: 'Where is he now?', 'What a flop he turned out to be!', etc. However, I know from the inside that Shayne has been breaking America, which is what some music stars, such as Robbie Williams, for example, have struggled to do for years. Shayne's hardly a flash in the pan and is now worth a serious amount of money!

How long can these shows last? This is a question that I'm frequently asked and I have to reply with the answer, 'I don't know, but one thing's for sure, they've made me a good living over the last few years!'

Streetmate

Tiger Aspect Productions hit gold with the Channel 4 series *Streetmate*. It not only proved to be an extremely popular show, but it also launched the presenting career of Davina McCall. The *Streetmate* series was based on a simple concept of a 'dating show on the streets'. Davina would run around a city looking for someone who was unlucky in love and currently single. Once found, she would then take on the role of Eros by trawling the streets hunting out a 'date' for her new friend. Over the entire three series spanning three years, none of the people were pre-arranged and none of the dates were rigged. The *Streetmate* crew would literally pull into a city, charge around the streets (for as long as it took!) and make the whole show happen. The proof that the show wasn't rigged was that on a handful of occasions, no matter how hard we tried, we couldn't find anyone who was single and wanted to play along. In some cities it would take us an hour or two to find the *Streetmate* match, while in others it would take ten hours of running around!

The *Streetmate* Team comprised a director, producer, assistant producer, researcher, runner, two cameramen, two sound recordists and a camera assistant. It was quite a sight to see all ten of us running around the streets, following Davina with our cameras blazing! All who worked on *Streetmate* loved it. It was not only a trend-setting show (as it proved to be in the style that we shot and edited it) but it was also a blast to make. As with all long-running series, it is favourable to keep a level of continuity within the crew and team, as friendships are formed (we all love to work with our friends) and 'If it's working well ... why change it?' Seven years on I'm still in regular contact with most of the team, and some have become my closest friends.

When a TV show of this nature is born, due to the expense involved in the filming and producing of it, it is essential to have every tiny detail nailed down before steaming ahead. I remember the run-through that we shot in Brighton with Tommy Tiernan – an Irish comedian who was auditioning for the presenter's role. Tommy is a very funny man and had the makings of a capable presenter, but unfortunately for him he was up against (a practically unheard of) Davina McCall. It didn't take the producers long to realise that this new girl on the block seemed born to present *Streetmate* – and they were right! It was amazing to watch how Davina's fame grew throughout every series. Series one, we would run around the streets with people shouting 'Carol!' out of their office windows, thinking she was Carol Vorderman! The second series we seemed to do far less running as people had watched the first series, recognised the girl from the show and were, therefore, far easier for us to approach. By the time we were shooting the third series things had changed dramatically. As we arrived in a city, almost before we had our cameras on our shoulders, we would be surrounded by people who had heard that 'Davina' was in town! The power of the media machine is quite phenomenal!

Having tried and tested the show format in a couple of pilot shows we were ready to hit the UK!

I shall never forget the first time we filmed *Streetmate* in Cork, Ireland because, without me knowing anything about it, they turned the cameras on me! We had found a very pretty girl named Eileen, whom we had run around the streets of Cork with, stopping and asking blokes that she liked the look of, 'Are you single?' If they were, Davina would then ask, 'Would you like to go on a date with Eileen?' When we first found Eileen, all the guys in the crew nodded at each other approvingly, as not only was it going to be a pleasure running around looking at another pretty girl, but also, with such a cute girl, we stood a better chance of finding her a date easily, thus giving us an early lunch! However, all did not go according to plan. We must have asked hundreds of men, but most were in a relationship and the few that were single were not willing to go on TV. This was proving to be a problem.

We were in Pizza Express (a crew favourite for lunch!) and I was just returning to the dinner table from the toilet, when I crossed Davina on the stairs. She stopped and said, 'I don't understand why this is so difficult, Mungo. What do you think of Eileen?' I replied, 'I know, I can't believe we can't find her a date as I think she's stunning!' Davina then asked me a loaded question, 'Would you go out with her?' Not realising the consequences of my answer I said, 'Of course, I would! At the drop of a hat!' Apparently during the morning Eileen had mentioned to Davina that she liked the look of me and asked if I was an option. She was told no, but a seed had been sown in the heads of Southern (Director) and Claudia (Producer). We continued on with the shoot for the whole afternoon, desperately trying to find a genuine date for Eileen, but alas to no avail. Unknown to me, it was time to put the contingency plan into action – and I was it!

Everyone had been briefed, but me. I was asked by Southern to stand in the doorway of a shop opposite a pub, ostensibly to get a shot of a guy that was coming out of the door in the next few minutes. The guy didn't exist and as I stood there, completely unaware, the rest of the team were re-grouping around the corner. They filmed Davina telling Eileen that she had remembered how earlier in the day Eileen had said that she fancied Mungo the cameraman and how then Davina had said that he wasn't an option, etc. Well, now nearing the end of the day ... you guessed it, he had become an option! So they came running around the corner towards me, which instinctively made me keep filming to cover whatever was happening. As I filmed them, they ran up to me! James (the other cameraman) turned his camera on me, then Davina joined me and, with a smirk on her face, asked me if I would take Eileen out on a date. I had no idea what to do or how to react, but going along with it as best I could, I agreed to the date and said that I knew of a great restaurant just down the road (one that I had visited earlier that day to do a technical check on it before it was booked for filming the impending date!). So, that was it: the day was over, but it was me that was going on the date!

As you can imagine, the team thought it was hilarious and the crew were on to me like vultures – taking the mickey! I stopped for a moment and thought, what have I done? I took Claudia aside and said that I was worried that it may have a detrimental effect on my camera career: if people took me for a bit of a clown, they may not employ me. She assured me that it would be the opposite – that people would see that I was a team player and up for a laugh! It was also pointed out that by saving the shoot in Cork from being a disaster I had saved the company a great deal of money, and obviously that was in my favour. It then dawned on me, what would I wear? Due to the nature of the shoot, running around the streets of a city, come rain or shine, we chose to wear sensible outdoor clothing, rather than making some fashion statement. All I had was a few pairs of combat trousers, some t-shirts and fleeces! The restaurant that we had pre-booked was one of the best in Southern Ireland, so I couldn't turn up looking like the grounds man! Claudia arranged for Southern to take me shopping for a new outfit the following morning, at the company's expense. We found a great clothes shop and, an hour or so later, I walked out with a new outfit worth over £250! On arriving back at the hotel, I found Claudia and apologised for spending so much money – she didn't bat an eyelid!

The following evening, filming of the date started with one crew in Eileen's house interviewing her and her friends while she got ready to go out, and another in my hotel room! Being the second cameraman, my taking part in the date meant that it gave Jules (our camera assistant and my best mate) his first chance to shoot for broadcast TV. This was an important break for Jules, and he was understandably nervous, but then, when he found out that as my best mate he was also going to be interviewed about me, he really had something to worry about! Eileen's best friend was suitably complimentary about her as, to my relief, was Julesy about me – although, never one to miss a trick, he managed to wield his wicked sense of humour and get some jovial jibes in.

The date itself went like a flash – partly due to drinking champagne on an empty stomach and partly due to enjoying myself immensely. It was certainly surreal. Having sat, hidden behind plants, bookshelves or partitions, in numerous restaurants all over the country filming the two people on their date, now I was on the other side! I actually felt very comfortable being on the date even in front of the hidden cameras. In retrospect, it must have been due to my understanding of what was going on behind the scenes and also knowing those in control. I can't imagine how it would have felt to be there, being filmed by complete strangers. I couldn't help but use the opportunity to make a few jibes on camera at Southern and the boys behind the cameras, etc. – after all I knew that most of it would be edited out. I remember poor Eileen saying to me over the meal, 'How do I know you're not an actor?' I think my reply was, 'Maybe I am.' Which I'm sure wouldn't have helped the poor girl. As the meal went on, it was clear that she was very nervous, so I attempted to ease her nerves by telling a joke ... which I ended up getting completely back to front, before prematurely telling the punch line! I remember hearing stifled guffaws from the crew hidden behind the plants, delighted by my calamity!

After the magnificent meal we had a few customary interviews away from the earshot of each other, during which we were encouraged to bare all about what we thought about each other, etc. Eileen was sweet, and I was honest about the fact that although she was cute, with her living in Ireland and me in London, the relationship could never have a future! The cameras followed us on to a nightclub and, being fully aware of what they were after – filming a kiss – I kept my wits about me and stayed at a distance from Eileen. Cottoning on to my awareness not to give anything away, Southern eventually backed off and retreated to the hotel. That's when I knew I was safe, so I kissed her!

A few weeks later, back in London, we were shooting the 'update' interviews when all the couples who had taken part in the show would come back and tell Davina about everything that had gone on since their date – some had worked out well, some had been disastrous! The location for this day's filming was to be a beautiful, big house that had been hired. Once set up, we would work through five or six couples in a day. My update interview was left until last. Unfortunately Eileen was unable to come to London on that day and so was unable to defend her corner, which seemed a bit unfair, but she did have the advantage of having Davina on her side! It was all done in good humour, but Davina had a bit of a dig due to the fact that I had said that I was willing to stay in touch with Eileen and had then used the excuse that I didn't have her phone number. I thought that I had worked my way out of it, but Davina wasn't having any of it: she rightfully stated that since I work with the people who make the show I could have got in touch with Eileen at the drop of a hat, should I have really wanted to! She was right; I confessed and Davina said how I amazed her, because I was so honest! It ended with me telling her a joke that I'd made up:

Mungo: Knock, knock...

Davina: Who's there?

Mungo: Cock a doodle...

Davina: Cock a doodle who!

Despite my poor joke-telling, I am aware that appearing on *Streetmate* actually helped my camera career. After my 'fifteen minutes of fame', for the next six months people stopped me in shops, bars and airports saying that they recognised me from the show. This was the same within the TV industry and, up to four years later, I was being employed for jobs on the back of *Streetmate*.

The success of the first three series of *Streetmate* led on to a couple of special shows: *Beachmate*, shot in Barbados and the Greek island Mykonos, and *Skimate*, which was shot in Courchevel (French Alps).

Beachmate (Barbados) was opened by Davina walking out of the ocean dressed as Ursula Andress in *Dr. No*, in a bikini and holding a knife! It was a mouth-watering sight, which in the heat of the Caribbean sun was a good thing!

Later in the week our second 'date' had fallen through, so after having filmed some 'Pick Ups' to explain the story to the viewer, we had a few days off! Not surprisingly, the opportunity was made the most of by the crew, who were being paid to be in Barbados, windsurfing, snorkelling and drinking Mount Gay Rum! It was on one of these idyllic evenings at the resort's beach bar that Julesy and I were caught out!

Streetmate was always shot over the summer months, and it had become an after-hours' tradition, whenever we were in a city on the coast, to skinny-dip! This had become a challenge that we had kept going all the way through the series, and up to this point we had never disappointed. Even when the British summer had failed us, we would grit our teeth, summon up some 'Dutch courage', and strip off and swim under the moonlight. Barbados was not much of a challenge, rather more of a joy! Needing no encouragement at all, Julesy and I had stripped off stark naked and were running towards the beautiful, warm, shimmering moonlit ocean. Yet, while we were diving into the water, the inevitable was happening ... yes, Davina and co. were stealing our clothes!

After half an hour we had frolicked around enough, so with our 'manhood' cupped in both hands (Julesy's in one hand!) we jogged back up to the bar to find that our clothes were missing. We then had a long walk of shame back to our hotel rooms. However, we still made it back for last orders!

A year or so later, Julesy, Diddley and I were on a shoot in Tenerife. Still keeping up the tradition, it wasn't long before we were naked in the water again. Two Kiwi girls who were staying at our hotel, seeing us skinny-dipping, quickly ran out and stole my clothes, only this time I wasn't left completely naked. In their friendly antipodean manner, they had left me one of their little summer dresses in return for my jeans and t-shirt. I had no option but to squeeze into the summer dress as best I could and head back to the hotel, trying somehow to keep my dignity intact. Julesy and Diddley were giggling like a couple of schoolgirls, as I had to run past the night security guarding reception. It was like a scene from a *Carry On* film!

On the *Skimate* series, shot in Courchevel in the French Alps, we filmed Davina having a skidding competition down the pavement with the punter for whom we were trying to find a date. She put so much exertion into the skid that she let out a ripping fart! To our delight, it was so loud that we picked it up on camera. With embarrassment she sprinted off down the road, as we mercilessly chased her. Finding her hiding, crouched behind a small wall, we all cried with laughter as we filmed her rather rouge complexion! What a beauty!

4

Sport and Music

The Big Match

Being a huge rugby fan, filming a football match didn't really interest me very much, but one particular offer I received seemed far too good an opportunity to miss.

It was the infamous, epic clash of two of the biggest hitters in the English Premiership: Arsenal versus Manchester United. I received a phone call from the producer of Manchester United Television (yes, this super club has its own cable TV channel!).

The offer was to meet the producer at Highbury, sit in the Media Box for the duration of the match, then stand in the tunnel as the players came off the pitch and seek a few post-match interviews with the Manchester United players. 'Was that all?' I asked, never quite sure how much to believe when offered such an easy job. 'And you'll pay me a full day's rate?' 'Yes, that's literally it … we'll just sit, watch the match and grab a few short interviews afterwards,' said the friendly voice on the other end of the phone. Well, I had nothing planned for the Saturday afternoon and it had been a while since I'd attended a live football match, so the answer was easy … 'Fine, great, I'll see you there.'

On the day of the match I picked up the camera kit from the facilities company and set off for Highbury in my Land Rover. One-man-band jobs (the cameraman operating both camera and sound) were not always the easiest of assignments. Logistically you have to transport all the equipment to the location, read the map of how to get there, lug it around all day, operate the camera and at the same time operate and monitor the sound, and then do the same all again in reverse when heading home.

Driving around the narrow residential streets surrounding Arsenal's former stadium at Highbury I prayed for a close parking space. I was in luck. A local primary school had opted to make some easy money over the sporting weekend and surrendered their playground to be a makeshift car park for the football fans. With only a short walk to the stadium I took what seemed like a good option.

Safely parked up within the school grounds I stood at the back of my Landy and began to unload and assemble my camera kit. I only had one pair of hands, so I was careful to take only as much as would be required: the camera, fitted with a wide angle lens, a few spare batteries, tape stock and a top light (small lamp fixed to the top of the camera's hand grip). But then, begrudgingly, there was the stick microphone, the XLR audio lead and a pair of headphones … never had a sound recordist been so valued! Loaded up, without any spare fingers left, I took a deep breath, braced myself under the weight, and took off down the road towards the Media Gate of the arena looming ahead.

On arrival, I asked a steward in his fluorescent jacket if I was at the correct entrance for the Media Box. 'No, mate, it's the fourth red door further up on the left,' he replied, as I grimaced while desperately trying to keep hold of the expensive kit in my over-stretched hands and almost dislocating my shoulder trying to keep the camera's strap hooked up. By the time I arrived at the big red doors I had already broken into a sweat. 'So much for the easy job!' I muttered to myself under my breath, straining under my load. Carefully placing the delicate gear on the pavement I unzipped my pocket and reached for my mobile phone in order to locate the producer amidst the growing swarm of the crowd. 'Hi Stephanie, it's Mungo here. How are you? Where are you?' Stephanie sounded cheerful and relaxed as she said she would make her way to meet me at the designated gate.

There is a running joke that I have with my sound recordists: when having a phone conversation with a woman (whom I had yet to meet), I would repeatedly say how gorgeous she would be and how we'd end up falling in love! As with most jokes, it was particularly funny the *first* time I played it out.

One time I was overseas with Shirley (my usual sound recordist) and I kept telling him how I was convinced the sexy voice, with whom I'd had numerous conversations over the past few weeks arranging the shoot, was going to be the love of my life. When finally meeting her, Shirley said my face was a picture as I came face to face with a woman who had the misfortune of looking like Margaret Thatcher's lost twin! Needless to say, as I greeted her, in the background Shirley crumpled into hysterics.

This time I was in luck. Stephanie came floating out of the door looking like a vision of beauty from a Timoté commercial. I couldn't believe my eyes. This *was* going to be a good day, I thought. After our introductions, we made our way up through the warren of stairways built under the grandstand and eventually found our way to the Media Box. Like any other 'Hospitality Function Room', there was the token blue carpet, a few chairs and tables dotted around, and to my delight a magnificent complimentary spread of food and drinks. Stephanie told me that we wouldn't be doing any filming until after the match, so I should settle down until it was nearing its end. This was great, I thought; I would find my way to a seat with a superb view of the pitch and sit hand in hand with Stephanie. But alas, no; Stephanie had taken off to some other seat and I was left for the full ninety minutes by myself. There was nothing that could quell my disappointment, except for some comfort eating, so I slowly gorged my way through the impressive selection of sandwiches, cold meats and cakes. I ended up getting so engrossed in my romantic dinner for one that I didn't even make it outside to the seats: I just remained in the Media Box watching the match on the wall-mounted television!

When it was nearing full-time, Stephanie re-appeared and said that it was not good news. Manchester United were 1–0 down, so the players would be reluctant to give interviews.

'And the bad news is ... ?' I thought, while stifling a rumbling belch. 'We'd better head down to the tunnel,' she said. I picked up the camera kit and we set off back into the labyrinth of stairwells and corridors, eventually popping out in the famous Players' Tunnel.

The sound was deafening as we stood awaiting the final whistle. The sight of the packed stadium really was something to behold and I imagined what it would be like to run onto the pitch as the vast crowds went mad at seeing you, their beloved player. The officials and stewards were all focused on the game, while all the policemen kept their disciplined eyes on the fans. It took all my discipline to stand in my position, desperately holding myself back from running out to my adoring fans!

The five minutes we were in the tunnel seemed like twenty. At the piercing scream of the referee's whistle, the tunnel was engulfed with a flash flood of people. First it was the 'magic sponge' and bucket carriers, then it was the Head Stewards who were followed by one or two players. As they walked in, I think part of me was expecting some hugely impressive gladiators retreating from their theatre, but instead their appearance was more like a few young lads from the Sunday League played on Clapham Common. Even the bigger names were really unimpressive and I'm proud to say that I was easily as tall as the 'mighty' David Seaman!

Stephanie was doing her best to attract the players and grab them for a quick soundbite about the match. However, not even her beauty would slow these lads down, let alone stop them for a chat. As the torrent of people grew, we dodged to the side, making way for the remainder of the football super-stars. The entire time my camera was loaded and locked on my shoulder, ready to start filming with the press of a button, but it was something else that grabbed my attention.

The referee entered the tunnel, flanked by the line referees and closely followed by a backwash of players. I couldn't quite see what was going on, but I could certainly hear it. The players were fronting up and screaming in the referee's face, using every expletive under the sun! The referee looked nervous as security guards pushed themselves in-between him and the feisty footballers. It was a horrible scene and one that left a very bad taste in my mouth. I'm sure the same event occurs after every match, but to me this was the epitome of bad sportsmanship. The match was over, the scores were set; Arsenal were ecstatic and Manchester United were distraught. That is what the game is all about. Of course, it's acceptable to have a fired-up rivalry between the two teams, but to verbally abuse the man who was officiating the 'game' was to me unacceptable! The over-inflated salaries of the offending players were obviously being matched by their over-inflated egos! Standing watching the foray as it continued into the changing rooms, I remembered how professional rugby players out of courtesy and respect address the referee as 'Sir'. That to me is true sportsmanship! Maybe that is also the difference between men and boys?

One of the last people to enter the tunnel was Sir Alex Fergusson, who miraculously heard Stephanie shout 'Manchester United TV' amid the Arsenal fans' celebratory chants. He stopped, listened to Stephanie's question, gave a thirty-second answer and walked off. 'That was good,' Stephanie said, knowing that she was batting on a losing wicket. 'Well, Mungo, that's it. Thanks for your help.' I knew

I must have heard her wrong as I had only recorded one minute of tape. 'Sorry, what did you say?' I said bending down to hear better. 'That's it. That's a Wrap!' she said.

Well, that was certainly one of the easiest day's work I have ever done since I started working in television and I remember it as a fond memory. Yet, I have to say that, for me, it has also left a nasty stain on the way I look at professional football.

More recently I have had the pleasure of working with David Beckham at his Football Academy in South-East London. To his credit he has restored some of my faith in professional footballers as, despite being surrounded by 'yes men' who all want a part of him, he came across as an incredibly nice guy. It was great to stand behind the goal and film him demonstrating how to curl a free kick into the back of the net. As he lined up his shot, he whispered into the radio mic which corner he would aim for. Having been given the heads up, I could frame my shot accordingly. Needless to say, every shot went exactly where he wanted it.

It was fascinating meeting the man behind the Beckham label. Two of his kids were there, and although shadowed by bodyguards, it impressed me that he made a point of spending all his down-time playing with them. Crouching down and pretending to be a photographer holding a camera, David watched as one of the sons ran on to the pitch. He would then shout, 'Over here, Mr Beckham, give us a wave', while mimicking the sounds made by a motorised stills camera. It was amazing to see the tiny kids acting out what they saw their worshipped dad do.

Later, we shot a few pieces-to-camera with him. After the first few attempts he became incredibly frustrated with himself for not being able to reel off the script. To set him at ease I reminded him that we had loads of time and tape and told him that he shouldn't expect to perform like a TV presenter, because he's a footballer! At the end of the shoot we shook hands and he apologised for being useless. 'You are actually one of the best footballers in the world,' I thought. 'Who cares that you're not as articulate as Des Lyneham!'

The Grand Prix

The pit-lane garage doors are shut; yet from behind the metal shutters there is a rumbling engine noise that occasionally erupts in a menacing roar. The sound is deafening. Lurking behind these barriers, kept well out of sight from the prying eye, are the super-cars of the Formula One Grand Prix.

These are some of the fastest cars in the world and the technology used to design and build the magnificent machines almost equals that of NASA. The vast amounts of money spent on running this man-size Scaletrix set adds up to tens of millions of pounds.

At the back of the garages is the Paddock, which plays host to some of the richest and most glamorous people on the planet. In short, the Formula One racing circuit is without a doubt the playground for the world's crème de la crème and wherever it is that Formula One Grand Prix lands, it can be said that the circus is well and truly in town!

My first real exposure to Formula One (F1) was to cover the Italian Grand Prix held in Imola. I was working for Total

World Sport, a British company who had been contracted to produce coverage for the Japanese company Fuji TV. Our small team consisted of about ten people including engineers, line producers, directors and cameramen. I was introduced to my Japanese director who, having duly bowed and grunted some version of hello, then beamed an enormous white smile and shook my hand. Our job over the race weekend was to grab interviews with various racing team members, including the drivers. Being Japanese there was an obvious interest in the Minardi team, but they had been having a shocking season and were a safe bet to be last over the finishing line, that is of course if they finished the race at all!

The motor circuit on the Grand Prix weekend is like Fort Knox. At either end of the Paddock (which is effectively a huge car park for the racing teams) are turnstiles, manned by dozens of professional security guards. There is definitely no welcome or means of entry for the uninvited. In fact, as we found out, it is hard enough to get in even when you hold an AAA (Access All Areas) pass.

The first time you walk into the Paddock on race weekend it is a sight to behold. As you enter through the sturdy security gates, you see stretched before you a huge strip of tarmac, not that dissimilar to an airstrip. Parked on either side of the grey strip are the racing teams' trucks and motor homes. On the side closest to the team garages (housed within the base of the main grandstand) are rows and rows of huge articulated trucks. You may be conjuring up the image that you would see as you pulled into the M1 Watford Gap motorway services, but these are no ordinary trucks. The incredible thing about the convoys parked here is that they are all spotlessly clean, right down to the minutest detail – even the smallest wheel nut has been meticulously hand polished. There they sit, impressively sparkling as though they are literally brand new, proudly dressed in the brightly coloured racing team livery. Another amazing aspect of this spectacle is that all of these vast vehicles are parked in perfect symmetry. On close inspection, you will notice that the tyres of each team's four or five trucks sit perfectly on the imaginary line drawn between them. This fanatical perfectionism permeates through every aspect of the sport.

Opposite the trucks are the racing teams' motor homes. These vehicles are also huge articulated trucks, which have had million-pound refurbishments. They are luxurious to the extreme. Within these luxury vehicles the drivers are able to have their rest periods, while in the adjacent motor home the rest of the team are lavishly catered for. The bonus that film crews like us have is that the team motor homes welcome the press, as it results in good PR for them and their precious sponsors. Throughout our day's work, we would drop in to various teams' motor homes and get treated to a decent coffee and cake. Another bonus feature that these motor homes have is that of the sponsor's occasional handouts. Depending on the nature of the sponsor's business, they give away everything from free packets of cigarettes to expandable earplugs (an essential piece of kit, considering the extreme levels of noise from the racing cars). I was particularly fortunate as an old friend of Simon and Sally's, Lindy, was the head caterer for the McClaren Team, so I was incredibly well looked after.

In the late 1990s, the leading teams were Ferrari and

McClaren. These two had heavily dominated the season and were leagues ahead of the remaining nine or ten teams. The two star drivers were Michael Schumacher and Mika Häkkinen, who were battling for the World Championship title. Being a casual follower of F1, like most fans I had grown weary of Schumacher's dominance of the sport and the majority of people were now rooting for Häkkinen. Even within the press circuit the Finn's popularity seemed to be at a height, due to his gracious press etiquette, compared to the German's distinct arrogance. However, we were in Italy – the home of Ferrari, so the grandstands were awash with red flags.

When filming the Grand Prix race weekend, you arrive at your hotel late Wednesday evening, have a meal and then get some rest before the onslaught of long working hours. Thursday is spent at the circuit, setting up base in the Media Compound (an area of the circuit designated for the media scanning trucks and satellite link-ups, etc.). While your whole team is busy laying the miles of multiple cable runs, setting up microwave links and generally putting everything in place, you also take this time to get your bearings around the circuit. Friday is the teams' practice day, so the TV companies use this time to test their equipment, practise shots of the cars as they zoom around the track and also grab the odd interview with the racing team members. At this early stage all are trying to predict what will happen come Sunday's race day. What will the weather conditions be? What tyres will each team choose? (Wet weather tyres or 'Slicks' for hot and dry conditions.) What will the re-fuelling strategy entail? (One long or two short pit stops.) The tactics planned by each team are guarded like a national secret, as this is a very serious business!

Saturday is Qualifying Day when in the space of one hour all the teams drive a limited amount of circuits – the best lap-time that each driver records will dictate his position on the starting grid. The overall fastest time is rewarded with the coveted Pole Position.

The Friday and Saturday are busy but sometimes tedious as they are the build-up to the main event, Sunday's Race Day. Having said that, these days are critical and it is exciting to watch the tension mount as engines blow up in a practice or a driver misjudges a corner and throws the highly honed racing car into the gravel pit – if this happens you can audibly hear the groan from the exasperated pit crew. This will mean them staying up and working all night (sometimes they literally rebuild the entire car in less than twelve hours!).

I'll never forget the test day in Imola as I was in the pit lane just outside the Ferrari garage. I was kneeling as I filmed a close-up shot of Michael Schumacher sitting primed in his fire-red racing car. As he sat looking at the TV monitor that is suspended from the ceiling over the cockpit, I zoomed in and held a fantastic close-up shot. The shot was so good that I concentrated hard on holding it still for a good twenty seconds. Holding my breath to minimise the movement of the camera, I noticed in my peripheral vision that the Ferrari pit crew were removing the tyre covers and preparing the car to leave the garage. The second I had captured my shot, I rose to my feet, pulled my lens to the widest that it would go, then went and stood very close to the car's front right wheel. I was intending to shoot the classic shot of the car leaving the pit with the front wheel close in the frame. As the car rolls out of the pit you hold the camera low and as steady as possible, while walking back with the same motion. Once the car is clear of the pit barriers it screams with acceleration as it is unleashed onto the circuit. On this burst of acceleration I have to spin the camera around in a 'whip' movement and film the rear tail as the car disappears in the heat haze, down the pit lane. So, according to plan, as Schumacher slowly rolled out of the garage I was right there with the camera in the low position, just a few feet from his front right tyre. With me walking backwards with him, to my horror he decided to rocket the car into life far earlier than I had anticipated. As the engine screamed I instinctively pulled the camera up, which was just as well since the bottom of the camera was literally millimetres away from the rubber of the tyre as it shot underneath. As the car zoomed past me and the front wheel literally brushed my lower leg, I spun with the momentum! Regaining my balance I quickly pointed the camera in the direction of the ever-decreasing red blob, yet eventually lost my shot and I gasped at how close that was to being a nasty accident. To be honest I was less worried about my ankle almost being broken, and more worried about what the consequences would have been of getting in the way of the current World Champion. The grief would have been monumental and I'm sure I would have instantly been black-listed from ever filming on the F1 circuit again. On the upside, despite it being a little embarrassing, I probably would have made the news in thousands of newspapers worldwide!

On Race Day we arrived at the circuit early and there was a tangible sense of expectation and excitement in the air. The crowds had turned up in their hundreds of thousands. The Paddock was crammed with celebrities, photographers and

TV crews and the racing teams were making their last-minute adjustments, as their smartly uniformed runners snaked their way through the crowds carrying out last-minute errands. The whole area was alight with colour, noise and movement. Having been allocated the pit lane camera, I was handed a set of Fuji TV fire retardant overalls, which were better sized for the average Japanese cameraman than for a six-foot-two European like me! With some careful adjustment I managed to customise them enough to be bearable, and as long as I didn't lift my arms above head height, my dignity would remain in tact. The only downside to this pit lane allocation was the fact that it was a freak day of cloudless blue skies and searing heat. It was hot enough in shorts and a t-shirt, let alone being wrapped up from head to toe in booties, a balaclava and a boiler suit! Still, it was better to be uncomfortably hot and in the thick of the action than to be tucked away behind the grandstand in the paddock where you really don't have a clue about what is happening in the race.

Before each Grand Prix starts all the racing teams and their respective cars line up on the grid (the boxed section of the track just before the start/finish line). It is here that the drivers climb into their cars amid the flurry of activity by the pit crew who are tending to the car, making those all-important tweaks and refining adjustments. There are literally hundreds of people on the grid, surrounding the cars. Certain TV crews with privileged accreditation are allowed on the grid to film last-minute interviews with the team owners and sponsors. Importantly, this is the last chance before the race to discover the thoughts of the drivers. The grid is always somewhat chaotic, as everyone wants a piece of a small amount of people. To film on the grid is always stressful as you are caught up in the ensuing bustle and it's easy to be in the wrong place at the wrong time.

After my 'wake-up call', courtesy of Mr Schumacher, I was fully aware that I must 'toe the line', so I went about my business more gingerly. As the countdown to the start of each race begins, a claxon horn is blown, which signals to all the TV crews and journalists that we must leave the grid and return to our respective race positions. Just as the claxon blew for this race, I had another fantastic shot of Schumacher. Again I was kneeling on one knee, this time literally two feet away from the Ferrari's front wing. The shot held a full frame of just his eyes looking straight ahead towards my lens. The eyes, being the window of the soul, tell a thousand stories and typically Schumacher's eyes were strong, steely and focused. While holding the shot, the thought did cross my mind as to whether he recognised me as the rabbit that he almost ran over those few days previously. Would this affect his concentration? (I secretly hoped so, as I was gunning for Häkkinen to take the championship this year.) Despite the claxon signal having blown over a minute ago, determined to capture my shot, I remained kneeling in front of the Ferrari. But then, suddenly, someone grabbed the collar of my overall and gave it an almighty tug! Not only did this prematurely end my shot, but my overall – being in one piece – thrust itself into places where the sun don't shine. I gave a high-pitched 'yelp' as I stood up and turned towards whoever it was that was pulling me. I shouted, 'What the ... ?', but stopped mid-sentence as I looked down to the little white-haired man that should have been picking on someone his own size – it was Bernie

Ecclestone! Since this diminutive man was the number one chief of Formula One, who owned and monopolised the entire motor sport, I figured that rather than drop-kicking him into the grandstand it would be wise to swallow my words and my pride. I turned away and, like a chastised dog, obediently walked off the grid. Due to my undersized overalls I displayed a distinctly uncomfortable gait, which must have meant I bore an uncommon resemblance to John Wayne!

The race was fantastic! I stood in the Renault pit for most of the race, keeping to the side so as not to get in the way of the pit crew as they buzzed around to prepare for when their cars came in for a pit stop. It was most impressive to watch them working with complete synergy, each one expertly carrying out his individual task. When there wasn't a great deal to film I stood with the mechanics and engineers and watched the race on one of the TV monitors suspended from the garage roofs. It was great to watch on screen as a car swung around the final corner and tore down the final strait, within seconds deafening us with the roar when it passed literally fifty feet from where we were standing.

It was a memorable race – one of the classic and dramatic F1 races. To my delight Mika Häkkinen took the chequered flag and later that year went on to win the championship. At the close of the day I was exhausted from the intense heat, the constant noise and the burdensome weight of my camera. As I headed back to the media compound, a few of my colleagues ran out and thrust a plastic white cup into my free hand . . . it was a cup of champagne. In the midst of it all, I had forgotten that it was my birthday! I smiled, thanked them and took an enormous gulp from the cup. That was it, game over: I had sweated so much throughout the day that I was significantly dehydrated and the champagne went straight to my head – as I walked the last one hundred feet to our truck, once again my gait changed, only this time it was less John Wayne and more John Cleese doing one of his funny walks!

Music

I've played Main Stage at the Reading Festival – admittedly, the imaginary guitar I played looked suspiciously like a camera! I've toured with a few bands and filmed hundreds of interviews with many big names in the music world: Manic Street Preachers, Primal Scream, Oasis, Elbow, Duran Duran, West Life, The Corrs, S Club 7, Mystique, The Sugarbabes, Rod Stewart, The Red Hot Chilli Peppers, and so on. Being a frustrated musician, I've always envied the big names of the music world. I've dreamed of playing and singing in front of thousands of adoring fans and once I even dated a singer.

One of my favourite perks of the job as a cameraman is being given an 'Access All Area' pass into the music world. This means I'm the lucky one who gets to go backstage at the end of a concert and meet the Artists, often joining them for a beer at the after-show party. There are not many people who get to meet their musical heroes in the flesh, but for me this has become a fairly regular event.

One Monday afternoon, sat on a bar stool in a closed bar on Clapham High Street, I looked down my camera viewfinder at some of my childhood musical heroes: Duran Duran. I smiled at the thought of how jealous my sisters would be to know I was meeting the legendary 1980s' heart throb John Taylor.

As a boy I would have never dreamed that I would meet these guys, but there they were sitting three feet in front of me. Now in their mid-forties they were promoting their new comeback album. Reticent to dwell on the success of the past, they wanted to talk about the future of their music. Even though they were very articulate, grounded and friendly guys, the thing I struggled with was their dressing a little younger than their age allowed!

Filming for the BBC I was one of the first crews to film Westside, a new Irish boy band. We filmed them in a small conference room within a hotel in Shepherd's Bush. I was dreading the thought of seeing yet another manufactured boy band come onto the music scene, although when they sang live and unaccompanied as I filmed, I had to admit they could sing! They could sing and they weren't ugly, so with that winning combination they stood a good shot at making it big ... and make it big they certainly did. A few weeks after the interview they renamed themselves 'Westlife' and took the charts by storm. Since then they have broken several records for album sales and made themselves and their record company a fortune, earning themselves the crown of being the biggest boy band.

In a flash Liverpool Street hotel suite my sound recordist and I sat with James Dean Bradfield from the Manic Street Preachers. We were filming an interview for the *Homecoming* series – where successful bands revisit their roots, culminating in playing a gig at their local music hall. I love the Manic Street Preachers' music and was excited to meet the band in the flesh. A number of years ago their original lead singer Ritchie had gone missing – it was a mystery as no one knew where he was and no body had ever been found. Being a larger-than-life rock star his disappearance had become a music legend – similar to that of Jeff Buckley, who was last seen swimming in the Mississippi river … tragically never to be seen again. The musical press feasted on the story, but being somewhat sceptical about what I read, I wondered how much of what they had documented in their numerous articles was accurate. This meeting was my opportunity to hear the story from the horse's mouth, his closest friends – the band. We broached the subject as part of the interview with James and then continued the discussion once we had cut the camera. He didn't really have anything to add to what we already knew from the press coverage. The one thing worth mentioning is the commendable fact that to this day the band still holds a bank account accumulating all Ritchie's share of royalties (which must be a huge amount of money), should he ever return.

After filming an interview with The Corrs, backstage at Wembley Arena, the sound recordist Rupes made me green with envy when he told me that he had managed to get a kiss on the cheek from Andrea Corr, who at the time was every man's dream girl! At first I thought this was a step out of line, as it could have come across as unprofessional for one of the crew to ask the artist for a kiss. However, the thought then crossed my mind of how envious my mates in the pub at home would be if I told them I had kissed Andrea Corr. Determined not to miss out on this opportunity and despite there being a sizeable pause since Rupes had made the move – even though we had already said our thankyou and goodbyes – I managed to muster up the courage to get my kiss. Well, to be honest, she was not expecting it and she didn't have much of a choice as I practically lunged myself at her. Still, technically speaking, I had been kissed by Andrea Corr and that was all that mattered!

About six months later I bumped into an old friend whom I hadn't seen for years and she said to me, 'I heard your name mentioned just the other day. A few guys were saying what a legend you are as you actually snogged Andrea Corr!' I just smiled smugly – Chinese whispers can work wonders for your ego!

Filming an interview with Bobby Gillespie from Primal Scream, Bobby stopped talking as the Director sighed, 'Cut'. The sound recordist had caught his eye, indicating that there was a low growling noise being picked up on sound. We all sat quietly trying to locate where the interfering sound was coming from. I realised that it was coming from under a pile of coats in the corner of the room. I was the closest one to the pile, so I carefully lifted the first coat up. To my amusement yet also embarrassment I saw my camera assistant curled up like a cat, fast asleep and snoring! Fortunately Bobby Gillespie thought it was hilarious; it was just a shame that the Director didn't. Needless to say, the camera assistant never worked for me again.

We watched the fans' curious faces from behind the blacked-out windows of the tour bus as we rolled through the backstage gates of the music festival in Cardiff. As the luxury bus pulled to a halt we could hear that the crowds were going crazy on the other side of the huge stage structure. I hopped off the bus and turned to film the Sugarbabes, whom I'd been travelling with for the last few days, follow me out and around to the stage steps. With a nod from the stage manager, my sound recordist and I ran out onto centre stage and the audience went mad at the sight of the large broadcast TV camera. I panned across the erupting crowd and then spun around to catch the three Sugarbabes strutting onto the stage. There were over ten thousand people going mental and the feeling of being on the receiving end of all that noise and energy was spine-tingling and slightly arse-twitching!

Later that night we ended up back at the hotel bar, where we hung out with the Sugarbabe girls and some of the other acts from the festival. I remember we shared a table with three really young guys, who at the time, to be honest, I thought were idiots. It was their first tour circuit and they were obviously very wet behind the ears. Still we finished our drinks and wished them well. 'Busted' did very well!

Filming the last series of *X Factor*, we stayed in the exclusive Lowry Hotel in Manchester. The week we were staying and filming in the hotel happened to coincide with the huge Take That comeback tour, and to our amusement they were also staying in our hotel. A few of the young girls on the Production Team were beside themselves with excitement and, as the Take That boys loved *X Factor*, we would join them at the hotel bar for drinks on their return from each evening gig. Even though we crew were hardened professionals and used to this sort of socialising with the stars, I think we were all secretly chuffed too. After a full day's filming of auditions for *X Factor*, we were all tired and enjoying a beer in the hotel bar as Louis (Walsh) walked in and said that he had been given eight VIP tickets to the final Take That concert, and there were three left ... 'Mungo, do you and the guys want to come?' Sound recordists Diddley (Sean) and Chatts (Julian) and I looked at each other, smiled and said, 'Give us two minutes to put a shirt on!' before running off to our rooms.

Minutes later we were jumping into the cabs waiting outside the hotel and on our way with the rest of our party: JJ, Julia and Trish, the make-up girls, Louis, and Kelly Osbourne, who was visiting her mum on set for a few days. We arrived at the Manchester City Football Ground as Take That were just starting their set. As we were being shown to our very own box, we could hear the screams of the fans packing the sporting arena. To our delight it had a complimentary bar, which we boys wasted no time delving into. A quarter of the way through the set we joined Louis and the girls in the outdoor seating area, where they were jigging around to the band's 1980s' anthems. I stood next to Kelly and Diddley was on the other side of Louis. It was odd to see how many people in the seats below us were turning their backs on the band they had come to see to take photographs of Kelly and Louis, as they looked on un-phased. A few moments later a girl from the corporate box besides ours leant over and said to Diddley, 'It's unusual to see you security boys drinking alcohol!' I guess that due to our size and our relatively conservative outfits we looked the part. When he shared this conversation with me we both agreed that we quite liked the idea of being mistaken for bodyguards!

At the halfway point of the concert we were all handed AAA passes and ushered downstairs, through the various tunnels and walkways, to the best position in the house, right in front of the stage. As we danced away in the pit we were with the chosen few hundred fortunate enough to get hold of VIP tickets. We were having a fantastic time. At one point Kelly rode on my shoulders and Diddley carried one of the make-up girls on his. Louis was grinning and jigging about as he does when having so much fun. All in all it was an amazing night. The music was great and the company was hilarious.

After the gig we all rushed back to the hotel for a few drinks before heading to an exclusive club in the city centre where the after-show party was to be held. As we arrived at the hotel it was weird to see the Take That boys pulling up in their police-escorted cars. They looked elated, though shattered, and headed into the lifts for a shower before the party.

The after-show party was typically full of glamorous people who were constantly looking at the door to see who was coming in next ... an 'A List' celebrity? Or Take That themselves? Over the years, having been to a number of these events, Diddley and I were completely uninterested in who was there, so we propped up the bar and enjoyed a few quiet drinks.

Just before Louis and the girls were due to arrive I was asked by a bulging bouncer to move three feet over to the left, in order to make space around the booth where Gary Barlow and his personal guests were to be seated. Being deep in conversation with Diddley, I chose to ignore the huge man, who subsequently changed his tone from asking me to telling me in no uncertain terms. I cannot repeat what he said, but his rudeness and swearing sent me over the edge, so I turned to him and unleashed a colourful retaliation insisting I was staying right where I was!

With that, I had the drink removed from my hand and my arm bent up behind my back, and I was frog-marched through the glamorous gawpers and thrown out of the club. The timing could not have been better as, just as I was being thrown out of the door, Louis and Kelly were arriving.

'Hey Mungo, what's going on?' said Louis, as I flew past him.

'Oh, nothing, Louis, I just had a little disagreement with a bouncer and I've been barred!'

'Really? Tell me, which bouncer was it?' he asked.

'That big oaf there!' I pointed to the mountainous shadowy figure standing in the doorway.

'Right, wait here and I'll sort it out,' he said as he and Kelly entered through the front door. From a distance I could see Louis talking to the hulk, but the body language was not looking good. As I had had a skin-full to drink already that night, I gave up, turned around and slowly walked back to the Lowry.

It turned out that I had argued with the Head of Security for the club and not even Louis' Irish charm could soften him up. In the morning Trish told me that Kelly had asked to see the club's manager to plead my case, but even that was to no avail. I have learnt that if you are a celebrity, you can get away with things, but if you are just accompanying them, no one seems to care – and that's just the way I like it!

The media spin around the Music Industry leads us to believe that being a music star is the ideal and that is what we should all aspire to. Yet, take a minute to think about the reality of what it is like to be famous and you will most likely come to a different opinion. Having a recognisable face certainly has its benefits: you can get into clubs and events without question; you get given free clothes and accessories from labels that wish to associate themselves with you; and the list goes on. But I believe that being so recognisable actually has more drawbacks than advantages. Imagine not being able to go to the supermarket without being stared at, or not being able to have a quiet drink without being interrupted and asked for an autograph or a photo. A few years ago I took my mum out to lunch in a vegetarian restaurant in Soho, only to notice that we were sitting at the table next to Kylie Minogue. Having had a huge crush on her ever since I can remember, I kept missing my mouth with my fork full of food, as my gaze was constantly drawn to her. I noticed that it was not only me who was transfixed, but practically all the other diners were staring at her too. A few of them had the courage to approach her table and ask her for an autograph and, of course, Kylie being both sweet and professional pulled a photograph of herself from her handbag, signed it and smiled politely. I couldn't help but think that it must be so exhausting constantly being the centre of attention.

With fame also comes the danger of being misread or misjudged. The press will be all too quick to pick up on the tiniest comment or error and blow it out of all proportion. This develops paranoia and intense insecurities, which forces one to be constantly guarded.

If you are famous, you are also forced to discern who are your genuine friends and who are the people who just want to be associated with you. It is not uncommon for some of the biggest, most well-known names in the world to have only a small handful of trusted friends. Often these friends are also well known and are in the same boat, or your safe friends are those who knew and loved you before you were famous.

We were warned that Rod Stewart was going to be a pain to work with. Shirley (sound recordist) and I looked at each other and rolled our eyes: this was going to be a long day of walking on ice, trying not to upset the Artist. Rod turned up and within half an hour of filming we were laughing and having a great time. The day flew by and we left extremely disgruntled that someone was spreading rumours that Rod was difficult to work with. He was a top man!

Similar to the stars of the sporting world, it is often the least famous names that are the hardest to work with. I guess it's their insecurity or 'small man syndrome', feeling the need to make a big noise in order to be heard. The new kids on the block like to turn up late for interviews and be rude or arrogant to the press and crews, as they generally lack maturity and experience in how to deal with their newfound celebrity status.

The reality is that all these famous pop and rock stars are human too. They still need to eat, drink, sleep and go to the toilet; they too get bored and have to cope with the very normal, mundane aspects of life. Of course, money can help take the pressure off certain material needs, but it can also become a hindrance. The more you have, the more likely it is that you will start mixing with those who have even more than you, thus rendering your own wealth unsatisfactory and unsatisfying.

Yes, their music is their passion, but it is also a job!

No matter how famous they are, when releasing a new record the band or artist have to traipse round the never-ending press circuit. After moving in and out of endless TV and radio interviews all day, they then fly or drive miles through the night to more meetings/appearances pre-arranged by the almighty Record Company. This is the aspect of the job that is extremely hard work, completely unglamorous and absolutely draining!

Having set up for an interview with Mystique in a night club in Central London, when the girls turned up I sat with them in front of the camera, showing them where I needed them to be. As I did so, Alisha put her head on my shoulder and pretended to fall asleep ... they had been doing interviews all day and were finished! Being used to the cameras the minute the red light came on (showing that we were recording), they dug deep and turned on the energy for the short while that it was needed. Yet, behind those perfect smiles were three very tired girls.

While filming the likes of *Pop Idol* and more recently *X Factor* I have found myself being challenged. Sometimes one has to think beyond doing a job purely for the money and think about the ethics of what is going on. In this case I have asked myself if it is fair to throw these young people into the jaws of the Music Industry Machine?

Some people are born with a talent and, if lucky, are snapped up by a major record label. Others spend a lifetime working at improving their art and then pray to be spotted by a scout. Most never make the big time. These days there is an alternative, quick-fix route that singers can take – the manufactured band. Young hopefuls can enter a long-shot national competition like *X Factor*, or respond to an ad in a paper to join a boy or girl band. Most of these youngsters end up being puppets, whose strings are operated by the master puppeteers who see them as a money-making machine. I have heard record company staff let on about how the lifespan of a particular fledgling boy band had already been pre-determined by the label's powers-that-be. Even before they had started, their break-up had been pre-ordained in order to get the maximum selling potential for the least outlay. Yes, I know this is 'business', but these businessmen are ruthlessly playing with the emotions, lives and futures of the young and impressionable.

The Music Industry is a cut-throat world in which only the strongest, most talented and 'luckiest' (?) will survive.

5

Round the World Ticket

As in most first jobs in any industry the new, low-level employee will inevitably be used as a 'mule' for some kind of delivery task. Camera assistants offer a fine example of this role. In between making tea, cleaning kit and other menial chores, the most common task for any camera assistant will be to drop off kit to a cameraman's house, or return kit to a facilities company that had probably been cross-hired for a particular job. On one occasion during my two years of assisting Simon at Eurocam, my delivery task took me further afield than the usual drop-off in Battersea or Fulham. This time it was *me* that was cross-hired to a neighbouring company!

Simon had received the call on the Tuesday morning and he shouted down to me from the upstairs office. I was keeping myself busy in the kit room. Asking me to come up for a minute, he wanted to know if I had any plans for the evening.

When I replied that I hadn't, he asked me if I fancied going overnight to Africa. I was obviously stunned, but in my usual enthusiasm for taking any opportunity, within seconds I had agreed. (Later in my career this kind of last-minute decision to do something radical would become normality and to shoot off somewhere overseas with such short notice would become a matter of routine.) My assignment was to fly to Kenya, Africa. Great! I thought, my first overseas shoot! Yet, even though it was for a television company, unfortunately it didn't involve me using or indeed touching any camera kit. I was to fly to Nairobi airport that night to deliver a passport to a cameraman who, for some reason, had either mislaid his, or required a visa that had to be issued in the UK. I was literally to fly out, meet the producer in the terminal, hand over the passport and then turn around and fly home!

I arrived at Heathrow in the late afternoon feeling decidedly naked without even an overnight bag. I was armed only with my passport, the cameraman's passport, my ticket, mini-disc Walkman and a book – never had I travelled so light – and I probably never will again! I distinctly remember sitting in the airport departures lounge thinking that I'd better get used to this environment – at the time I was purely thinking of the next twenty-four hours (little did I know that I would in the future spend half my working life in and out of airports!).

The flight was good (somewhere around twelve hours – of which I managed to sleep for nine!). As I landed I looked out of the window and saw the cars on the roads and groups of tiny people, like ants, dotted around. This was Africa! Over the years flying into a new country has never ceased to make me ponder. I wonder who the guy is driving that truck ...

What is he thinking as he's driving? I wonder what his problems and concerns are. To think that he lives in a completely different country, culture and 'world' to me and communicates in a different language, etc., makes my mind boggle! Embarrassingly, I have to confess that I also find myself wondering if the cow down there in the field speaks Swahili! I wonder what he would sound like if he could speak to us? (Weird, I know ... I blame the jet lag!)

I arrived safely in Nairobi, without too much trouble or delay. Before long I had found the producer who literally greeted me, took the passport, thanked me and then disappeared. So, that was it! Mission accomplished. That was easy enough, I thought. Only now that I had performed my duty, I had twelve hours to kill before my flight home. On the plane I had figured that I would just cruise around the airport reading my book, listening to my music and drinking vast quantities of coffee in the café, but on second thoughts as the reality of *twelve hours* had sunk in, I decided to take a quick trip into the city of Nairobi. Having been to Nairobi once before (taking stills photographs for a London-based charity) I knew that once I was through the passport control and customs, within an hour I could be in the lobby of the Hilton hotel drinking Earl Grey sat next to the grand piano.

Walking through the large glass doors of the arrivals terminal, I inhaled a deep breath of fresh air which instantly reminded me of the distinct smell of Africa (a warm, rich smell, tainted with a tinge of diesel). It never ceases to amaze me that you board an aircraft in grey, drizzly London and, a matter of hours later, you land in a completely different world!

Without a doubt, I was excited to be in Nairobi. What
would I see and do in the next twelve hours? Surely there
would be a story to tell the folks back home about my new jet-
set lifestyle? Not wanting to waste any time I headed straight
for the taxi rank. I had changed some money in the airport
with which to entertain myself, but I wasn't sure what the
charge would be for a taxi ride into Nairobi. What I did know
from my previous visit to Kenya was that there was a great
safari park en route to the city from the airport. A short safari
trip would certainly be a great use of a few hours, but how
much would a taxi charge me for that additional stop-off?
I was also aware, again from previous experience, that
taxis worldwide are infamous for ripping ignorant tourists
off. I was determined to be confident and hard-nosed in my
negotiations. As I walked along the taxi rank I subtly looked at
the drivers of each vehicle, searching for the one with the most
honest-looking face. I knew from London that this was an
un-PC thing to do as you should always take the first taxi in
the rank, since it's likely that he has queued the longest for the
right to ferry the foreigners into town. I noticed that on
the dashboard of the third taxi was a Bible – this was surely
an indication that the driver was God-fearing and would not
be out to rip me off? I smiled at the elderly man behind the
wheel and he beamed back at me with a warm welcome. After
a brief negotiation on the price, I agreed and he agreed that we
would spend the afternoon together – the reason I say the
afternoon is because he had informed me that you can only
drive around the safari park, but he had also insisted that 'for a
good price' he would be happy to be my guide. I remembered
that the price to the Hilton in the city centre, via the safari

park and back to the airport at the end of the day, came to around twenty pounds – a relative bargain! So off we went.

When travelling in cabs I have always made the effort to talk to the taxi driver, partly out of genuine curiosity, but also based on the theory that if I chat to them and they like me, then they will be less inclined to rip me off with the fare. It took about half an hour before we arrived at the safari park head office (a brick hut standing on its own). I entered and paid the attendant the money for two passes including the vehicle. Within minutes there I was, having left London fourteen hours before, sitting in the front of a tatty old black taxi with my new friend and driving into the vast plains of an African safari park! The world has indeed become a very small place.

We drove round and round for two hours and saw absolutely nothing at all! I was partly tired and partly depressed and disheartened, but I was still holding on to my hard-nosed determination to suck the marrow out of these twelve hours in Africa and therefore resigned to the fact that we would continue to drive around and around until we did see something!

After another half-hour we saw a stationary car, to which a couple of white tourists were just returning from a track that led behind a bush. 'Let's stop there and ask them what they've seen,' I said, and the driver did as I had asked. 'Crocodile!' they said. 'Just around the corner in a waterhole.' Good, I thought. I have seen many crocodiles in Australia and in zoos, so it wasn't the most exciting prospect, but I *was* determined to see at least one native creature and this could be it! I left the driver in the taxi and went off in search of the long-toothed beast. As I walked I recalled the Park's requirement that all visitors should remain in their vehicle . . . was this a good idea?

What would happen if I met the croc face to face and he wasn't as pleased to see me as I was to see him? Well, at least it would be a glamorous way to go!

Anyway I shouldn't have worried myself as there was no crocodile to be seen anywhere! This was not going according to plan! However, by this stage I was starting to see the funny side of it all.

Thankfully my luck hadn't run completely dry and eventually we struck gold. As we continued to drive along the dirt track I spotted a few dots on the horizon: surely this was big game? I conferred with the driver who agreed that this was big game, and not only that, but as we got closer, the small dots grew into two hulking adult rhinoceros and their calf. Amazing! I would never claim to be a wildlife expert, but I would hazard a guess that to see a family unit of rhinoceros must be fairly uncommon. I was thrilled at the sight and I'm pretty sure that my friendly driver was as relieved as I was thrilled (he must have been worried as it was starting to look as if he was leading me on a wild goose chase!). He was so happy to see the family that without stopping to think, he suddenly steered off the dirt track and headed straight towards them. I was still buzzing from finally seeing an animal and didn't really register the fact that what he was doing was extremely dangerous!

We whooped and chuckled as we approached the magnificent beasts. He swung the car round and stopped about twenty feet away from them, with the passenger's seat (where I was sitting) facing them out of courtesy, allowing me the best view. We sat and stared at them with great smiles on our faces. The rhinos stood completely motionless and stared back. We thought this was terrific! There we were within spitting distance of one of the most powerful and majestic mammals on God's earth. What we failed to realise was that we were actually in a stand-off situation with two tons of muscle and horn!

The male – naturally protecting his mate and offspring – began to fidget, shuffling his tree-stump-like legs to and fro. Then his head began to nod and I was actually close enough to see his gaping nostrils flare. I slowly began to feel uncomfortable and my smile morphed into a grimace as my chuckle turned into a babyish warble. My partner in crime was still smiling and giggling away, completely oblivious to what was occurring. The male rhino's patience had run out, and as his mate and calf turned their backs and jogged off, his fear and wrath trained on us. In a thumping whoosh, he burst forward transforming into a charging steam train that hurtled towards my passenger's door in a display of power and aggression!

Time seemed to slow down like a slow-motion scene from a movie. I was caught in the suspended animation of a nightmare. My head slowly turned, though my eyes stayed transfixed on the cloud of dust generated by the snorting hulk! Meanwhile, the driver continued to cackle like a mad man in a horror film, almost crazed and delirious in his uncontrollable hilarity!

With the beast charging towards us, I screamed a strained expletive, briskly followed by 'Drive, drive ... DRIVE!' My mouth stretched with the scream, my eyes stayed fixed on the rhinoceros, the driver's laugh echoed in the air. Closer and closer he came, so close in fact that I shut my eyes ready for the collision, waiting for the gigantic horn to impale the metal of my door and then me! Yet then, as the slow motion cranked back up to full speed and the eerie sounds of the slurred scream mixed with the cackling burst into clear, crisp sounds, there was the grinding of gravel, dirt and dust as the steam train skidded to an earth-shattering halt! The rhino stood only about six feet away from my door, still looking menacing as his great body heaved for air from the burst of physical exertion. The charge was for real, but he was fair enough to give us a false warning charge, and a chance to move away, before he reset for his second not so charitable onslaught.

By now the driver had come to his senses. He put the old taxi into first gear and carefully moved off. My relief was tangible as we rolled away from the rhinoceros and, realising our narrow escape, my smile returned. I joined the driver in laughter as we drove down the slight gravelly incline. He was pleased to see that I had enjoyed the experience and I was simply pleased to be alive. But then the car stopped. The driver changed gear, put his left arm over the back of my seat, turned his head back to look out the rear window and started to reverse at the rhino!

In disbelief, before I could muster any words from my speechless mouth, we were driving at a rate of knots towards the animal with the car horn hooting trying to cajole the great beast back into action! I had to physically grab the driver's arms, forcing him to stop the car. He then realised that I had severely lost my sense of humour as I was not wishing to die that day! After a few brief words (the likes of which I am confident he wouldn't have understood, though the tone alone would have transcended any language barriers) we took flight and headed for the park gates – I was physically and emotionally exhausted and I'd had more than enough adventure for the afternoon.

X Factor auditions with Kate Thornton

X Factor – The Last Supper before the final. *From left*: Matt Flack (Sound),
Shayne Ward, Tabitha (Producer/Director), Louis Walsh and me.

Streetmate – Davina, Diddley and myself on the Reading Festival Main Stage

Interviewing Mika Häkkinen (Formula 1 Motor Racing World Champion)
in the McClaren Motorhome (Imola, Italy)

Catching my ride
(Abu Dhabi)

Skimate – Julsey and I in the mountains of Courchevel (France)

Filming the one
sign of life in the
vast salt flats
(Abu Dhabi)

Muttley and I on the spire of Notre Dame (Paris, France)

Maccu Picchu (Peru)

Travelling light?
(Vietnam)

On the roof
of a truck
with Wrighty
(Cambodia)

Mekong River
(Cambodia)

The last Elephant King (Vietnam)

Richard Meredith and I before the flight from hell (Laos)

Paddling upstream on the River Namtha (Laos)

The Akka village – above the clouds! (Laos)

The Akka – ladies in waiting (Laos)

Before long we were back on the tarmac road that led us into the city, where he dropped me off at the Hilton Hotel for tea. Need I say that I took another taxi back to the airport an hour or so later?

India

I had visited India once before on a short stopover on a return journey to Australia where I was studying. Little did I know that the next time I would be in the country I would be filming for the BBC!

Accompanying me on this shoot was Tim (Producer) and Dr David Bull (Presenter). We spent our first night in Bombay and the following morning took a connecting flight to Hyderabad, Central India. We were filming *Newsround Extra*, the Children's BBC flagship current affairs programme. The story we were there to cover was that of 'The Flying Hospital'.

The Flying Hospital is an American charitable organisation that takes medical professionals to developing world countries to help those who are less fortunate than us. They are flown in in an aircraft which has been converted from a standard jet liner into literally a 'Flying Hospital'. Externally the aircraft looks normal, but on entering you see that it is far from normal. At the front of the plane the first-class seats remain in place, but as you work your way further up the fuselage you see that the economy seats have been ripped out and replaced by a small hospital ward – complete with beds and the latest medical equipment. As you continue to move through the ward towards the rear section of the aircraft, you enter two fully functional, state-of-the-art operating theatres! It is incredibly impressive, as are the staff that run the whole operation.

Being a Christian organisation, when flying into Muslim countries the Flying Hospital is not always made particularly welcome. It has been known for local extremists to fix bombs onto the plane at night when it is parked in the airport grounds. Such experiences mean that these countries have to be treated as potentially hostile environments, and so travelling with the plane there is an impressive security team made up of ex-Navy Seals (US Special Forces). The medical team comprises surgeons, doctors and nurses who donate their precious vacations to join the Flying Hospital, offering surgery and health care to those in the developing world who would never be able to afford it.

On arrival, as the ground staff busy themselves setting up on board the aircraft, the doctors and surgeons attend previously organised clinics in the surrounding districts. These local clinics offer an open door to all those who are potentially in need of surgery. Due to the relatively brief nature of the Flying Hospital's visit it is imperative for the surgeons to ascertain who, among the great numbers attending the clinic, is going to benefit the most from their surgery. Obviously it is very hard to say 'no' to any who are so desperately in need, but they have to be firm in order to make the best use of their time and resources.

It was at one of these clinics that Tim, David and I found two stories that we decided to follow. The first was that of an eight-year-old girl called Samiya who had been born with a squint (a crooked eye). This may seem to be a minor problem, but when you take into consideration the culture of the village in which she lived and the stigmatisation she suffered, its rectification would make a phenomenal difference to her social standing, confidence and future. Also, this is a relatively simple surgical procedure which is frequently carried out at the Flying Hospital.

The other story was of a six-year-old boy called Aadi who had been born with a severe cleft lip and palette. This condition dramatically hampered his talking, eating and particularly his drinking. The fact that the roof of Aadi's mouth had never fully developed meant that in order to drink water, he had to turn his head to one side and very carefully pour the liquid into his mouth. Even while drinking slowly, he spilt a great deal of water down himself, and if he rushed this delicate procedure it resulted in water spilling down his throat and into his lungs, causing him to choke violently! These two lucky kids were about to have a life-changing experience, under the knife of the skilled surgeons of the Flying Hospital.

In order to tell the full story for television production you have to paint the whole picture. If an artist only painted a vase of sunflowers on his white canvas without putting in any of the background, the result would be a floating vase with no context, no grounding! The same goes for story-telling through film. If we just showed Samiya and Aadi having their operation it wouldn't tell the whole story of what was going on. We needed to paint the background to the story, before applying the main point of interest.

We asked the parents' permission for us to follow each child home and film their home, their school and general way of life pre-surgery. They agreed and were excited, though also nervous at the thought of this BBC film crew coming to their home.

We visited Samiya's house first. It was set in a suburban sprawl of very basic dwellings, an hour or so outside of the city. We were driven in a clapped-out white minibus through the traffic jams, the like of which you can only experience in India. The heat was unbearable and the noise was torturing to the ears. After an hour or so of bedlam, we pulled off the main road onto a dirt track. Following the labyrinth of increasingly sandy roads we arrived at Samiya's home where we were greeted by the entire family and welcomed into their home. The house was extremely basic, with the walls made from mud and the roof from fragmented pieces of corrugated iron. The two rooms were dark and relatively cool, offering shade from the intense Indian heat outside. The floor was compounded soil, covered with thin bamboo mats.

Although basic and by our standards impossibly small, these buildings are the most common form of housing found in developing countries. The luxury of a three-bedroomed house with a kitchen, lounge, dining room and bathroom is easily the exception, not the norm!

Within these two tiny rooms the entire family (including extended family) eat, sleep and live, and the children play. In my travels I have seen up to fourteen members of the same family sharing one tiny (four-metres square) room. It was cramped, to say the least, so the cooking was done outside the door along with the washing of themselves and their meagre supply of clothes.

Despite their poverty, the family was jovial and seemingly happy – which is typical of many who live in such circumstances. People count themselves lucky to own what little they have and ultimately happy to be alive! We sat around the fire and ate with them. The food was curried meat served with a little rice – magnificent! After our meal Samiya led us to her school, which was a few lanes away. Through an interpreter she told us what her favourite subjects were and also how her squint affected her life. This gentle-natured young girl spoke very quietly as she told us of the bullying and name-calling that was part and parcel of her everyday life. She accepted her lot, as she had no other choice ... That was until now!

Aadi's house was a considerable distance further out of the city and when we arrived at his home, it was obvious that his family was extremely poor and was living way below the poverty line. The dwelling they called home was literally a mud hut. One room. No windows. It was dark, smelly and terribly overcrowded. Again, we were offered food, yet having already eaten we humbly declined. We sat and talked, and I filmed as the family ate. I subtly filmed Aadi struggling with his eating and drinking, to illustrate to the kids viewing back in the UK just how difficult living with a cleft palette is. After an hour or so, I went outside and took some exterior shots of the hut and the area where Aadi's family lived, as David and Tim said their goodbyes.

That night back in the city, eating an evening meal at our palatial five-star hotel, we found it hard not to think about those we had spent our day with. The contrast between our material lives was stark. We had showered, changed our clothes and sat at the bar before being shown to our table, where we had a fine choice of a dozen or so dishes. We are privileged beyond belief!

I was sitting opposite David. As we talked I saw over his left shoulder that the man sitting on the table next to us, with his back facing us, had doubled over. His wife's face turned ashen as his head lay motionless on the table. Letting out a cry for help, she got up and leant forward, reaching her arms out to him. Interrupting David mid-sentence, I stood to my feet and quickly moved towards them. What happened next almost seemed to take place in slow motion. As I was rushing towards the collapsed figure, in my head I was running through the first-aid training that I had taken a few years previously. I thought: if he's choking I should perform the Heimlich manoeuvre; if he's having a heart attack I should check his airwaves, give CPR … 'Hang on a minute,' I said out loud. 'David! Help!' It had suddenly occurred to me that I was sitting having supper with an Accident and Emergency doctor! David swivelled in his chair, saw what was going on and calmly dealt with the situation in the professional manner he was so accustomed to.

It turned out that the man who collapsed was a doctor himself. David diagnosed that he had a heart condition, which the patient doctor admitted that he knew about, but had been keeping from his wife so as not to worry her. Later, rejoining us at the table, David said how weird it was to deal with such an incident without being able to call an ambulance, or being immediately able to administer drugs!

The following day was spent filming around the city of Hyderabad. We filmed the sites and tried to portray the smells, as David performed pieces-to-camera – all adding to the stories of the children that we were featuring.

The fourth day was the day of the surgery. Leaving early in the morning, after a rushed breakfast, we headed straight to the airport. The Flying Hospital was already buzzing with life.

Nurses were carrying instruments around the plane as the anaesthetists wheeled their equipment to the bedsides in the operating theatres. The administration team set up a seating system in a marquee on the grass by the side of the aircraft and the security team swapped shifts and stood with a watchful eye. This was the day when the well-oiled machine proved its worth.

Patients (the chosen few!) turned up in dribs and drabs. They were ushered into the marquee where the friendly-faced American nurses took their blood pressure, temperature and weight, etc. Then one by one, as the senior nurse read out their names, they were called to board the aircraft where they were taken through pre-surgery checks and preparation.

I worked my way around the aircraft, inside and out, trying to capture on film the whole sequence of events. Tim and David flittered backwards and forwards from the plane to the marquee anxious to be present when Samiya turned up. Samiya was scheduled for surgery in the morning and Aadi for the afternoon. I had just enough time to grab a coffee in the old first-class section of the plane, before I received the call from Tim – Samiya had arrived. I filmed as Samiya was checked over by the nurses in the marquee. It was obvious that she was feeling really mixed emotions – part excitement, part fear! There was a tearful farewell when she and her mother said goodbye to the rest of the family, having been called to board the aircraft. Put yourself in their shoes and you can begin to imagine the uncertainty of their situation. They would never have been on an aeroplane before, they almost certainly would never have met Americans before and not only that, but these strange people were taking Samiya on to the 'spaceship'-like machine, to cut into her eyes – supposedly making them straight. I don't know about you, but I would be petrified!

Not long after Samiya and her mother had boarded the aircraft, David and I got dressed into surgical gowns, enabling us to enter the Theatre and film the operation. For David this was normal routine; for me it was quite exciting – I had been under the knife once or twice, but I was yet to witness an operation while being awake. I moved around the operating table finding different shots as the surgeon skilfully cut into the eye muscles. So spellbound was I by the skill of the man in front of me that it did not even occur to me to feel squeamish. As the surgeon cut and stitched, David stood next to him and spoke to the camera explaining the procedure. He was carefully loosening the eye on one side by cutting the muscle and then stitching the opposite muscle to strengthen and so straighten the eye. The whole operation took about half an hour and before we knew it Samiya was back in the recovery area, where the anaesthetist patiently waited for her to come around.

Tim, David and I were extremely excited about the outcome of this story. We knew it would translate well to the young viewers back in the UK so all in all it had been a roaring success. When Samiya woke up she was given a huge pair of 'Stevie Wonder' sunglasses to wear, as her eyes would have been extremely sensitive to light following the surgery. A few hours later she was transported to a children's ward in the local hospital. We thanked the Flying Hospital staff and left for our hotel. It would be a few days before Samiya had recovered enough to give us a final interview and show us the end result.

Later that day, on arrival at our palatial hotel that served as an oasis amongst the chaos of the Hyderabad streets, we headed straight for the bar to have a celebratory drink. Throughout our week's stay we had frequented the bar most nights and by now had struck up a good banter with the Indian barman. His grasp of English was very basic and the few words he did speak were so obscured by a thick Indian accent that I found him incredibly hard to understand. Despite the language barrier I warmed to this character and found it immensely frustrating not being able to hold a proper conversation with him, so I tried to think of a common interest. Every Indian man I have ever met loves cricket, so I gave it a go ... As he handed me a cold beer in a frosted glass I said to him, 'Shayne Warne?' He smiled, and replied with 'Alan Border'. The universal language of sport had worked, so I thought of another cricketer. 'Alan Lamb,' I said. He wobbled his head and said, 'I like your bottom!' Thinking that I had misheard him, I said, 'I'm sorry?' To my surprise he repeated, 'I like your bottom!' Somewhat taken aback and starting to feel uncomfortable as to what he was suggesting by this comment, I began to slide off my bar stool and edge away to the more distant bar tables. Tim then piped up, 'Botham! ... He means he likes your Ian Botham.' Bursting into laughter, partly out of amusement but also out of embarrassment, I resumed my position at the bar and we all enjoyed a few more drinks.

Two days later we packed our bags and checked out of the hotel. On the way to the airport we returned to Samiya's hospital to say our goodbyes and complete our filming. This was the moment we had been waiting for, the 'reveal', showing the transformation of Samiya's crooked eyes made straight.

We entered the children's ward and scoured the beds for Samiya. It was her mother whom we recognised first sitting on the edge of her bed. We went over to say hello. After a brief chat Tim explained that we were so grateful to them both for letting us follow her story and as we were on our way home, he asked if it would be OK for us to conclude our film with a final interview. They agreed and as I stood filming, Samiya raised her hand, took hold of the comedy sunglasses and lifted them up onto her hairline ... I was looking through the viewfinder, but had to lift my eyes to see first hand what I thought I saw ... I then looked at Tim: his mouth hung open. I turned and looked at David, who in turn looked at me. To our horror, her eyes were still crooked! Desperately trying to stifle our shock, we each in turn said, 'Wow, Samiya, you look amazing', when deep inside we were coming to terms with what a disaster this was. As Tim and I kept up the positive feedback David slipped away and managed to speak to one of the American medical staff, who explained that it would take a number of days for the muscles to fully adjust to the surgery. This was a blow as far as our film was concerned, but it was a relief to know Samiya's dream would come true.

There's a phrase that all cameramen know very well, 'You can save it in the edit', meaning that there is always a way to correct what happens, with clever editing. Sometimes this phrase is vocalised due to human error, but other times something happens, which is completely out of your control. Fortunately what happened in this case was completely out of our control and, without a better understanding of the healing process, it was unavoidable. After some clever editing and with the use of Voice Over, the story remained as powerful as we had hoped. The BBC was happy, but more importantly there was a very happy little girl in India!

Aadi's operation also went well and, in his case, there was an instant improvement to his face. However, he would require a few more operations to fix his cleft palate fully, which would have to be done after the Flying Hospital had left Hyderabad. We were told that as these further operations would be performed by local surgeons, Aadi's parents would have to pay. As a gift Tim, Dave and I clubbed in together to cover these costs.

6

Venturing Off the Beaten Track

Cambodia

I was incredibly excited to be asked to shoot the Lonely Planet Guide to Cambodia, as it was my first fully-fledged travel documentary. This to me was 'real' camera work: being out in the wilds for weeks on end taking part in a proper expedition. I felt as if this was my shot at the 'big time'. Although it was really out of my depth at this early stage in my filming career, I was not about to turn down the opportunity to leap a few rungs up the ladder. I was called into Pilot Productions based in West London for an interview before they accepted me for the job. I had a meeting with Leanne Richardson and Angela Gourley who ran me through some questions to see how suited

I would be for the job. Within ten minutes they clearly saw my enthusiasm and didn't hesitate in signing me up.

I had worked with the director, David Tiballs, on a series of *Streetmate*, so we already knew each other and got on incredibly well. I was thrilled to know that David was confident enough in my ability with a camera to take me on his first shoot for Pilot Productions.

My sound recordist Roger had started his working life in the Royal Navy serving time as an officer on nuclear submarines. When he left the Navy, he found his way into sound recording, which offered him a degree of technical interest, but more importantly took him to some weird and wonderful places. The first time I met Roger was at the airport on our departure along with Ian Wright, who had been presenting Lonely Planets for a number of years. We all got on famously and within minutes we had a good banter going.

Ian Wright, not to be mistaken for the football player, is a short, cheeky East London boy with a wicked sense of humour. Formerly a drama teacher, he randomly auditioned for the Lonely Planet TV series and soon became the anchorman. It seemed to me that Wrighty's fame was ideal, as no one in the UK seems to recognise him. However, when boarding a plane it was a different story. After taking off from Heathrow, within a few minutes of the pilot turning off the seatbelt sign, there was a queue forming of travellers who wanted to speak to Wrighty. It was amazing to witness and I will never forget the grace with which he handled it. He joked with them and signed their Lonely Planet guidebooks, occasionally glancing at me as if to say, 'I hope they all go away soon, so I can get some rest.' Despite having never met these two guys before, I felt completely at home with them and so settled into the flight, looking forward to the adventures that lay in store for us.

Later in the flight I chatted with Wrighty about Cambodia. He told me that out of all the places he had been in the world, he was most nervous about this trip, as we were the first non-News TV crew to be allowed into the country since the terrible Khmer Rouge regime. It was said that western tourists were still a target for bandits and a few had recently been shot dead for their money while travelling on a train. Although the British Embassy had cleared the country as a tourist destination, it enforced strict recommendations not to go out at night, wear any military-style clothing or travel to remote areas on trains, etc. My knowledge of Cambodia was very limited: I had heard of Pol Pott and the Khmer Rouge, but knew very little about the details of what had happened. What we would learn over the following three weeks would shock us to the core.

We had been officially invited by the Cambodian government to make the travel guide programme. After the recent history of war and famine, they were desperately keen to re-introduce Cambodia as a popular tourist trail in South-East Asia. To achieve this they would have to show the world that the country was no longer dangerous and that they had exorcised their dark demons. Being guests of the government, when we had landed we had been privileged to be ushered through the VIP area of the airport, thus avoiding any queues for passport control or customs.

Before the crew and presenter arrive on location, the director and producer travel the whole three-week trip that we are about to shoot. The purpose of this recce is to prepare and set up all the necessary logistics, as well as pre-empting and ironing out any problems that we may encounter. When they met us at Phenom Phen's International Airport, David and Binni (Producer and David's partner) were somewhat weary from the previous three weeks' travel, so they were glad to see some fresh, keen faces. Although tired from the flight, we were raring to go. We headed straight to our hotel where we would be spending our first night.

Early the next morning we kicked off the shoot by filming Wrighty zipping around Phnom Phen on the back of a moto-taxi (a chauffeur-driven moped). After that we filmed some opening pieces to camera, in front of the Royal Palace and on the banks of the River Mekong. We also visited the colourful Central Market, which is housed under an enormous concrete dome and is said to be one of the largest single-structure domes in the world (later in the trip we were able to hire a military helicopter which enabled us to get a most magnificent view of the superstructure). Before too long we were ravenous, so we stopped for a basic, but fantastic lunch. This set the precedent for me of the fantastic Asian food that we would be eating over the next three weeks. I love my food and the staple diet of rice and chilli chicken with vegetables and soy sauce suited me fine!

Later that day we headed off to our first rural location – Phnom Dah – travelling by longboat. It was dusk when we arrived and the low sun bathed the temple ruins on top of the hill in a rich golden light. Wrighty's mood was sombre as he recounted the story to camera of how a large group of peace-loving Buddhist monks had been slaughtered right where we were standing. This horrific tale was to become all too familiar throughout the trip – anyone who got in the way of the Khmer Rouge's tyrannical revolution was simply wiped out.

That night was spent with the re-formed monastery of monks. At the foot of the hill, not far from the banks of the river, stood the hut they used for worship, teaching, eating and sleeping. Constructed from solid dark wood, it balanced six feet off the ground on stilts. We joined the monks in the hut and shared their meal which was a basic rice dish served in a bowl, which we all ate with our fingers.

We were tired after a long day but very happy to have begun our adventure. We sat outside in the dark and chatted about each other's lives at home and mercilessly took the mickey out of each other, often resulting in stifled giggles. This was aided by a large bottle of Jameson's whisky which David pulled out of his rucksack. After a long, hard day in the sun, the potent poison soon took effect. Before too long the one bulb that offered a dim halo of light to over fifty shaven-headed men was extinguished, engulfing the entire area in pitch blackness. We continued to sit and chat outside the hut for a few more hours until we were seeing double and needed to seek our own rest.

We were bedding down on the wooden floor with the monks, so all we had to do was find a spot and lie down. Normally this would have been an easy manoeuvre, but I had left my head-torch by the camera, which was on the far side of the hut. Hampered by a spinning head from the whisky I stepped out into the darkness before me, wobbling from side to side. It seemed that every step I took I trod on a monk! It was literally like finding your way through a minefield. There was snoring, groaning and the occasional muffled explosion of wind, which had me sniggering like an adolescent. Eventually I found the camera, which I had fixed onto the tripod during daylight. Unaware of how far we could trust the locals here, I decided to sleep with my head within the tripod legs, so that the large camera balanced above me. Aided by the whisky, within seconds I had slipped into unconsciousness. I was out like a light. It must have been an hour or so later that I woke up choking. I literally couldn't breathe. Jerking myself into a sitting position I hit my head on the tripod and wretched. I grasped for my head-torch and quickly turned it on. Lying a foot away from me was Wrighty with his back turned to me; he was in a deep sleep. What I discovered was that, in the dark as he found his sleeping spot, just by his back and what would have been a few inches away from my face, he had placed a smoking mosquito coil – the vile scent and smoke of which I had been sucking in for the last half hour or so. Disgusted, though relieved that I wasn't going to die, I moved the coil well away from harm's reach and lay down again taking in big lung-fulls of warm, but clean air.

Over the next few days we drove south through the Cambodian countryside in a Land Rover. For safety we decided to take with us a motorbike, which our local fixer[2] and I would take turns in riding in convoy. If the Land Rover broke down, or something more serious took place, we would be able to ride off for help. You didn't want to be left out in the middle of nowhere for too long in the current climate.

Whenever I had finished my stint on the motorbike I would join the others in the cramped conditions of the Landy, crushed between kit and bags. We whiled away the hours by talking, laughing, reading books or listening to our mini-disks (how funny to think that Ipods were not invented then!).

[2] A 'Fixer' is a person on location who sorts out the shoot logistics, organising accommodation, hiring local people, etc.

One day Wrighty paid me the huge compliment of telling me that working with me was just like working with Si (Niblett). This, I guess, was inevitable as Simon had nurtured me into the TV industry, but to hear the likes of Wrighty say it made me think that I was doing OK and moving along the right lines. I didn't show it, but I was very chuffed.

We stopped at numerous spots on the long journey south to the coast and filmed Wrighty walking down roads and crossing bridges, etc. We also stopped at significant towns and filmed some 'tips' for future travellers. One event that sticks in my mind was a Thai boxing competition, which was being held just outside the window of Wrighty's hotel room. As we didn't have permission to film in the rustic arena itself, we settled for shooting a piece-to-camera from the window, with Wrighty looking down on to the ring and making hilarious comments as he pretended to commentate. When we had finished the sequence we left the camera kit in the hotel and went down, brought some tickets and spent the remainder of the evening watching the various fighters beating each other to a pulp under the murky orange lights.

Our last stop before reaching the coastal town of Sihanoukville was a magnificent derelict hotel, which served as a reminder of the French occupation of Cambodia. Set on the crest of a huge hill, from which you could see the hazy coastline in the distance, the once-opulent hotel had been built to offer the wealthy French a place to holiday. The architecture, though now ravaged by time and war, was impressive and the cooler temperatures high on the hill offered a welcome relief from the searing heat in the valleys. I spent a few hours walking around the palatial ruin, shooting it from every perceivable angle. I focused not only on the angles and aspects of the design, but also on the bullet holes and damage inflicted by the war.

It was here that David and Binni had arranged to meet and interview a French ex-pat who had lived in Southern Cambodia for a number of years. In looks he reminded me of Jean Reno. He was a tough man, unshaven, and with a questionable history – later we all agreed that he was a somewhat 'dodgy' character, though his knowledge and history of the area was invaluable to us. We learnt from our French interviewee that when the French had fled the region, the Khmer Rouge had moved in. Pol Pott himself had resided here and this hotel on the hill famously became his final stronghold before being overthrown.

In the grounds around the back of the building, on the left-hand side, was a steep cliff. At this very spot, prisoners were offered an alternative to the slow death by torture that would otherwise have been their fate: they were permitted to throw themselves off the cliff to a bloody and certain death as their bodies hit the rocks hundreds of metres below ... such was the savagery of the Khmer Rouge's methods, hundreds took their own lives.

Even though there were solemn aspects to the story of this hotel, we also felt it necessary to convey the original purpose of the building, before it was corrupted. Standing in the enormous shell of what was once the grand ballroom, Wrighty with a smile on his face suggested to David that we could film a locked-off shot (a static camera angle) with him and the French ex-pat dancing a waltz around the room. In the edit they could blend the swirling dancing couple as they floated around. David intuitively knew that this was Wrighty's way of making the Frenchman look like an idiot and, due to his arrogance and attitude, we all agreed that he deserved exactly that. 'Great idea,' said David. I took the camera to the far corner of the room to get the widest shot possible and locked off the tripod head so that it would not move. As David explained to our guest what he wanted them to do, Wrighty looked at me and smiled like a Cheshire cat. I started the camera recording and David, Binni, Roger and I stood and watched with wry smiles on our faces as Wrighty took the Jean Reno lookalike by the hand and the waist and started waltzing around the room. In order to keep a rhythm Wrighty hummed loudly a tune that sounded like the ones you used to hear in the old black-and-white movies. It was hilarious, even though a little cruel to our French interviewee. (To our surprise David kept the sequence in the final programme and even though it was a bit odd seeing two grown men waltzing around a huge empty ballroom, it also came across as quite eerie and actually spoke of the hotel's history very well.)

We eventually made it to Sihanoukville where we spent a few days hooking up with travellers, interviewing them and taking them on a boat trip to a deserted island a mile or so off the coast. Being halfway through our trip, it was great for us all to spend time with some different faces. For their part the travellers were so excited at the prospect of being featured in the Lonely Planet Guide of Cambodia that it led to a few days of fun and laughter.

As we headed North again, the next leg of our trip was to become distinctly less jovial. After a hard day's travelling we hit the outskirts of Phnom Phen and arrived at the famous

Killing Fields. What happened in this god-forsaken place is enough to make your blood run cold. The Khmer Rouge, led by Pol Pott, had plotted to rid Cambodia of any resistance to their murderous cause and so began a brutal mass slaughter of its people. With an extremist communist agenda they wished to create a perfect state with an obedient nation that would jump when told to (literally at times!) or play ball with their twisted ideology. They started by wiping out any person who would pose a threat to their plan and so all the rich and the educated were faced with the choice of whether to flee their homeland or stay and be killed. People fled in their thousands. The Khmer Rouge then began to recruit young children to command their armies. A child with a gun knows little about either responsibility or morality, so these young leaders proved to be ruthless and thoughtless. The gun ruled, and anyone who dared to question or to stand up to them was simply exterminated. The country rapidly disintegrated and crumbled under their new, self-appointed leaders. The rules they imposed upon the Cambodians were fanatical and oppressive. If these rules were broken, there was one punishment – death!

When we drove into the fields, we were hit by a mysterious sense of peace, yet also a palpable feeling of sadness and distress. We walked around the pits that were each the size of a large allotment found in England (five metres by twenty). Each pit had obviously been dug out and then filled with earth. Tragically it was not only earth that filled these trenches, but hundreds of mutilated corpses. It was common for the killing squads to line their victims up alongside the graves and, to save bullets, machete or stab them to death with sharpened bamboo. The bodies would slump into the pits and form a mass grave.

Young babies were held by the feet and violently swung against the trunks of trees, repeatedly smashing their heads and killing them outright. They would then join their mothers, fathers, brothers and sisters in the grave. It was a horrendous story of genocide and one could not help but feel moved.

While filming a shot low across the grassy pits, trying to establish the location geographically, I noticed in my peripheral vision a small figure sitting in the distance on the far side of the field. I swung my camera around and zoomed in to see Wrighty sitting with his head in his hands. The single image of the grieving figure encapsulated the entire scene: I held the shot for thirty seconds before resting by the tripod and taking it all in for myself.

When filming around the site that day, I remember there were literally hundreds of pure white butterflies fluttering over and around the mass graves. While I am sure there is a biological explanation for the phenomenon, for me it spoke of the innocent souls who tragically lost their lives in the merciless massacre.

That was not the end of the trauma of that day, as we then went on to visit S21. S21 used to be a school, but was taken over by the Khmer Rouge and transformed into a prison where the prisoners were tortured to death. In fact, over the course of its existence S21 held over twenty thousand prisoners and less than one hundred survived. Some of the instruments of torture were still in evidence in some of the old classrooms, such as a wooden structure which clamped its victims, stretching them to death and steel bed frames where the prisoners were chained in a star position and beaten to death. On the floor, besides two of the beds, there were still bloodstains.

An hour or so after arriving and filming this museum of murder, we were introduced to an elderly man who was one of the few remaining survivors. We filmed a long interview with him, in which he told us of the horrors that he had experienced in that place. He had shared the small room which served as his cell with thirty other people. It was so cramped that when they lay chained on the floor, their shoulders would literally touch the person beside them. The physical condition of the prisoners varied depending on how long they had been imprisoned there. Whilst the newest arrivals were relatively fresh, most of the men were badly beaten and lay groaning in a pool of their own blood and excrement. Worst of all were those who were literally about to die: they may have been there for months and were slowly festering and decomposing.

The old man told us about the methods the guards used to torture and kill their victims, one of which was to pour cement powder down the prisoner's throat and in his nose, followed by a good douse of water. Slowly the cement would set, causing him to suffocate. The reason this old man had survived the death camp was thanks to his ability to paint. Pol Pott was obsessed with the desire to portray in history both his own face and the faces of his partners in crime in portraits as well as illustrating the achievements of his regime through paintings. This artist was granted privileges within the prison to work as a painter for his enemies. He wasn't stupid; he embraced the offer and his life was spared. Years later he turned his propaganda-style painting into pictorial accounts of what really happened. He told the story as it was, with no restraint. The paintings were graphic and disturbing, but served as an education to the new generation of what really went on. Interestingly, Binni asked Roger and I how old we thought the man was. We thought about it and said, 'Early seventies?' She told us he was in his late fifties ... the toll of those terrible times will be etched on his face for the remainder of his life.

While filming an interview, as a cameraman you have to keep a mental note of what has been discussed so that after the interview you can take shots of the relevant subjects to illustrate the point visually. On this occasion one of the points that I picked up on, was the fact that the cells in which many of the prisoners were held were the size of dog kennels. After the interview I told David that I would like to get a shot of those cells. He agreed. We climbed the stairs to the top floor, which turned out to be a warren of these cramped box cells. On my hands and knees I looked in a number of the cells and eventually found a chain secured to the floor at the far end of one of them. I crawled in and took a close-up shot of it. I then squeezed my body around and sat bent over as my head hit the roof. The view I had out of the one-metre-high and two-metre-long box was exactly the same as the prisoner would have had. As I pointed the lens out, pulled focus and opened up the iris, I asked David to swing the door shut as though he was going to lock me in, which he did. As I went to press the camera to record, the camera battery ran out. Thinking I would only be a few minutes, I hadn't brought a spare one up, so David said he would run down and get a fresh battery.

While David was gone, I sat in the cell, with my body hunched over and the camera on my lap. I was in near darkness. There were bloodstains on the floor. It was the first time I had ever smelt death, and the vile stench was nauseating. I could not help but wonder who the last occupant had been. He would have sat exactly where I was seated. What would have gone through his mind? How long did he live? How did he die? I shall never forget that experience. What must have been five minutes seemed like twenty! It was horrid. When David returned, I finished the shot, crawled out and left the building. I had had more than enough sadness and death for one day. We left for that night's hotel.

The next day we were going to head North for the penultimate location of our trip – Siem Reap and Angkor Watt. The bulk of our journey was to be by boat, up the Mekong River, but en route to the river we were to film Wrighty travelling on a train and a motorbike/van-like conversion carrying people, chickens and goats! The train journey was hilarious as Wrighty and I pushed David into allowing us to travel on the roof. This is often the locals' preferred method of riding on a train as it allows them to avoid the crush of the overpopulated carriages. Wrighty sat on the roof of one carriage and I sat on another with the camera on my shoulder. Suddenly he shouted over the noise of the train engine, 'I've always wanted to do this, but remember it's not big and it's not clever', and leapt from his carriage over the gap to mine! He practically fell on to me and we both skidded towards the edge of the sloped roof. Fortunately there was a tiny ledge on the edge, which I managed to grip with my foot. That was the only thing that saved us from falling from the moving train. We laughed together as we knew we had got away with it and it was a classic sequence for the programme. Eat your heart out James Bond ... here comes Wrighty.

The van/motorbike scenario was equally as funny and could also have easily ended in disaster. Undeterred by the train experience, again Wrighty and I opted for the roof of the trailer. Roger fed his curly umbilical-cord-like sound cable (that connects the sound mixer to the camera) up through the open window of the trailer, where he was sitting, to me on the roof. Wrighty sat on the edge of the roof with his legs hanging over the side, with a local on either side. I was on my knees in the centre of the roof with the camera on my shoulder, following his movements as he talked to the amused locals. We were driving up a dirt road through some fields heading towards the river. David and Binni followed in the Land Rover a good distance behind so as not to be in my shot. A few minutes into the journey, as I filmed, Roger, below us, said, 'Mungo, I need to stop to go to the toilet.' I could not hear exactly what he was saying as he was surrounded by farmyard animals and I had the wind blowing in my face, so I ignored it. A couple of minutes later I heard it again, though this time considerably louder, 'Mungo, I *need* to stop to go to the toilet!' I shouted back, 'Just hold on, Rog', we'll be there in ten minutes.' 'No,' he screamed, 'you don't understand, I *need* to go *now*!' With that the van/bike juddered to a halt and in a flash I saw Roger's bald head shoot from under me as he ran into a field towards a bush. Since the war Cambodia has had a huge problem with unexploded ordinances – mines – left buried beneath its soil – the week before we had even been filming with MAG (Mines Advisory Group), showing their teams painstakingly sweeping the land for mines and carrying out controlled explosions of the mines they found. The explosions were massive. From the first day of the shoot we were advised never under any circumstances to wander into a field, but always to stay on the road. Now, there was Roger, having had the 'one-minute warning' of diarrhoea, running full pelt across a field. Both Wrighty and I screamed, 'No, Rog, *no*!' But this man was on a mission! To our relief, but more importantly his, he made it to the bush, where the world fell out of his arse! As he, more gingerly this time, carefully stepped his way back to the vehicle, he found Wrighty and I in wheezes of laughter and floods of tears as we recounted the whole event. Eventually, after chewing on some Imodium, Roger came around to see the funny side of it with us.

Angkor Watt is as magnificent as all the guidebooks say. The towering, majestic temple after which the whole site is named is quite breathtaking. Then you realise that over the surrounding ten square kilometres there are hundreds more ancient temples of the Khmer people, mostly smaller, yet equally as impressive. Being a huge tourist pull, this vast site is well kept and well policed. In the past bounty hunters have stolen and ransacked some of the stones and statues, but now this precious place has become a World Heritage Site and is well protected. As the hundreds of temples are spread out – some over a mile apart – there are bicycles available for hire, which add to the fun of the visit. It was at one of the bicycle rental shops that we found 'Ice Cream Sandwiches' – literally a few scoops of ice cream in a baguette. Bizarre, but fun.

We spent two days scooting around the site, visiting and filming in a number of the temples, some of which were used as a set in the *Lara Croft – Tomb Raider* movies. While there we were hampered again by Wrighty's world celebrity status. In between takes and locations we would have to wait as he faithfully had his photograph taken and signed autographs, etc.

On the last night of our trip we decided to celebrate, so we went to the Raffles Hotel and treated ourselves to some cocktails – after a few long weeks on the road it was a welcome break and, needless to say, we had a lot of fun.

Vietnam

Following the success of the Cambodian shoot, I was invited back to work on a *Pilot Guide to Vietnam and Laos*. This time my presenter was an American called Zay and my director was called Lucy. I requested to take Richard Meredith as the sound recordist, as he had operated on a previous Amazon shoot and we had got on famously.

The aim of this shoot was to cover both Vietnam and Laos, back to back. We began our trip in the beautiful city of Hanoi in Northern Vietnam. We spent our first few days covering all that backpackers would need to know for their travels. We presented tips for the traveller and showed the best places to stay for the most competitive price as well as the points of interest that must be visited.

I loved Hanoi. There was an incredible atmosphere of excitement in the city and it was so elaborate in colour, smells and sounds. The roads were full of small dark-haired people hastily going about their business, some in old, battered cars, most on foot or on bicycles. The noise of the traffic was deafening, with its concoction of horns and screeching engines. In order to cross the road as a pedestrian in Hanoi, you literally have to take a leap of faith!

These days most cities around the world have a 'China Town', an area which has been taken over by Chinese immigrants – literally creating a little piece of China in that foreign city. As you walk through China Town, you are hit by some strange and exotic sights, such as ducks hanging by their necks in restaurant windows, cooked and battered yet fully intact. The little grocery shops sell an impressive variety of foreign-looking vegetables, accompanied by sauces and spices that are tangy and often hot – definitely not for the faint-hearted. No matter how much I love the vibrancy of these Chinese home-from-homes, it always proves to be just a poor reflection of the real thing. Granted, Hanoi is not China, but once you have experienced the intoxicating culture of Asia, there is nothing that quenches the thirst for the real deal.

One of our featured 'places of interest' in Hanoi remains with me. It was called 'Seeing Hands', which was founded by a man named Steven, who told us his remarkable story. Previously a moto-taxi driver, one sad day Steven was mugged and his moto-taxi stolen from him. The horrific part of his story was that the muggers had thrown acid into his face! Steven's burns were so severe that he lost both his eyes and due to the rudimentary plastic surgery where his eyes used to be there were now skin grafts. Now he was not only blind, but was very disfigured, looking as though he had never had any eyes. The positive side to this tragic story is that rather than dwelling on his misfortune, he had been taken under the wing of a charity that taught him to be a masseur. Through losing his sight, as with most blind people, his sense of touch had been heightened, which made him able to give the most incredible massages. Not only had Steven made a name for himself as a top-class masseur, but he had also set up a massage company called 'Seeing Hands', which only employed blind people to perform the massages. After spending a morning filming the Seeing Hands operation, we all stayed behind and had a massage ourselves. Over the years, due to filming with heavy equipment, I have had countless massages all over the world, but I can safely say that the one at Seeing Hands was among the very best!

Steven's story spoke to me of the character of the people of these South-East Asian countries. They have been through so many traumas, yet with resilience they get on with their lives and make the most of what they have, no matter how little that may be.

Over the last ten years Hollywood has focused its full attention on Vietnam, resulting in numerous blockbuster movies on the subject of the Vietnam War. As a result one of the main pulls for tourism in Vietnam these days is to see where the events took place and, therefore, it was inevitable that in our programme we would have to touch on the subject. It is tragic to see such a beautiful country, rich with history and culture, being reduced to a museum of the damage man can do to his fellow man. We had to include the war in some aspect of our film but, rather than take the obvious story-line, Lucy cleverly decided to cover it from a far less obvious angle. We were to follow Zay on a motorbike tour of the central highlands – the main war zone. Our tour was to be led by a guide named 'Mr Hahn – the man that can!'

With the dark features of the Vietnamese and sporting an enormous grin, Mr Hahn was not only fascinating to look at but proved to be a real character. During the late sixties and early seventies, he had fought on the side of the US during the conflict. With first-hand knowledge of the war zones Mr Hahn's motorbike tour would take the tourists to the sites where some of the most famous battles of the war occurred. Having been there when it happened, he could give a deep insight into the facts and tell the story like no other. He was immensely proud to have fought alongside the Americans and to our great amusement he had adopted some of the slang phrases used by the GIs. The reason this was so funny was because he spoke as if he was still in the sixties – spouting phrases such as 'Groovy Baby!' It was like being on the set of *Happy Days* or an Austin Powers' mmmmovie! He loved the fact that this tickled us and so we laughed along with him, rather than at him.

As we rode through the central highlands, our guide would stop and point out vast areas of scrubland that had been decimated by napalm or sprayed with Agent Orange (brutal chemical warfare). We visited numerous wrecked bridges and buildings that each had its own terribly sad story. One particular church that we stopped at was situated on a plateau surrounded by paddy fields, a few hundred metres away from a snaking main road. Mr Hahn recounted how he had been there when a large US military convoy had driven up that road. A few forward scouts had noticed a surprised group of Vietcong who, on seeing the huge US military convoy approach, had fled and taken refuge in the church building. Tipped off by the scouts of the Vietcongs' hide-out, the heavy artillery had slowly rolled to a halt. Like a giant laboriously turning his huge head, the enormous hulks of the armoured vehicles gradually turned their guns and drew aim on the church. With the flick of a switch the huge guns bombed the holy place to near oblivion. Mr Hahn told of the many men that had been killed in the merciless attack and, despite having sided with the US, he tried to explain how horrific it had been to witness so many men being obliterated before his eyes. We then walked down to the church ruin where we filmed an interview about the story. Halfway through the interview we had to stop for a few minutes as Mr Hahn became over-whelmed with emotion. The horror of that day will never leave his memory and seeing this brave man shed tears over his fallen countrymen drummed home to me the unimaginable amount of damage that war leaves in its wake. On the landscape you can observe broken bridges and demolished buildings, but on a closer look you can see the ugly, haunting scars of a broken people.

Calling these locations 'places of interest' for the tourists may sound somewhat gratuitous, but there are definite lessons that can be learned by visiting such sites. For me whether or not it is appropriate to visit such places depends on the spirit in which the visit is carried out. Mr Hahn makes a frugal living from sharing his past experiences, but he does so with taste and a sensitivity and respect that is most admirable.

A few days later we were invited to visit the last living 'Elephant King' in Vietnam. A few hours' drive out of the central highlands we arrived seemingly in the middle of nowhere. Leaving the vehicles at the side of the rural road, we were directed on foot down a dirt road that led to a stereotypical Vietnamese grass hut, which was built on stilts to avoid flooding by the neighbouring river. To get to the entrance to the hut you had to climb up a set of rickety steps.

As we were climbing the steps, we met the Elephant King himself. Despite being well into his seventies this dark-skinned, wiry old man had kept up traditional methods for taming wild elephants and magically transforming them into useful workhorses. Over the years he had 'broken' hundreds of the magnificent beasts, making them a great labour-saving resource for the local villagers.

Amazingly for us, a rogue elephant had very recently been caught after rampaging and killing its *mahout* (elephant driver/rider). The Elephant King had been contacted and asked to tend to the rebellious beast, to see if it could be tamed for the second time. Since it was not a common occurrence, this was a stroke of luck for us! The Elephant King invited us to join him as he travelled to the neighbouring village to carry out the ancient ceremony on the animal.

On arrival at the village we saw two enormous elephants tied with thick ropes to a sizeable tree trunk. The animals were obviously agitated and were not happy about being restricted in this way. I asked Mr Hahn, who was translating for the King, which elephant was the offender. He pointed to the large one which was pacing up and down, head nodding and muscles twitching. I wanted to get some establishing shots before the ceremony began, so Richard and I carefully skirted around the elephants taking shots of the scene.

Soon after this Lucy came bounding over to tell me that the ceremony was about to begin. I left the tripod where it was and went in with the camera hand-held. The brief ceremony involved the King sacrificing a chicken and throwing its blood onto the elephant's forehead. For the next three or four minutes he spat on the beast and chanted in an unrecognisable tongue. After a few more spits and shouts, that was it ... job done! It was time to find out if the ceremony had worked. Had the two-ton lump of muscle been successfully tamed? 'Let's not wait to find out!' I said to the others, who nodded and we all hurried to pick up our kit and get out of there! The thing that amused me no end was that as we scurried around, keeping a sharp eye on the poor elephant, who now stood brooding and humiliated, covered in chicken blood and spit, the King himself was hurriedly getting himself out of there. He was off like a shot and there was obviously no way he was going to stick around to test the result.

Having said a hurried goodbye and thankyou, we returned to the King's house where we found him sitting on his porch, chortling away as he sipped on his lethal rice wine through a straw. He was no fool. We sat and laughed with the old man and purely out of obligation we sampled some of his special brew (which incidentally he swore was a homeopathic form of Viagra!). Feeling a little groggy after the vile liquid, we were told that the King wished to show us what truly tamed elephants were like. He led us down to the nearby riverbank, where he invited me, with my camera, to ride with him on his elephant. Never one to pass up a unique opportunity like that, I readily agreed and watched as the old man, despite being half drunk, carefully and gracefully took control of the huge elephant. The hulking beast had no quarrel with the King and without hesitating humbly knelt down. Following instructions I carefully straddled the chair, which was secured to the elephant's back by means of thick straps fastened around its belly, and onto its mammoth back, sat down in tandem with the King. Once on board, with a word of command and a subtle kick, the elephant rolled up onto its feet and we were off. He had been telling us earlier about the fact that elephants are so strong they are able to act as a bulldozer. To illustrate this we approached a medium-sized tree and with a 'cry' of command the elephant dipped his head and pressed it against the tree trunk. As the King continued to 'whoop' and 'cry' the elephant rocked a bit, finding its footing, and then with an enormous push, it seemingly effortlessly pushed the entire tree over onto the ground. He then manoeuvred the animal around and gave more orders and kicks. Obediently the elephant wrapped its trunk around the tree and slowly walked back-wards, in one movement tearing the entire tree out of the ground, roots and all! It was a magnificent display of strength and my heart was pounding with excitement as I filmed. Unfortunately I was concentrating so hard on filming an over-the-shoulder shot from behind the King that I didn't see the enormous branch of a neighbouring tree directly in front of us. Before I could reason why, the King had ducked out of my shot. 'Thwack!' – the branch hit my camera with an almighty thud and it knocked me right over onto my back. Thankfully I managed to keep hold of the camera and just stay on the elephant's back, so all I lost was some pride – much to the amusement of the Elephant King who proceeded to chuckle loudly all the way home.

We often bump into the most extraordinary people along the way on such shoots and this one was no exception. While going up to a local festival in Northern Vietnam we shared a hostel with Graham, a teacher from the UK who, after an argument with his girlfriend, had packed a bag, thrown it onto the back of his motorbike and driven off. Almost three years had passed since that day and Graham was still going. Since our story was all about following Zay on his motorbike tour of Vietnam, Graham's advice to travellers was incredibly valuable. I remember his greatest word of advice was to take it slowly as, particularly in countries like Vietnam, you never know what is going to be in the road around the next corner – a chicken, pig, cow or even an elephant!

After our quick tour through Vietnam we said goodbye to our fixers and boarded a small plane to Laos.

Laos

Arriving in Vientiane, the capital of Laos, I was mortified to find out that we had just missed Kylie Minogue who had been holidaying there. 'Like ships in the night,' I thought to myself. 'One day our paths will meet and we'll live happily ever after!' Not only was I distraught at missing Kylie, but I was also very surprised to realise that hardly anybody knew about Laos, let alone visited the place.

Laos is the forgotten country of South-East Asia. Mountainous and landlocked, it is the size of England but has a population of just five and a half million. Despite being one of the least-densely populated countries in the world, it is one of the most ethnically diverse with over sixty different tribal groups. It may be one of the poorest nations on the earth, but in culture it has to be one of the richest! There was so much to show about this untouched country that no one seemed to know about. We started by flying up to Xam Neua.

We boarded a small ten-seater plane for the flight up to the mountain ranges of North-East Laos. The old plane was so basic that the pilots had to fly without the luxury of radar or GPS, using purely their experience and knowledge to get us to our destination safely. I have flown all over the world in numerous types of aircraft, but this trip was the closest I have ever come to crashing!

I was seated next to Sascha (Producer) who would admit herself that she is a terrible flier, but I would go further than that and say she suffers in fact from a serious phobia of flying! The question did cross my mind as to why she was on a shoot in which she would be required to make close to fifteen flights! As we took off she tensed up ... nothing that unusual there. Then, an hour or so into the flight, we hit some cloud turbulence, causing our little aircraft to be thrown around like someone being given the bumps on their thirtieth birthday. Noticing the panic on Sascha's face, I quietly said to her, 'It's fine, Sascha, this happens all the time ... you've got nothing to worry about.' She smiled sweetly at me and I believe took genuine comfort in the fact that someone like me who was such an experienced flier was completely unflustered. However, about thirty seconds after I had sworn that all was fine, the aircraft dipped its nose and we began to drop out of the sky like a stone! Despite having left my stomach one thousand feet above us, I deliberately kept a calm expression on my face. With Sascha now squealing in horror as we kept charging head first towards the earth, I turned to her and forced a smile, which was actually a grimace. She couldn't smile back. At this point the dive we were in was so severe that the plane began to whistle like a bomb. I pushed myself back into my chair and braced myself for what I hoped would be quick (smashing into the mountainside). We've probably all heard of people in near-death situations who speak about having experienced a moment of calm as the events took place – I can't say I experienced anything like that: all I remember is wondering, since the place was so remote, how long it would be before my family found out that I had died. Probably a few weeks, I thought. Death doesn't scare me: it's more the dying that unnerves me. At least this would be quick. It was a terrifying number of seconds before the plane pulled out of the dive and returned to a horizontal position again. All the passengers without exception were panting for breath, having not dared to breathe for the duration of the dive. Zay turned around and caught my eye as if to say, 'We made it!' I responded by lifting my eyebrows and subtly nodding toward Sascha. He winced. Sascha was in pieces: she was crying and looked absolutely distraught. I tried to comfort her by telling her that we were nearly there and she didn't need to worry any more. She looked at me blankly with utter disbelief.

Ten minutes later we were safely on the ground. I asked the grounds man (well, grass cutter on the overgrown mountain runway) why we had gone into the steep dive. Had there been a problem with the plane?

'Oh no,' he replied, 'they would have been in thick cloud and then, in a break of blue sky, realised they were going to overshoot the landing spot, and so dived to lose altitude.'

'Oh,' I replied, 'that was lucky!'

'Luckier than the people on the plane that crashed two weeks ago – they all died,' he said, chuckling to himself. As he walked off to go about his duties, I told the boys never to tell Sascha what we'd just heard!

We had (safely) arrived in Xam Neua, which is built on a high plateau within the mountains of the Laos Golden Triangle. Still a communist stronghold, this city is relatively well organised and well built, especially considering its geographical position. One less attractive feature, however, is the propaganda which is blasted out from the loud speakers that adorn every street corner and from which there is no escape. Another is the rats! Being extremely poor, this city has become known as the world's rat capital. They breed them, live alongside them and even eat them! At first we thought that this was just a novelty tourist label, but soon found out that no, it was literally the case!

The guest house where we spent our first few nights consisted of several little rooms each with a thatched roof. At night these roofs came to life! While you attempted to sleep, the noise of thousands of rats moving around sounded like a herd of stampeding ponies! It was amazing. Every night my soap was completely eaten up and items in the room would be moved around. I noticed on the first night that my toothpaste had been tampered with and my toothbrush looked as though it had been disturbed. Having thoroughly washed it, I made a point of zipping it up in my hanging wash bag from then on – interestingly, whenever travelling I still go through this routine to this day! Apart from finding hundreds of rat droppings all over your room in the morning, it was quite rare ever actually to see one of the creatures – a fact I was very glad about when I woke up on the last morning to find that there were bite marks in my pillow!

After a few days in the city we headed by road further north to Vieng Xai. Between 1964 and 1973, as part of their struggle against the Vietnamese, the US had raged a secret war on the communists. With their stated aim to 'Bomb the enemy back to the dark ages', they attempted to cut off the 'Ho Chi Minh Trail'. Since most of it ran through Laos, this small country became the most heavily bombed country in the history of warfare. In the space of nine years more than two million tons of ordinance were dropped upon the Lao people – more bombs than were dropped during the whole of the Second World War!

We were to be the first film crew to be allowed into a large complex of over eight hundred caves which had been used as the nerve centre for the communists' campaign against the Americans – for many years a top military secret. What we saw at the caves and the stories we heard about them were unbelievable.

For nine years Lao people, seeking safety from constant bombing by the Americans, had lived in these caves, working in the paddy fields in the dark of night and sleeping in the safety of the caves by day. They literally became nocturnal. One survivor of those hard times whom we interviewed said, 'It was like lightning and thunder every night although it rained bombs!' Amazingly, it was this nocturnal way of life that was the key to their survival. They transformed over eight hundred caves into housing, banks, schools, hotels, hospitals and even factories. The resilience of these people was outstanding.

I later heard from military sources that another reason why the bombing over Laos was so severe was because sometimes the US jet fighters flying over the Central Highlands of Vietnam couldn't drop their ordinance, so rather than risk landing with the bombs attached to their planes, they would divert over Laos and indiscriminately offload their deadly cargo. Nine years of terror and suffering engulfed the Lao people. Like Cambodia Laos is still littered with buried unexploded mines and bombs, which continue to ravage the people.

Leaving the sad stories of Vieng Xai we continued to head north, travelling by boat up the mighty Mekong River, to reach the home of the Akka people. We boarded our boat at Luang Prabang, which was once home to the Lao royal family and is now a World Heritage Site due its magnificent colonial French architecture and Buddhist temples. This city is one of my favourite places in Laos. It was here that I came to realise that one of the greatest legacies I think the French have left their colonies is their bread-making skills – in Northern Laos you can eat some of the best croissants in the world!

Having negotiated the Mekong, we then continued up the Namtha River, this time in smaller long-tail boats. Eventually we arrived at Luang Namtha where we were told by Lucy and Sascha that there was now a three- to four-hour walk up a mountain to the Akka village. Noticing that they were both wearing plimsoll trainers, I enquired what the terrain was likely to be. They said it would be a long but relatively easy walk and that trainers would be fine. Richard and I opted for our sturdy walking boots, just in case – thank God we did. As we would be filming at different stages of our ascent, I decided to carry the camera in the Portabrace rucksack on my back, with the tripod straddled across my shoulders. While practical, this was absolutely exhausting ... especially as the walk turned out to be a serious climb which ended up taking almost eight hours! The terrain was wet and slippery, and at times the bridge crossings (small tree trunks laid over sheer, deep gullies) were extremely dangerous. I told Richard that we should take it easy as if any of us slipped, fell and broke a leg, we would be in serious trouble. We were in the middle of nowhere with very little communication to the outside world.

With our heads down concentrating on every step we trudged on until eventually we arrived at the top of the mountain. Despite our exhaustion we were all stunned by the view that awaited us. As we walked around the final corner of the track, we looked out over a village that seemed to be floating in the clouds. We all stood in a group and gawped in awe at what we saw, before making the final push and traversing down into the village.

The village was literally like the land that time forgot. The people were tiny in stature (making Zay and I seem like giants!) and the young women were dressed in incredibly elaborate tribal clothing with brightly coloured head dresses and stark pink circles painted on their cheeks, resembling a Victorian toy doll. The Akka were incredibly warm with their welcome and immediately invited us to take part in one of their traditions ... being massaged! Since there is no other way of getting to the village apart from the long, laborious climb, whoever arrives is in a state of physical exhaustion and that is how the tradition of offering a massage started. The young Akka girls clothed in their traditional dress take turns to stand on you, stretch you and rub your tired muscles. It was simply bliss. We all found it fascinating listening to their strange language as they giggled and chatted away – it sounded like a form of Elfin from *The Lord of the Rings*.

That first night we desperately needed some time to recover
from the climb, so we literally crashed on the wooden floor of
one of the Akka huts on stilts, where thin mats had been laid
out as our beds. We were so tired and our leg muscles were so
achy that we could barely unravel our sleeping bags and climb
into them. One by one we all started to pass out.

In the morning we were told a festival was being thrown to
celebrate the marriage of two young people in the village. All
day preparations were made: we filmed head dresses being
polished up, songs being practised and even a special hut being
built especially for the consummation of the marriage. On
the menu was chicken, pork and *dog*! We then witnessed the
slaughter of the animals and I filmed the entire process, from
them walking around minding their own business, to being
held down, throat cut, skinned and cooked. Never one to be
squeamish it really didn't bother me, that was until they cut off
the dog's penis and peeled it like a banana! I later found out
that dog's penis is considered a delicacy by the Akka who also
believe it has the effect of an aphrodisiac!

As the sun went down the music and singing started. By
firelight I filmed the marriage ceremony and then Zay eating at
the festival table. We all tried dog, just to say we had and,
guess what, it tasted like chicken ... just more bitter. We then
tucked into the local rice wine, which was lethal considering
we were running on empty stomachs and we weren't going to
eat a great deal of the dog!

Eventually Lucy called 'Wrap' for the evening's filming and
we all headed straight for our beds. As we lay slightly drunk in
our sleeping bags, it gradually dawned on us that we weren't
going to get a wink of sleep until the Akka men, who were

having the time of their life outside, called it a day. Then Zay came up with a novel game which he called 'Caterpillar Jumping'. He got us all to lie in a line with our sleeping bags tucked up to our necks while one of us would roll down the line and everyone had to jump over him or her ... it was hilarious! Have you ever had one of those moments in life where you stop, pinch yourself and think: can I really be here doing what I'm doing? That was exactly one of those moments: playing Caterpillar Jumping in a wooden hut in a village above the clouds up a mountain in Northern Laos!

The next morning somewhat bleary-eyed, we packed our bags and film equipment, ready to head back down the mountain. Sascha came up trumps and pulled a packet of porridge from her rucksack, saved for such an occasion as this ... perfect. On top of that, the girls had arranged for a few of the local men to help carry our kit back down the mountain for us. To my amusement the guy who was going to carry my rucksack was only just as tall as the bag itself – literally! I asked him, 'Are you going to be alright, mate?' He just nodded and gave me the thumbs-up and a smile. 'OK,' I thought, 'let's see just how long you last!' With that thought, he was gone. He'd almost literally sprinted off. I burst into laughter and told Richard that I was going to try to run down with him. Off I went with the much-lighter camera on my back. That two- or three-hour journey down the mountain was one of the most memorable times of all my travelling experiences.

As I chased my little friend I was taking huge paces and every time I hit some wet mud, I would fall over onto my arse. While my Akka companion was only wearing flip-flops and was having no problem in the mud, I was wearing some state-of-the-art walking boots and I was all over the place. What was his secret, I thought? Just experience? After I slipped and fell a few more times, the Akka man stopped, turned to me and motioned with his hands that I should take small, pitter-pattering steps. We couldn't talk, as we didn't speak the same language, but through sounds, hand signals and facial expressions we were practically having a conversation. As we continued to run, I adopted his pitter-patter method and I didn't fall over at all. Looking back, the theory behind it is the same as the new Automatic Braking System, 'ABS', which effectively pumps the brakes of a car to prevent skidding. That was exactly how it was working for me. We were practically running now, rapidly descending the steep edges that had so hampered us on the way up. We were now miles ahead of the others who were walking carefully behind.

A few hundred feet further down the mountain he stopped me again. This time he held his ear and gently pushed it forward ... he wanted me to listen. I could hear an unusual bird call coming from somewhere far away in the canopy below us. He put his finger in the air as he registered that I heard it. He then cupped his hands together and blew through his fingers, perfectly mimicking the bird call. I broke into a smile and raised my thumbs in approval. Gesturing first that as he made the call, the bird would come to him, he then acted out drawing back an arrow in his bow, releasing it and shooting the bird. That was it: he was a hunter. It was one of those magical moments – being halfway up a deserted mountain in a very remote country with a perfect stranger who was not only looking after me but was also teaching me. I felt honoured to have spent that precious time with him. I'll never know his name and it's highly likely that I'll never see him again, but one thing's for sure: I'll never forget it and I sincerely hope that he won't either.

Zay's closing piece to camera said it all: 'Mention Laos and you may never have heard of it. Research Laos and you'll read about war and poverty. But come to Laos and you'll discover a beautiful countryside, full of happy people who are simply proud to be Lao.'

7

Down the Amazon – Without a Paddle!

One day whilst I was at home in London I got a call from Jim at Pilot Productions asking if I was willing to shoot for them on a new series called *Treks In A Wild World*. Having a history with Pilot (who produced the Lonely Planet TV series) I knew all too well that the jobs they offered would provide the perfect opportunity for my favourite extreme travel. I asked Jim where they were going this time. He replied with a long list of countries. As he rattled off the list I listened for a location that I had not yet visited, somewhere that I would not only love to go to but would also look good on my CV. The location that immediately caught my attention was 'The Amazon'.

A month or so later, I was sitting on a plane heading to Brazil. Joining me on this adventure was Ian (Director), Richard (Sound Recordist), Ollie (Assistant) and Aisles (Presenter).

Ian and I had met briefly once before, Ollie was on staff at
Pilot, and I had met Richard for the first time at the airport.
My relationship with Aisles was a little more complex. Pilot
pride themselves (and rightfully so) on their new, unheard-of
presenters. Partly, I think, because they are young, fresh and
enthusiastic, but also because they are cheap! Not only was this
Aisles' first major presenting break, but it was her first trip
outside the UK apart from a brief trip to the USA. The Amazon
was going to be a challenge for those of us who had travelled
extensively, and I had my concerns on how well she would cope.
On top of this, she had recently been dating my flatmate Danny
and their romance had ended just before our trip!

On our arrival into Rio, we had a nightmare getting our
fifteen or so equipment cases through Customs. Despite the
Brazilian Embassy in London handwriting a note in my
passport, instructing them to let us through unhindered, it
was proving to be just a little more complicated. We sat in
the Customs Hall for over three hours, until finally the Chief
Customs Officer readily accepted a cash bribe and, with a
smile on his face, finally stamped our carnet papers! Relieved,
yet exasperated, we were able to carry on with our journey.

For the final leg of our trip we had to transfer onto a light
aircraft for the relatively short flight up to Manaus, a small
city in the North-East corner of Brazil, built on the banks of
the River Amazon. Our journey from London to Manaus had
been epic and we were all shattered! We desperately needed to
rest and it was already getting late. We were spending our first
night in a small and basic hotel in the centre of the city. The
heat was unbearable and the air was heavy with humidity. We
piled our cases into a room on the top floor that would be

locked overnight and then we retreated to our rooms for a cold shower and a well-deserved rest. Later that evening we found a pizza bar where we ate and went through the schedule for the coming weeks.

Early the next morning we loaded up a van with all our kit and headed down to the riverside where we caught a ferry to our next destination – a floating hotel a few hours further down the river. On this journey I pulled out my camera and we began shooting. The first shoot is always an interesting one, as most of the team have never previously worked together, so each has to find his/her own way of doing things. The more experienced the crew, the quicker this process is. This time we all gelled together within the first few minutes ... a good sense of humour being the key! As we steadily floated off down the Amazon River we filmed, sat, talked and laughed!

The Ariau Amazon Towers Hotel is truly amazing. The only access to the hotel is by boat, which carries the hotel's guests along the main artery of the river before turning down a watery side-road. As you approach the large wooden structure you feel as if you are entering a Hollywood studio set. The main building is like an over-sized tree house, which is linked by a web of rope bridges and walkways seventy feet above the ground to the guest accommodation. It's exactly the kind of place you would expect Tarzan to live in, had he lived to see the year 2000! There is a great circular dining room made of polished tropical woods and the bar is like an eagle's nest. The honeymoon suite is built 110 feet up a mahogany tree! Everywhere you look there are monkeys scampering all over the place and the raucous sound of macaws and parrots fills the air.

Although our rooms were as crude as those you would expect to find in a tree house, they were clean and relatively comfortable. To our great amusement we found an open-sided games room, with the river lapping below. There we could play table tennis and drink cold beers. As with nearly all remote shoots, after sun-down there isn't a great deal to do, so needless to say it became a frequent haunt.

After an hour or so to settle in, unpack the camera equipment and get ourselves together, we met Samuel who was to be our guide for the next few days. Samuel was a 'jungle boy', by which I mean that he had grown up in the Amazon jungle. He was small in stature, though solid in build and had a friendly face with a warm, welcoming smile. Soon after welcoming us he led us down to the main jetty where a long-tail riverboat was waiting for us. We hopped in and sped off down vast waterways to our designated 'places of interest'. The feeling of zooming down the river on this long, narrow boat was so exhilarating that we all whooped and smiled at each other as we went. After our short introductory boat trip it was back to Ariau for supper, table tennis and bed.

The next few days were spent filming in various locations in the surrounding area. On one of the days we re-housed a sloth from one island to another, apparently to improve its chance of survival. As I stood filming the sloth, which was latched onto a branch curving down in a great arch from the top of a tall tree, I wondered how Samuel would physically get to it at such a height. Maybe this was where he would do his 'jungle boy' circus act and shin barefooted up the trunk? But no, to our surprise, he pulled on the end of the branch and catapulted the sloth into thin air! It honestly looked like a scene from

The Simpsons! We were all stunned into silence and stood in disbelief – not knowing whether the poor air-borne sloth would have survived. Samuel skipped through the bushes, bent over and picked the animal up. It was hard to know whether the sloth was dazed or not as they live their entire lives in a comatose state! With an almost audible sigh of relief, the test pilot had survived the flight and the crowd burst into cheers and laughter ... it was one of the funniest things I had ever seen.

The only way of transporting the heroic beast was to take it with us on the long-tail boat. Since I was already sitting in the boat, Samuel laid the sloth in the foot-well area in front of me and then climbed into the rear of the boat. I looked at the sloth, then turned around and looked at Samuel ... was he serious? What if it became angry? Samuel's mouth burst into a huge white smile and, before anything could be said, we were off!

A few minutes into the journey, as the speeding boat bounced over the choppy water, the sloth started to stir. It was surprisingly large (about the size of a medium-sized dog), and if you looked closely, you could see that its matted fur was literally crawling with life. Samuel told us that because they move so slowly, sloths are home to thousands of insects, offering them free, centrally heated lodging. I spread my feet out to the sides of the boat in order to give the animal room to stretch – hoping that it wouldn't touch me with its infested skin. But, to my horror, it slowly attached its large clawed paws to the side of the boat and began to lift itself up, obviously intent on getting out! Aisles, seated behind me, saw what was happening and squealed. 'Samuel!' I cried out,

'It's trying to get out!' However, the noise of the engine was so deafening that my cry for help went unnoticed. *'Samuel!'* I screamed again, as the sloth now moved its leg further up the side of the boat and was literally about to tip over into the water! 'Pick him up, Mungo,' shouted Samuel calmly from behind me. 'What? … Pick him up? … How?' I mumbled to myself as I stood up very unsteadily and stretched my hands out over the sloth, not knowing where to grab him. I quickly glanced back at Samuel who motioned with his hands to hold out two fingers and let the animal hook them with its claws. There was no time to stop to think or else the sloth would have experienced air and sea in one day – enough adventure for anyone, let alone a sedentary sloth! I hooked my two index fingers under its claws and pulled its long arms up into the air. It was like holding a toddler's hands up as you teach them to walk, although this was one heavy, grubby toddler! As the boat skimmed its way across the Amazon River, I rocked back onto my wooden bench-seat, still holding onto my new friend. I held him for another ten minutes until we reached land, where Samuel took over and expertly placed him into the tree canopy – releasing him into his new home.

Later that day we realised that we had been filming for eight hours without stopping. By now we were getting tired and hungry, so I asked Ian (Director) what he planned for us to do for lunch. 'Ah, well, I thought we'd get into the spirit of things and get Samuel to source us some food from the jungle!' I could have cried. Ask any of my colleagues and they will confirm that I am like a bear with a sore head when I'm hungry. The analogy I like to use is that of a car which, when it runs out of petrol, judders … then stops! That's what I'm like.

Seeing the look on my face, Ian then asked Samuel if we could stop for lunch. 'Sure, we'll drive the boat under the tree canopy over there,' he said as he pointed to a shaded area of water under the low-hanging trees. Our boat driver tied the craft to a tree trunk that disappeared into the murky depths. Then from under a tarpaulin he dragged out a small cool box. My mouth watered with the thought of a chunky filled roll, but to my disgust he pulled out a section of cow's tongue! My heart sank. This wasn't exactly what I had in mind. As I sighed in desperation he reached into the side pocket of his shorts and pulled out a rolled-up length of fishing tackle. Samuel then piped up and said that this was the perfect spot to fish for black piranha! We were each handed a length of tackle, a hook and a slice of tongue. Tying one end of the tackle to our fingers we dipped the other end, with the tongue hooked onto it, over the side of the boat and into the water. Despite feeling weak with hunger, I have to admit that I loved the idea of fishing for our piranha lunch with hand lines ... presuming that it would be good fun, the fish would be easy to catch and would be the size of a small whale! Fun? It was. Easy? It wasn't too bad: we caught about five fish each in about thirty minutes. Large? Unfortunately not! They were not much bigger than sardines. Samuel demonstrated how vicious their bite could be by catching one, holding it firmly in his hand and brushing a rubbery leaf against its lip. Like a hole punch, its mouth opened and closed in the blink of an eye – leaving a perfect cut-out of its razor-sharp mouth.

He then went on to explain to us that the piranha has had bad press. People have been led to believe that a school of piranha fish could strip the carcass of a cow of its flesh within a matter of seconds, leaving behind a clean skeleton. While apparently piranha have been known to feed in such frenzy, this only occurs when there is a large school that is cornered and close to starvation, for example in a pool of water that is cut off from the source and is drying up. It seems the ferociousness of their feeding has been dramatically exaggerated by Hollywood. I really was genuinely interested in the lesson being given, though I have to admit that at that moment all I could think about was taking part in my own feeding frenzy!

When we had caught our fish, we made our way to shore, moored up the boat and Samuel lit a fire. I sat like a dog transfixed by a juicy bone, watching my fish cook and drooling over the smell of fresh fish on a wood fire. When we had eaten our catch, before I could blurt out that I could eat another seventy of the little swimmers, we were joined by the driver of the boat who came over with a couple of prepared chickens and some bread. I could have kissed him! The joke was on me ... lunch was prepared!

The Amazon is a mecca for all wildlife enthusiasts. Since it was crucial that we portrayed this fact effectively in our programme, I was required to film as wide a variety of animal life as possible. As you can imagine, some animals are easier to film than others. For example: trying to film the Amazon's famous pink dolphins is easier said than done. Sitting on a moving boat you have no idea where to point your lens as you have no way of knowing where they will pop up for breath next! Birds are just as tricky since they are either twisting and turning in flight or incredibly shy of humans, therefore requiring a long lens to photograph them. Wild monkeys are particularly skilled at being elusive to the camera lens, due to their playfulness and rapid movement. That is, of course, if they can be bothered to turn up at all!

In the third week of our trip we travelled deeper down river to find a particular point of interest: miniature marmosets. Standing at only three inches when fully grown, this is the smallest species of monkeys in the world and is incredibly rare. Through some clever networking Ian had found an eccentric Belgian conservationist who had been living in Manaus and studying the miniature marmosets for a number of years. He took us, by boat, to one of the most remote places I have ever been in all my years of travelling – a tiny village located on the banks of the Amazon, halfway down its length. Due to the remoteness of the location and our tight schedule, we only had two full days there, so there was no time to waste. First we set up camp, which was as basic as it comes and consisted of suspending our hammocks between two tree trunks. Then, as directed by the local villagers who claimed to see the rare miniature marmosets on an almost daily basis, we set up a hide. I swopped the wide-angle lens on the camera for a long lens (the monkeys' tiny size was going to stretch the capabilities of my equipment to the maximum), and then Ian and I climbed into the hide where we settled, sat and waited.

Waiting in a hide is an odd experience as you go through different phases. For the first hour or so you are alert and full of anticipation, but after a while you slowly begin to lose concentration. Hours in, you begin to grow sleepy, bored and, without even realising it, you start to daydream. Ian and I went through both these phases, first conversing in whispers about such topics as life at home, TV, religion and politics and then lapsing into daydreaming. After several hours of sitting and waiting we decided to take shifts. Ian would go and talk with the villagers to try to develop pieces-to-camera we could film with Aisles, etc. When he eventually came back I took a break.

I love to take photographs of the people I meet in all the different circumstances that I experience and countries that I travel to and this trip was no exception. The people in this village were beautiful, with big brown eyes, bronzed skin and dark, straight hair. The children were particularly stunning, though even at their young age they were already beginning to show the physical strain of years of living in such a remote environment. Through an interpreter I asked if the chief would allow me to take a photograph of his son and daughter. With a huge smile which revealed his broken teeth, he agreed, called them over and introduced me to them. I shall never forget the little girl's name as she was called 'Diana'. He explained to me that she was named after 'Princess Diana'. It was phenomenal to think that Diana's fame was so widespread that even a child in the middle of the Amazon Jungle was named after her! Yet, it also saddens me to think that the world has grown to be such a small place that you can't go to the very ends of it without finding a piece of rubbish with a Coke logo on it!

For two whole days Ian and I sat in the hide without seeing or filming a single thing! It was frustrating, but wild animals don't play to schedule or to a script. We did end up getting some footage of the miniature marmosets, but that entailed me standing in a cage with several of them back in Manaus. Once cleverly edited the viewer would never know the difference – that unfortunately is the harsh reality of TV! At least we tried!

On our last day, by now back at the Ariau Amazon Towers, we filmed late into the evening as Samuel took us on a tarantula hunt. At dusk, after covering up with long-legged trousers and long-sleeved tops, we applied plenty of mosquito spray before departing from the jetty of the hotel and heading towards a remote corner of the jungle where the boat was pulled up in a thin muddy gully and left tethered to a stump. Richard and I rigged the camera and sound kit with torches, checked our batteries, replenished our tape stock and mounted our water supplies before we all trekked off into the jungle to see what we could find! Or what could find us!

Anyone who has visited a jungle will know that once the sun goes down and darkness falls, it becomes a whole different world. A legion of hidden creatures crawl out from under stones or out of their holes, hides and nests. It is in the darkness that nocturnal species play, hunt and go about their business. Together, the rubbing of legs, the buzz of wings and the croak of throats compose a cacophony of sound that must be heard to be believed!

As our boots crunched through the pitch-black under-growth, we shone our torches in 180 degree sweeps – partly looking for tarantulas and partly to see where on earth we were going! In this dark world I had the added problem of the bright viewfinder of the camera shining in my right eye. It is amazing how the human eye can adjust and cope in varying light conditions, but it does take time to adjust. If you are in darkness, as long there is a tiny amount of light (such as moonlight) your eye compensates and gives you a degree of vision (often surprisingly good), which we call 'night vision'. However, if the darkness is polluted by bright light, this brightness will cancel out one's night vision, leaving you temporarily blind.

Before too long we spotted our first mammoth spider, which was motionless and disturbingly well camouflaged against the bark of a palm tree. It was a beauty – literally the size of a man's hand! After an initial squeal of terror, Aisles managed to compose herself and whisper a few questions about the spider to Samuel. I held my breath and concentrated while filming to reduce the movement of the camera. When the spotlight from a torch swept off the spider as the interview finished, the creature unnervingly disappeared back into the black of night. We moved on, crunching again through whatever lay underfoot and sweating profusely in the heat, our torches swinging like wartime searchlights around the jungle undergrowth. Having already found two or three more large spiders on the trees, Samuel who was leading up front stopped dead in his tracks. As we followed suit, Richard and I walked into one another with a bump and a groan. Samuel called me forward so that I could film what he had spotted: a Black Widow Tarantula. It was sitting on the ground by the entrance of a hole, like a hairy black glove that someone had discarded during the day. As I focused in on the beast, Samuel silently crept forward, gingerly pointing his large knife towards it. 'Watch this,' he said. 'Are you ready, Mungo?' 'Yep,' I replied, holding my breath to keep the shot steady. With a flash he lunged the tip of his knife over the entrance of the hole, trying to beat the spider to it, but it was gone – it had bolted down the hole before Samuel could even get near to it! A perfect demonstration of the creature's speed and reflexes!

After an hour or so of trudging around this sweltering, dark, eerie world, we agreed that we had enough footage of the spiders. The only bit of filming remaining was a closing piece-to-camera from Aisles. We decided to film this back by the boat, so I took the camera off my shoulder and carried it by my side for the trek back. As we walked Richard and I discussed our yearning for a cold beer, while Ian and Aisles went through her lines for the closing link. Eventually we found the gully and thankfully the boat was still there. We lightened our load by stowing some of our bags in the boat and then I hauled the camera back onto my shoulder for the last time.

The first few takes Aisles fluffed her lines. That was fine. But then it continued . . . take five, take six, seven, eight, nine! (This is not to blame Aisles – she was an inexperienced presenter at the time and the conditions we were in would have made even Kate Adie fluff at least a few times!) It was hot, and I was sweating from every orifice God gave me! It must have been the tenth attempt, and this time she was getting it right . . . As she spoke I was willing her on . . . But then something buzzed around my ear . . . I ignored it. Come on, Aisles . . . come on! She was doing well and I decided that, whatever happened, I would keep filming . . . Just as I was thinking that to myself, whatever had been buzzing around my ear flew straight into it! Despite a little jolt of shock, I kept still and kept filming . . . Come on, Aisles. Yes! She finished. I threw down the camera and gave a girlie squeal at the same time as tilting my head and banging my ear! Letting out a number of expletives I danced around like a Red Indian having just made a kill.

No matter what I did, it wouldn't come out! By now I was feeling so exhausted and the thought of cold drops dripping down the side of a glass of beer was seeming so attractive that I tamely resumed my seat on board the boat and we headed into the black of the night. The taste of beer was never sweeter and after necking a few I was past caring about anything anymore, let alone the insect still in my ear, so I went to bed.

The following morning the little critter was still there and to my dismay it was doing a rendition of Mr Bojangles! That evening, unable to stand it any longer, I went to see the hotel's nurse and she placed a few drops of warm olive oil into my ear, which successfully drowned it. I thought that was too easy, and I was right. In a matter of hours, as we were making our way to the airport, without any warning I projectile-vomited a bright pink liquid. It was so bizarre that at the same time as I was being violently sick, I was half-laughing! After that, almost on the stroke of every subsequent thirty minutes, I would have gastric convulsions and then throw up – until inevitably there was nothing left in my stomach to come up! At the airport I worked out that if I was the last person on the plane, then I would have enough time for the plane to take off, for it to settle into the flight and for the seatbelt signs to be taken off before I would need to get to the toilet to throw up again. So I sat by the departure gate until they were about to shut the doors, then ran to the toilet, made myself sick and then ran straight onto the plane, knowing I had thirty minutes … Once in my seat, although feeling like death warmed up, I was so physically exhausted that I immediately fell into a deep sleep. When I woke a few hours later, to my utter relief the nausea had gone. I wasn't sick again and by the time we landed at Heathrow I felt fine.

Having heard horrendous stories about bugs under the skin, etc., as soon as I could I made a point of visiting St Thomas' Accident and Emergency Department to get my ear checked out. It turned out that during its swim for life, whatever it was had scratched my eardrum, which in turn had blown up into a nasty infection. For the next few weeks every morning I checked my pillow for any eggs that may have fallen out during the night!

My office! Sunrise – 5 a.m. (The Amazon)

Charging off to save a sloth! (The Amazon)

Waiting for the marmoset monkeys to arrive (The Amazon)

Lads Army with Joe and Nookie

Bad Lads Army final exercise (Sailsbury Plain)

Bodyguards – perched for a great shot!

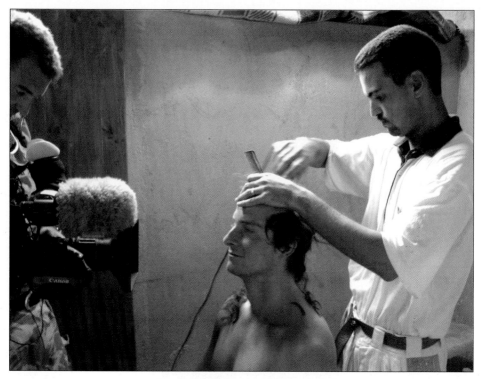

Bear bares all! (Escape to the Legion)

Shirley and I next to our
beloved Land Rover *Santa*
(Sahara Desert)

Escape to the Legion (Sahara Desert)

Playing soldiers (Bosnia)

Happy faces (Africa)

Danny and I SAS? (Bosnia)

'Crusty' portrait – Chadden Hunter (Ethiopia)

Grazing Gelada baboons (Ethiopia)

Breakfast at 15,000ft in the Simien Mountains (Ethiopia)

8

Action Man

I have been told on numerous occasions that I am so fortunate to be a 'Jack of all trades'. '...But a master of none!' I am quick to add. I am lucky enough to be able to do lots of different things well ... I can draw, paint, play the guitar and the piano; I can act; I can perform above average in most sports; I can turn my hands to most practical skills; and to some degree I can translate my thoughts onto paper (I leave this to the reader's discretion!). Yet, the taste left in my mouth is bitter-sweet as my greatest asset proves also to be my greatest hindrance! I often say that if I could live my life several times over, I would be an artist, musician, actor, sportsman and writer ... Agreed, all the above can be dipped into within one lifetime; however, not to be master in any one discipline leaves me frustrated beyond explanation. Am I sounding like a spoilt brat? Perhaps. Some people's path in life is clearly laid out – if you are good at maths, you become a banker or an accountant. If you excel in science, you become a scientist or a doctor. Here lies my quandary: I am able in various skill sets, but which do I choose to follow? Mercifully I seem to have found the middle ground in camerawork, within which I can draw from my various faculties in order to perform well. My art background has developed my eye for composition; music has taught me timing and rhythm; sport has developed my body to sustain a physically demanding job; and my performing arts have rounded my personality and communication skills. Yet, as I continue to spit out my dummy ... there is one more life that I would have loved to have experienced: life as a soldier.

At an early age, I remember one of my three older sisters, Clare, vocalising her fear that I might end up joining the Armed Forces. 'If you join the Army or Navy, you'll sell your soul,' she said. Of course, she was speaking from a doting sister's viewpoint, thinking of her little brother having to live in barracks and work abroad for months on end, as well as the (at that time) remote chance of going to war! Yet being a young lad and having attended the stirring 'Royal Tournament', I had dreamed of being able to call myself a 'soldier'. In retrospect I fantasised in boyish naiveté. I loved the idea of running around with my mates, shooting guns, fast-roping from helicopters and generally getting dirty! At such an age one doesn't consider the harsh reality of soldiering: immense hard work and strict discipline, not to mention the potential danger! In camerawork, once again, I have found the middle ground. Over the last five years my work has brought me in contact with the military on various levels. Being with them, yet not being one of them,

I have been fortunate enough to have had exposure to the military without having to 'sell my soul'. To this day, Clare stands proud!

Bizarrely enough, my first meeting with real soldiers was while filming a celebrity's fortieth-birthday celebration, which took place over a weekend.[3] The brief given to the party planner was: 'My friends have more money than they can spend, they've been to every imaginable party: I want to give them a weekend they'll never forget!' Even with a limitless budget, this was a formidable challenge but, being the best in the business, the party planner went to work.

The invitations that were sent out to the forty or so friends and family read as follows: 'Meet at this address, bring your passports, Black Tie outfit, trainers and some old clothing!' The address was a barn in a field in Surrey. As they turned up in their dribs and drabs, they were escorted into the barn, where their personal items were taken from them. Somewhat taken aback by the rudimentary welcome, they stood and chatted, murmuring with excitement over the unknown events that lay in store. When the role call was complete, the guests were uniformly dressed in blue 'Guantanamo Bay'-style overalls and training shoes. The tension built as the huge barn doors on the opposite side were opened to reveal six twin-squirrel helicopters, whistling as their rotor-blades began to turn methodically.

While this was going on in Surrey, I was in Herefordshire in a makeshift army camp. Set in a stunning valley, the camp was

[3] Note: As I signed a confidentiality agreement, I am unable to mention names, though I can say that he was an owner of a Formula One racing team and extremely rich!

surrounded by tall hills, creating a bowl effect. The team had been working day and night to complete the construction of the camp, which consisted of two enormous military marquees and twenty two-man infantry tents. There was a fire pit and scattered around the site there were a number of Land Rovers and, just to add a bit more reality, there was a checkpoint-style barred gate, complete with a manned security hut! It was literally like walking onto the set of *MASH*. The military team was led by Lofty Wiseman, who had completed twenty-six years' service in the SAS (Special Air Service – British Special Forces). Having written a number of best-selling books, Lofty is now a legendary figure. Alongside Lofty were six other SAS personnel, four retired, two still serving. My introduction to them was over a cigarette: when one of them asked me for a light, I sat with the group and made my acquaintance.

Like most guys I had read a plethora of SAS books, some biographical, some fictional. From those books I had formed my stereotype of what Special Forces' soldiers would be like – big, steely and as hard as nails! However, I was wrong. The first serving Trooper I met was a small, wiry 21-year-old! I was blown away by how 'normal' he looked and was perplexed by how such young shoulders could carry such weight (both in heavy Bergans – rucksacks – and in responsibility!). Either way they were nice guys, very welcoming and seemingly looking forward to the weekend.

I took up my first filming position on a hill, setting up the tripod and fixing a long lens to the camera. Minutes later the walkie-talkie crackled into life as we received our warning that the 'birds' were almost at the landing zone. I trained my lens onto the horizon of the adjacent hill and started recording. In my head I could imagine hearing the *Apocalypse Now* theme music, as the six helicopters all rose together over the horizon. It was a truly magnificent sight. As they flew towards us, I quickly changed to a wide-angle lens and ran to get a shot over Lofty's shoulder, framing his towering stature in the foreground and the helicopters landing right in front of him. As the helicopters' wheels touched the soil Lofty and his men burst into action, running over to each of the aircraft and ducking under the spinning blades. They grabbed the doors and then the guests. One by one they pulled them over to the edge of the field where they were instructed to form a line. The soldiers screamed orders at the bemused guests, who floundered, not really knowing what was happening. The shock on the faces of the new recruits was priceless! Some were giggling like kids, others were horror-struck. Any back-chat was stamped on by Lofty and his unit with the command, 'Give me ten!' Seeing the Formula One World Champion with his face in the dirt doing press-ups was a picture. With the air full of dust and dirt, still being churned up by the growling helicopters, it was pandemonium.

On arrival at the army camp, the guests were given refreshment and then a pep talk from their new boss, Lofty. He explained that they were now on a Special Forces' Training Weekend and they would be required to work hard and listen hard as the training they were about to receive would culminate in a real-life situation! In the group there were titters of laughter and some nervous-looking faces. Lofty revelled in the job, being part serious and part jokey, as after all this was a birthday party! Having instructed at Stirling Lines (SAS HQ in Hereford) during his service, Lofty had perfected the art of banter and quick one-liners to counter any heckling or negativity. Filming him as he talked was most captivating.

The Mess tent was run by a leading catering company, so the evening's banquet was far more extravagant than normal and, needless to say, the alcohol flowed freely! That first night the army games were paused to let the guests enjoy each other's company and familiarise themselves with their new surroundings ... or so they thought!

While the revelries continued, a few of the army boys tipped us off that at around 1 a.m., a few hours after the new recruits had been ushered to their infantry tents, there was going to be a surprise! They told us where the best vantage points would be and we made sure we were in position at the strike of one.

At 00.50 a.m. I headed up onto the hill, from where I could look down on the camp. It was a glorious night – warm despite no cloud cover. Bathed in the moonlight below me I could see the twenty small infantry tents and a few twinkles of torch-light from the odd swaggering fellow trying to find the toilets. It was a quiet, serene scene and quite pleasant to behold. But then, suddenly, the air exploded with the most deafening explosion, then another and another! One after the other, about ten bone-shaking booms shattered the night's peace! From the tents came screams, both from the girls and the guys! You could almost see the small tents jump several feet into the air with shock at the barrage. Surprise! The entire camp had been rigged with huge explosives! Standing up on the hill I felt my backside twitch with the impact of the noise, and I was one of the few who *knew* it was going to happen! I couldn't imagine what it would have been like to be woken from a deep drunken stupor by what must have sounded like an air strike from within the camp. As the echoes subsided, the drone was replaced by the sound of loud expletives from within the tents, followed by one or two heads emerging through their tent-flaps to see what was going on. It was a fantastic demonstration of things to come as the party (?) continued.

Saturday was a full day. Woken at around 6 a.m. the guests had a harsh reality check: this was no dream ... it was really happening! After breakfast they were ushered to different areas around the camp where, in a number of teams, they were instructed in various Special Forces' disciplines: mortar firing, driving tracked vehicles, riding on a zip wire, mine clearance and blindfolded runs through an assault course. As the day went on, they swapped areas until they had all completed the circuit.

In the early afternoon they were served a soldiers' lunch around the campfire, during which Lofty gave a pep talk. I remember him saying, 'What do you do if you and your mate are confronted by a ravaging dog?' A few brave individuals threw out some ideas, but we were all then told the answer: 'Agree to run in opposite directions on the count of three. One ... two ... THREE! You stand still as your mate runs off like a mad man, not knowing that a dog will always chase a runner!' The group burst into laughter and the atmosphere relaxed. Despite the interruptions during the night, the morning had been great fun and certainly different from *anything* anyone had ever done before. As the fire hissed and cracked, Lofty continued speaking but, then, from the other side of the camp came the loud rev of an engine. As they all turned towards the sound, even Lofty appeared shocked. An army Land Rover came screaming over the field towards the fire pit and, as it screeched to a halt, two men wearing balaclavas burst out of the back and dived onto one of the female guests at the same time as another masked man from the jeep fired a handgun into the air and screamed, 'Everybody stay down ... STAY DOWN!' The guests were dumbstruck as the men grabbed the girl, physically threw her into the back of the jeep and then jumped in behind her before the vehicle sped away into the woods. Pulling the focus back onto the group session, Lofty instigated action. He said that he had received intelligence that the enemy group were housed in a wood a few miles from the camp and it was now time to implement their training to secure the release of the hostage. It was not by chance that the hostage was the girlfriend of the other Formula One driver among the guests, who seemed alarmingly thrilled by the idea!

The group, led by Lofty and a few of the other lads, split into two and made their way to some troop-carrying vehicles that were by the camp gate. These took the fledgling warriors up to a farm outhouse where they were issued with high-velocity paintball guns. Masked and ready for action, the two groups cautiously stepped into the woods, nervous of what was awaiting them. There was one person in particular who was more nervous than the rest – and that was me! Having played 'Paintball' on many stag weekends I had plenty of experience of getting hit by the spherical paint pellets and, believe me, it hurts! One time I had been shot at point-blank range and my cheek had exploded, rendering me unable to shave for a few weeks until the wound had healed. This time, the only thing I was armed with was a camera and, in order to get a good composition of shot, I would have to stick my arse out and get in the right position. Knowing that I would be a huge sitting duck for an accountant from Slough, let alone one of the world's most elite marksmen, was somewhat terrifying! As the group blended into the foliage I struggled to find a shot ... Trying not to give their position away to the enemy and at the same time trying to keep myself away from the danger of getting hit, I stepped stealthily around the bushes. It was a matter of seconds rather than minutes before I stood on the fatal twig that snapped loudly and gave my position away. Within a flash I was pelted with shots from every direction. I swear that among my yelps and whimpers as the pellets burst onto my body, I could hear the wheezes of the army boys as they took delight in painting me from head to toe!

The onslaught of fire also gave away the positions of the enemy, so in the furore the guest troops engulfed the makeshift camp and, in true fairytale style, it was the hostage's boyfriend who found her sitting in a small Hessian-covered hide. With covering fire from his fellow troops he lifted her onto his shoulders in a fireman's carry and ran out of the woods. The game was over. The woods looked like a Pollock painting and I walked out looking like Joseph in his Technicolor coat!

Regrouping at the army camp, Lofty congratulated the team and then invited them to the final event of the weekend's itinerary: a Black Tie dinner and dance at the local Manor House. You could hear the sigh of relief at the news, but everyone without exception had thoroughly enjoyed themselves. All credit to Lofty, his outstanding team and, of course, the party planner who had pulled off the fortieth birthday party of a lifetime!

Lads Army

How many times have you heard an elderly person say, 'It wouldn't have happened in my day ... What young people need today is discipline! I think they should bring back National Service!' The whole idea behind *Lads Army* was to put that theory to the test.

By transporting a Ministry of Defence army base, located just outside Southampton, back into the 1950s, the television series aimed to test how effective basic military training could be. No expense was spared: the billets were re-painted; fifties' props were shipped in; all the personnel were clothed in genuine Second World War uniforms, with haircuts to match. Walking around the set was literally like stepping back in time.

The military staff were all ex-service men, most of whom had only recently left the forces after long serving careers. The recruits were volunteers from various walks of life: young lads between the ages of eighteen and twenty-four. It was a genuine experiment in which traditional military methods came face to face with our modern culture. The end-result was a roaring success, with the majority of the lads experiencing a radical turn-around in their lifestyles and attitudes. A number of them actually went on to join the regular British Army. The older generation had been proved right!

Since the viewing public had clearly lapped up the concept, the following year another series was commissioned, only this time the stakes were raised. The second series' recruits were still volunteers, but had been head-hunted for the programme as 'Bad Lads'. This time the programme makers wanted to test whether the tight military machine would still work with tyrants and troublemakers from our streets. Reigning in these young offenders was considerably more challenging but, no stranger to such individuals, the heavy hand of the army prevailed. The startling outcome of series two was that an even higher number of the 'Bad Lads' joined up after participating (two or three even winning commissions to Sandhurst for officer training). Making the programmes was hard work, but an immense amount of fun.

With my interest in the military I found it fascinating to hang out with the military staff and to hear their stories, usually while taking their money on the local pub's pool table! They were genuine, sincere men who knew their craft and acted with precision and discipline. I got on particularly well with the two corporals, Joe and Nookie. Maybe it was because I showed interest in their careers or because I share their dark humour that we hit it off. I revelled in the more physical aspects of the shoot, running along with the camera with a big goofy smile on my face, and I think they secretly approved!

Filming on a period set is an art that together as a team we perfected. The ultimate plan was to create a 'bubble' in which the recruits genuinely forgot that they were on a film set and started to believe that they were in the 1950s. As unbelievable as it sounds, this transition actually took place within the first five days of the three-week training. To help matters, we as a crew and a production team adopted various rules and methods. The crews were the only people allowed onto the set in modern-day clothing, but even we had to wear dark, military-looking clothing (many of us wore combat fatigues which proved very useful – despite being modern-day issue). If, within the intensity and distraction of their training, the lads didn't see 'normal' people, they would soon forget that they even existed! We also adopted a harsh no-talking-to-recruits policy. At first, turning your back and walking away from a lad who had just asked you something, was tough and felt rude, but when you saw the bubble building within their minds, you knew it served a purpose. Occasionally, within the confined spaces of the billets, we would unintentionally get in the private's way and, if it resulted in him getting bollocked by his corporal for being late, he quite rightly complained about it! This issue was brilliantly dealt with by Joe and Nookie, who referred to us as 'Ghosts'. The boys soon cottoned onto this and, before too long, if they had to refer to us, they would also use the term. On one particular occasion I remember crying with laughter as my sound recordist Mick had silently farted while we filmed in the Section Two billet, and one of the lads had said, 'I tell you what, boys ... You may not be able to see those ghosts, but you can bloody well smell them!' Being the consummate professionals that we are (?), both Mick and I stifled our laughter until we got outside, but then we fell on our knees in hysterics! (I had to leave the room anyway as the camera was shaking so much from my laughter that it rendered the footage unusable!)

There are countless moments of hilarity on a shoot like *Bad Lads Army*, but they are always matched by the 'lump in the throat' moments. To witness a young man being broken down to 'nothing', sobbing and almost vomiting due to physical effort, and then to see him find his worth and pride as he is built back up by the skilled military staff and eventually blossom into a straight-backed man: such a transformation would move even the coldest of hearts.

Bodyguards

It was a brutally cold December morning as I hitched a one-ton generator up to my Land Rover and headed down the A3 to the Territorial Army SAS camp, which was to be my home for the next month. I was part of a crew filming a group of wannabe bodyguards being taken through their paces by two ex-Special Forces' soldiers and one ex-Royal Protection squad officer.

There were three crews: the usual faces. Everybody was staying in the main barracks building, a larger version of a basic, post-war house. The contributors resided in two dormitories on the ground floor and the crews shared one big dormitory upstairs. For the duration of the month we would be running around the expansive grounds of the army base, performing various physical tasks and mocking up various security scenarios. In fact, the crew would do pretty much everything the contributors did (but with camera and sound kit!). Furthermore, we would be up an hour earlier than them and go to bed a few hours after them! We would eat the same food and sit in all the lectures that were given. There were times when we asked ourselves, 'Who are the recruits here? Them or us?'

The recruits came from a variety of backgrounds. Among the ten who started the course there were working doormen/ women, a couple of martial art enthusiasts and a fireman. At the beginning most of the contributors fancied themselves as good candidates to become professional bodyguards, but only one would win the prize of further training and a potential position working as a bodyguard for one of Britain's leading private security companies. If you fancied your chances, this was an opportunity to be trained by the best and fast-track your way into a very competitive specialist industry.

The series *Bodyguards* had been commissioned by Channel 4 and my great friend Simon Tucker had been employed as Series Producer. When Tucker briefed the crews about the shoot, we were very keen to be involved as we knew it would mean we'd get to do some exciting filming and it would also be fascinating to dip into the worlds and minds of the professionals who would run the course.

As I walked into the main building on the base, I said hello to a few of the production team that I had worked with before. Because Tucker was in charge of this shoot, there was no doubt that the entire production team would be great people (another good reason for agreeing to do it). After saying hello to Jen (Production Secretary), I noticed a man whom I had never seen before. Assuming that he was the Executive Producer, I thought it important that I should introduce myself to him straightaway, so I said, 'Hi, I'm Mungo, one of the cameramen.' The man smiled, accepted my outstretched hand and shook it, saying in a mild Scottish accent, 'Hi, Mungo, I'm John, pleased to meet you.' Still confused as to what role John played in the team, I asked, 'What do you do, then, John? Are you the Exec?' (meaning Executive Producer). John replied, 'No, I'm the Course Instructor!' To be honest, I was expecting a hard-looking, rugged man with a broken nose and a scar across his eye, but instead I was facing a slight, ginger-haired, softly spoken man ... a 'grey man'.

In the early stages of the course, the recruits were taught that in top-level bodyguarding it is considered a hindrance to 'look' like one. If you looked like a big, beefy thug, you were more likely to be employed by a pop star, who wanted to put over the image of being 'tough'. We were told that the American rapper Eminem, for example, had a 'bodyguard' who was a mountain of a man: he was so fat, in fact, that he couldn't physically walk up the steps at the side of a stage, so he had to stand and protect from below it – while this was fine as a 'deterrent', it was no good if there was a real threat on your client's life. On the other hand, if you were a 'grey man', looking like a normal businessman or 'Executive Producer', you could do your job efficiently and covertly, without being detected by potential threats. In a life-threatening security situation, this is imperative. Makes sense!

John, who had served for a number of years in the Special Air Service, shared with us some stories of situations he had experienced while in the field and they made our blood run cold! Since leaving the army, he had started his own private security company and had operated in close protection and security consultation pretty much all over the world. His client list was not particularly impressive if you looked at the number of people on it, but extremely impressive if you considered their calibre. He would give close protection only to those who faced a real threat to their lives, be it from a kidnap threat or a genuine death threat. John admitted that he wasn't cheap, which again acted as a filter of the class of client that he would be employed by. It was clear that John was the consummate professional and had 'been there and done that'.

Assisting John with the running of the course was an older, shorter, fair-haired man, Paul. Paul had served for over twenty years in the Royal Protection Squad – a specialist unit of the

Metropolitan Police Force, providing a team of personal bodyguards to the British Royal Family. Working in shifts, this crack police team (trained by the SAS) accompanies, watches over and protects each individual member of the Royal Family for twenty-fours hours a day, 365 days of the year. Being the final line of security surrounding the Royals, these elite police officers are granted the rare permission of operating within the Royals' personal space. During his service, Paul had been assigned to Princess Diana, whom he spoke of with an incredible fondness ... tainted only by a twinge of regret. Even though he had left the service way before the time of her tragic, untimely death, he obviously still felt an almost paternal sense of responsibility for her safety and protection.

It was interesting to observe that there was an evident difference in the professional approaches of John and Paul. It wasn't necessarily that one was better than the other: they were just from different schools of training. As a policeman, Paul was trained to the highest standard possible, yet his skills were purely honed to protect. In John's case, however, his training in protection was just one aspect of his role as a Special Forces' soldier and ultimately he was trained to kill!

A few days into the course we were introduced to another instructor who completely stole the limelight. Pete, who is of Maori descent, is close to six foot tall and appeared six foot wide! A colleague of John, he too was working in the private security sector, although his career background and current position were to a large extent kept under wraps. As far as the crew was concerned, this surrounded him with an air of intrigue, and we constantly tried to wittle out of him any information that would help us to build up a picture of this gentle giant's background. With regards to his army career all we knew, as a fact, was that he was from the Special Forces. He did divulge some stories about his close protection work, but we knew that he never really gave the whole game away.

The one aspect of his life that Pete would talk about was his heritage. In Maori tradition, in order to prevent tribes going to war and losing men in battle, it was customary that each individual tribe would put forward one warrior who would fight one on one with a warrior from the opposing tribe in order to settle a dispute. The first-born son of the current warrior would take on this terrifying mantle from his father, and Pete was that baby boy. His warrior father had dedicated his life to training his son in the ancient arts of Maori hand-to-hand combat (a raw, aggressive and often deadly version of the more common martial arts). Pete told of how, during his childhood, he had landed up in hospital over one hundred and twenty times as a result of his father's heavy-handed fighting school. This was obviously controversial, but it had the desired effect as this firstborn baby boy was slowly turned into a force to be reckoned with. Later when he joined the army, he had become recognised as an expert in hand-to-hand combat and had quickly been assigned as an instructor. One of Pete's mates, 'Mongo', a six-foot-eight Kiwi giant, joined him in helping out on the bodyguards' course. I'll never forget meeting Mongo, not only due to the similarity of our names, but because I'm six foot two and when I shook his hand, which is literally the size of a shovel, and then craned my neck to look up at him, I felt like a six-year-old boy! Pete proudly told us of how Mongo had become a student of his, and to this day, when the two of them climb into the ring, Mongo says to him, 'Please don't hurt me today, Pete!' As I imagined the scene, it reminded me of David and Goliath.

The Bodyguard Course began and we steadily fell into the filming routine for the month. It was fascinating to watch the various individuals being put through their paces and especially to see the so-called Hard Men slowly going soft under the intense pressure. The freezing early-morning runs had the recruits vomiting; Pete's hand-to-hand combat training left people lying on the deck, winded with pain. In the lecture room you could almost smell the grey matter burning and see the steam coming out of their ears! We carefully reconstructed past 'security scenarios' that had taken place, using extras who played the part of rioting crowds, smoke machines and blinding spotlights. A dog handler was brought in, who set his two enormous Alsatian dogs onto the recruits as they sprinted through a dark, derelict warehouse trying to rescue a mannequin dummy that had been taken hostage.

Nevertheless, it was not all dramatic and exciting. Ask any professional bodyguard and they will be the first to admit that the large majority of the time the job is actually incredibly dull. Most of it will be sitting in cars or standing outside a hotel-room door in an empty corridor throughout the entire night. Your preparation work before travelling with your subject will be clinical and monotonous, yet essential. You will work hard to try and ensure that you never see any trouble, which effectively means (with regards to the firearms and hand-to-hand fighting) that you should never have to use what you are trained for! Quite strange when you think about it. I couldn't imagine being highly trained to film with a camera, but never shooting one tape throughout my entire career!

If a bodyguard is doing their job correctly, they should never place their client in any danger. John and Pete both said on separate occasions that in close protection a bodyguard's job is not about picking a fight, but rather running away from it! If a shot is fired, they do not heroically stand and shoot back: they bend their client's head down low and run them out the back door to a pre-arranged safe room or the getaway car. It's all about diversion and extraction.

The Hollywood film *Bodyguard*, starring Kevin Costner and Whitney Houston, paints a typically sensationalist picture of the profession. In the scene when the bodyguard (Costner) hears a gunshot from the audience of a theatre, he launches himself in front of the pop star (Houston), taking the bullet in his shoulder, thus saving her life, and they all live happily ever after ... oh yes, and they fall in love – of course! Personally I enjoyed the film, despite its fiction, as I think it portrays the innate essence of women wanting to be looked after and men wanting to protect. Being intrigued about the subject, over dinner one evening I asked John, 'Would you really take a bullet for a wealthy businessman or someone who had just employed you?' His reply was, 'Well, you should avoid ever getting into that position, but to be honest there is only one client that I would not hesitate taking a bullet for.' He infuriatingly then refused to disclose who that client was.

As the days and weeks of the series went by, we witnessed broken men and women opting out of the course until only a minority remained. As with most courses, the higher the stakes get, the more exciting the course becomes. This one was no exception and the stakes were getting higher ... literally!

We set up to film at the Trapeze Course, located in the lower section of the army base. On arrival you entered through a tall cross-wired fence. When you trained your eye up the towering tree trunks, you could see that there was an expertly-built high-rope course within the tree canopy. The order of the day was that each recruit was required to navigate his or her way through the disturbingly high rope course. Sometimes they would work as a team, but mostly each person would be by themselves. I loved this part of the course, as it meant that I could don my harness and climb with the camera into some hair-raising positions. What made me laugh was that Tucker, being generally more office bound and a frustrated Action Man, pulled me aside and said, 'Mungo, you've got to make it sound as though you need me to come up with you ... there's no way I'm missing out on this!' Of course, I wanted my mate to ascend the timber giants with me: for a start, it would more than likely be a while before the recruits arrived at my best vantage point, so it would be good to have a laugh up there while we waited. Also, filming in precarious positions can often be disorientating as your eye through the camera's viewfinder is doing one thing at the same time as your body is doing something else. Sometimes, even when you are on the ground, this can lead you to lose your balance, so the consequences of such disorientation when you are 100 feet in the air are somewhat more significant! I swung around and said to our camera assistant, Johnny, 'Mate, I need a spare tape and battery to come up with me ... Simon, do you think you could join me, bring up the spares and be my spotter?' In a comedy tone Tucker replied, 'Oh, go on, then!' With the camera strap slung over my shoulder, I began the climb. Tucker followed close behind. We found a ledge that would give me a great shot as the recruits edged their way across a long section of rope. The remaining cameras on the ground would portray the perspective of the height, but my position would enable us to see a close-up of the fear on the individual's face. It was bitterly cold and the ends of my fingers were so numb that I had lost all feeling in them. I asked Tucker to warm them up for me, but he sarcastically suggested that I should shove them where the 'sun don't shine'!

One of the recruits, Darren – a big, black hulk of a man – admitted to suffering from acute vertigo, so all eyes and camera lenses were trained on him. As he approached our high ledge, you could hear his laboured breathing before you could see him. As he arrived into my shot I zoomed the lens to its greatest length in order to capture the terror clearly etched on his face. As he shuffled his way along the ropes, you could hear the bellowing encouragement from the instructors far below: 'Come on, big man, you can do it!' Despite the biting cold weather, sweat poured out from under Darren's climbing helmet as he inched his way, murmuring and talking to himself. Eventually he reached our end of the rope where he erupted into 'whoops' and 'shrills' with the relief and satisfaction of having overcome one of his greatest fears. Yet, the final test was about to become apparent. There was a telegraph pole that jutted into the air, the top of which was only just large enough for a man to stand on with both feet pressed closely together. Standing on this small circle would have been hard enough if it was one foot off the ground, but this end of the pole was a good 80 feet in the air. Climbing the pole was going to be difficult enough, but in addition the exercise entailed contorting your body to lift it up high enough to be able to stand upright with both feet on it. If you made it this far, you would then notice a trapeze bar suspended from the tree opposite, and the aim was to take a leap of faith and catapult yourself out and up another eight feet to grab hold of the swaying bar. From the ground this looked nigh-on impossible but, according to the instructors, achieving it was more a case of mind over matter (easily said with your feet firmly on the ground!). The colour drained from Darren's big black face, and his 'whooping' was silenced. The 'shrills' were replaced with expletives as he began to heave his bulk up the telegraph pole. You could have heard a pin drop on the crisp leaves frozen to the soil, as all below stared in disbelief that he was even willing to attempt the climb. The silence from the crews and instructors was spasmodically shattered by a gasp of air from the climber. As he reached the top of the pole more expletives were let out. 'I can't believe I'm doing this ... what am I doing?' Despite his grumbling, he miraculously swung his feet up onto the end of the pole and with a groan he slowly, carefully stood upright. The instructors below, hardly believing their eyes, began to shout encouragement and tips about what to do now. Following their instructions, Darren gradually bent his knees and, as the pole swayed under the weight of the great man, with a cry he threw himself out into the air. One of his hands touched the trapeze bar but the other fell short. The velocity and the weight of the man combined were too much for the one hand to sustain and he rapidly fell towards the ground. Fortunately, within a split second of falling, the safety rope kicked in and Darren was swung upside down as the rope tightened and took the weight of his body. Swinging from side to side, suspended a good 60 feet from the ground, Darren burst into 'whoops' of elation at his achievement. He may not have completed the task, but the fear that he had overcome had taken a monumental effort. The instructors were thrilled at what they saw. This attitude, courage and determination was exactly what they wanted to see in their recruits.

This was the most outstanding display of bravery yet from the recruits and, sadly, from that high things went steadily downhill. John and Paul became more and more disappointed with the results of further tasks and, on the final task, John pulled the remaining wannabe bodyguards into the lecture room and gave them a good rollocking!

This final assignment was a full-scale close protection exercise involving a man and a woman (actors) who were coming down from London on the train. The recruits, dressed in suits and driving two seven-series BMWs, were to meet them at the local station, see them safely into their cars and take them to a hotel, where they would spend the night before the man would attend an important meeting the following morning. Due to threats on the man's life the protection was of critical importance. This exercise gave the finalists the chance to put all their training into practice, work as a team and secure the VIP's safety. The job required, as taught, a recce of the station, hotel and meeting place, which would entail checking the personnel at all the locations to ensure that they were genuine employees. Had anyone randomly joined the staff in the last few weeks? These people could easily be

potential plants and a definite threat. What routes would the
BMWs drive? Were there any areas of weakness, which could
lead to a roadblock and possible ambush? Could there be a
hidden 'IED' (Improvised Explosive Device)? Were the hotel
and meeting room secure? Where were the emergency exit
points? Was there a safe room available for use? Generally,
what were the weak links in the chain of events?

The recce, carried out the day before the arrival of the VIPs,
was a complete disaster. The team fell apart, major aspects
of the security checks were missed or ignored and, to top it
all, the BMW convoy even got lost on the way to the station,
heading the wrong way up the A3 towards London! On
returning to base that evening John asked a few of us crew
how it had all gone and we listed about twenty fundamental
errors that we had mentally noted. In John's rollocking he
included (off camera) that even the camera crews, while busy
filming, had taken in more than they had, and it was clear that
we crews would have done a better job!

The next day things came together a bit more, but there
was still a poor amount of effort on the part of certain
individuals. The two-day exercise concluded with the woman
accompanying the VIP being kidnapped by Pete, who had
dived out of a moving transit van, grabbed her and physically
thrown her into the van as it sped off! Late that morning, the
debriefing of the finalists was intense and, despite an overall
poor result, there was one young Scottish lad, Stuart, who,
although being the youngest of the recruits, had made enough
of an impression to win the coveted prize.

It was a fabulous shoot, full of surprises and plenty of
exciting activities and set-ups to keep us as crews busy and

amused. It was just unfortunate that, despite the great content and moody footage, the powers-that-be in Channel 4 at the time insisted on cutting Tucker's well-produced programme to pieces with the result that the end-product was a slightly disappointing series of programmes. Yet, because we enjoyed filming it so much, the disappointment was short lived. At the end of the day we had great fun and we were paid well for it, so the memories outweighed the final result.

Escape to the Legion

'How do you fancy five weeks in the Sahara Desert, filming basic training with the French Foreign Legion?' The voice on the other end of the phone belonged to Richard Farish. He had just spoken to Rupert Smith, who had recently secured the job of Series Director on *Escape to the Legion*. It was not a difficult decision. 'I'm there!' I replied without even having to think.

Before we knew it, we were on a plane to Morocco, arriving in Agadir in the Western Sahara Desert and driving down to a derelict Foreign Legion fort just outside of a small coastal port named Tan Tan. The crew was hand-picked by Richard who was Camera Supervising with Rupert's approval. Richard and I were to operate the cameras; Diddley (Sean Taylor) and Shirley (Mark Owen) were on sound. We took a young Irish lad whom I called 'Irish' (Anthony Dalton) as our camera assistant. Then there was another young guy, whom we had met on *Bodyguards*, called Muttley (named by his sister as, when she would tickle him as a boy, because of his asthma he would wheeze like the dog from the cartoon *Wacky Races*). Richard managed to get Muttley on the shoot as the Location Logger (someone who watches all the rushes – shot tapes – and makes notes of the content). It was a small but close-knit team and we were all kitted up and ready for the challenge ahead.

On arrival we were met by Duncan Gaudin, the First AD (Assistant Director), whom we all knew from *Bad Lads Army* and were very fond of. We were shown around the location by Duncan and Rupert who were up to their eyes trying to solve all kinds of logistical problems – which tend to hamper shoots of this sort in very remote locations. They were warm in their welcome despite being somewhat stressed out by the haggling and dishonesty of the Arabs. When we felt the intensity of the searing sun, saw the harsh environment of the desert, heard about the countless set-up problems and had our first 'Tagine' meal, that's when we knew we were in for a tough five weeks!

A few hours later we met Bear Grylls, who was both presenting and going through the arduous basic training of 'The Legion' with ten other contributors. Bear was a friend of a friend at home, so I had learnt a lot about him before the trip, including his phenomenally impressive Curriculum Vitae.

On leaving school at an early age, Bear joined the British Army. Within a few years he had successfully joined 21 SAS as a Trooper. While on a training exercise in Africa, however, he suffered a shocking parachuting accident when his parachute became twisted and then failed, causing him to freefall to earth. On impact, his body was shattered into pieces. Yet, despite these major injuries, including breaking his back in three places, after extensive surgery and a long period of convalescence, Bear was still able to walk. Not long afterwards, Bear became the youngest Briton to reach the summit of Mount Everest! No small feat. On the back of this incredible story of success, tragedy, grit and determination, he became one of Britain's youngest 'Adventurers' and now makes a good career on the corporate speaking circuit, recounting his daring feats at company dinners and corporate team-building conferences. Since then he has continued his crazy stunts, including circumnavigating the British Isles on a jet ski and crossing the treacherous North Atlantic Ocean in an open, rigid inflatable boat. Now married to a beautiful woman, Shara, with two fantastic sons you would expect him to slow down a bit and take less risks, but on the contrary he recently broke the world record for the highest open-air formal dinner at 24,262 feet while being suspended from a hot-air balloon, before free-falling back down to earth – this time landing safely! In between these mad stunts, Bear has now found a niche as a TV presenter within the more adventurous side of programming. Being a relatively young, good-looking and articulate SAS soldier, adventurer, TV presenter and dad, he's every young boy's hero. On top of this incredible resumé, Bear is an extraordinarily nice guy, which quite frankly makes one sick! Meeting Bear at the fort that day was a real boost as he immediately gave us all a warm welcome and we could see he was definitely going to be one of the boys.

Running the Foreign Legion Basic Training for the filming were three ex-Legionnaires. First there was 'Sutter', a Brit who had completed his five years in the Legion and was now working in personal security in Baghdad, Iraq. Standing six foot tall with gingery hair and of medium build, he constantly made us laugh as although his French (learnt in the Legion) was acceptable, he still spoke with an incredibly strong East End London accent, which at times made him sound like someone from *'Allo 'Allo!* Joining Sutter was Glenn. Barely five foot five, this small but perfectly formed American had joined the Legion as a form of rebellion against his family back home. Having also completed his five years of service, Glenn then joined the US Army where he did well, ending his military career as a Ranger. Now settled in France with a wife and six kids, he is constantly toying with the idea of signing up to a private security company and joining the likes of Sutter in Iraq. Not long into the shoot Glenn would be nicknamed 'Good Shit Glenn', as every day, whether looking at a recruit on his face begging for mercy or at a coveted can of baked beans, he would make the comment, 'That's good shit!'

Leading the two ex-Legionnaires was a Frenchman called Peter who would act as 'The Chef' (the Legion's commanding officer). An unassuming individual, Peter was fairly tall and wiry, with tattoos, short hair and a pair of round 'John Lennon' glasses. He had served with the Legion as a professional soldier, treating it as a career as opposed to a form of escape, which led to him joining (as he called it) 'The Crap', the French Foreign Legion's Special Forces Unit. He was quietly spoken and very nice – later even Bear agreed that Peter had nothing to prove, as he had obviously been there and done that!

We had one week on location before the recruits arrived. The plan was to use this time to prepare and test our technical equipment. However, after a few days our camp's water well, which supplied us with fresh water, became infected. I was the second victim of the dirty water and the disease hit me like a ton of bricks! For three days in a row I was projectile-vomiting and crapping through the eye of needle. It was horrendous and I wanted to die as a form of relief. One by one most of us went down with a debilitating form of Giardia. Even our medic, Mark, was walking around treating people with a drip hanging from his own arm. It was a miserable week and compounded the problems that we were still having with the corrupt locals. At one point there was talk of us having to pull the entire shoot and claiming the loss on insurance, as around 80 per cent of us were in our beds sick.

To counter-attack the sickness we all took a course of strong antibiotics; even those who weren't sick took the pills in an attempt to wipe it out. Fortunately it worked, and by the time the new recruits arrived on location we had all just about recovered. The ten volunteers were a motley crew, including a boxer, a debt collector, several ex-cons, several ex-drug addicts, a French entrepreneur and one Etonian lay-about. The ex-Legionnaires had their work cut out and as the crew we were particularly interested to see how the Legion would succeed with such candidates, compared to the success of the British Army that we had witnessed on *Bad Lads Army*.

From day one the training was physically hard, with numerous push-ups, star-jumps and pull-ups repeatedly dished out as punishment for the slightest out-of-turn comment or wrongdoing. At first the Chef (Peter) would address the new recruits solely in French but the only person who could understand him was the Frenchman, Luic. As we only had three weeks in which to convert this rabble into Cappe Blanc potentials,[4] reluctantly, the Chef began to give his orders in a mixture of French and English.

It was compulsory for all the new recruits to have their head shaved into a grade-one crew-cut by a local barber who, I am sure, was really the local butcher. This was one of the first scenes that I had to shoot with Bear, and I stood in front of him with my wide-angle lens practically in his face as he was shorn like a sheep. The look on his face was one of serious contemplation, the idea being that he was shedding his normal life for the Legion. Yet, while I was filming, I couldn't help but smirk when I saw that his 'Old Chap' was hanging out of his shorts! In a serious, dry tone I quietly said, 'Put it away, Grylls', at which his eyes fell to his shorts and his face broke into a big grin. That was the end of that sequence as we both got the giggles and I couldn't hold the camera steady any longer.

The heat was oppressive and the desert terrain was punishing. On day one of training we had our first casualty. Thankfully it wasn't through a physical accident, but a mental breakdown. The recruit in question was just not cut out for the military and although it was a nuisance, having flown him all the way out, it was actually good for the show, as it set a tough president. This was definitely not going to be a walk in the park!

Compared with the British Army basic training, the Legion's methods seemed more focused on physical endurance than on discipline. Every morning there was a long run, followed by a sprint test. The familiar 'Drill' was paced out around a makeshift sandy parade square. Weapons' training and hand-to-hand combat took the recruits into the afternoon.

[4] 'Cappe Blanc' is the infamous white cap traditionally worn by the French Foreign Legion.

All this was interspersed with the daily chores of washing, ironing and cleaning the billets. At the end of each day the recruits were shattered. But so were we, as whatever they did, we were there holding our cameras!

In the oppressive heat we were saved by our invaluable 'Camelbaks', which is a system that enables you to carry a water supply on your back, constantly feeding you fresh water through a tube straight into your mouth. Re-hydration in such countries is essential to survival. We would drink even if we weren't thirsty and we would constantly be analysing the colour of our urine. If it was darker than a light-straw colour, it indicated that we were dehydrated and needed to drink more. For the first few days of drinking so much water, you constantly need to urinate, but a week into the routine your body adapts and begins to retain the fluids, helping to keep you well watered.

One thing I can say for sure is that human beings are not designed to live in a desert. It seems that everything in that environment is against us. The desert is deadly dry and human beings are made up of 90 per cent water. There is hardly any vegetation – only those species tough enough to withstand the heat, rendering them inedible. There are no trees, so there is no shade from the searing sun. On top of all that there are a number of dangerous insects and reptiles, which make life very uncomfortable. The derelict fort was host to numerous rats, flies, mosquitoes, spiders, scorpions and snakes. Many of the creatures that on first sight seem harmless are in fact more dangerous than the more renowned creepy crawlies, as they carry disease. For example, malaria, which is the greatest killer in the world, is carried by mosquitoes with bodies the size of a pinhead.

Despite the fact that on an almost daily basis recruits were dropping out, the filming was running relatively smoothly. The recruits were taken on their first route march and were soon covering up to twenty kilometres a day. In theory, their fitness was vastly improving, although they were also accumulating injuries. The standard-issue Legion boots were creating vicious blisters and sores, and the men's tired muscles were stiff and aching, leading to inevitable muscular pulls.

Having survived our shaky first week, mercifully we as a crew now seemed to be on good form – apart from the occasional bout of diarrhoea and other internal grumblings. We had been careful to come prepared, with US-Army-issue desert boots, British Army desert combat trousers and light-weight Rohan safari shirts. We knew all too well that when working in such environments it pays to have the appropriate kit – no matter what the expense. To their credit the camera and sound kits were surviving relatively well, partly due to good covers but also due to Anthony's elbow grease at night. The constant barrage of sun and sand can play havoc with such sensitive high-tech equipment and only a sustained routine of care and maintenance enables it to continue working. Owning their own sound kits, sound recordists are notoriously meticulous in looking after their kit: it tends to be only in these extreme locations that we cameramen tend to follow suit.

After the first week of shooting everybody slips into a routine. The problems are slowly ironed out and each person begins to have a fair idea of what to expect from each day. As the recruits were put through their paces on the assault course and relentless marches, the stories of endurance, defiance and failure were piecing together nicely. It is very moving to see how far a man can push himself before his body or mind gives in. To witness the pain etched on the face of a recruit as he crawls on hands and knees up a vertical sand-dune for the tenth time. To stand silently filming in the corner as a corporal screams and spits a millimetre away from a recruit's nose, pushing each man to his limits of tolerance. This is an experience and insight that I revel in and, without a doubt, while filming you yourself participate. You experience your own pain while holding the heavy camera in what are effectively stress positions for hours on end. You develop your own mental discipline when working in such an environment for long hours, acquiring the physical endurance and mental toughness to keep going. The main difference is the fact that you are being paid to be there and, at the end of a long day, you can go back to your camp, have some decent food and get a decent night's sleep ... and all this without someone filming you do it! But, as we often say to the whinging recruits, 'You're the ones who chose to be here!'

We had some amazing days pushing our four-wheel-drive vehicles to their extremes over the baron landscape. We spent nights sleeping on the desert floor in the middle of nowhere under an enormous blanket of stars. I can't deny that we did have fun, but a lot of the time it was just plain hard work.

As the course progressed we lost another recruit, Dean, who twisted his testicle on the assault course. Realising the serious-ness of the injury, our medic Mark scrambled a jet from Heathrow bringing over a team of specialist medics. Within four hours the jet landed at Tan Tan's basic airstrip, where one of our four-by-fours met them and drove them out to the fort.

The diagnosis was that unless Dean got surgery within the next seven hours, he was likely to lose his testicle! Thanks to the professionalism of the medical team, they had him under the knife of a surgeon at the Chelsea and Westminster Hospital in London within five hours!

What we weren't aware of at the time was that Mark's brother – an ex-Royal Marine – was part of the medical team. When Mark had put in the call to scramble the jet, he had told his brother to bring out some food snacks for the crew. Having secured Dean in the high-tech stretcher, the two brothers exchanged their gifts. We had traded a wounded soldier for a huge sack of Ginsters pasties, scotch eggs, Pringles and baked beans. That night we dined like truckers! After a staple diet of camel and rice it was like heaven on earth. To our amusement, even Bear got wind of the treasure chest, abandoned his fellow recruits, sneaked out of the billet and joined us for the feast!

Closing in on the last week of the training, we were about to enter 'The Farm'. This is the part of the course when the recruits get to put their training into practice. Designed to sort out the wheat from the chaff, it is tough. The test was to be held in the Vallée de Sable (The Valley of Sand – and that is exactly what it is). As a child, when you imagine the Sahara Desert, you picture a scene from *Lawrence of Arabia*: miles and miles of sand-dunes. And in this instance that was exactly the view laid out before us. Somewhere in the middle of this vast valley was a Bedouin tent, which would house the final recruits. A few hundred metres south of that was a modern-day army tent, which was to be our crew tent.

The schedule for the Farm was more like real soldiering. The recruits would patrol and sweep large areas of the dunes, practising their formations with their weapons at the ready and responding to various types of attack. At night, a patrol would climb the dunes and set up look-out posts. As always, whatever they did, we were with them, just a few steps in front or behind.

I remember the night Shirley and I accompanied the two-man patrol up an enormous dune which overlooked the camp. It was very dark, since the patchy cloud cover limited the moonlight reaching the sand. I had abandoned the heavy Digi-Beta camera for a lightweight camera with an infra-red capability. It was about 2 a.m. and it was still very warm. As we approached the Bedouin tent we were accosted by an armed dark figure on watch duty. As we got closer, we realised it was Bear, so we hurled some friendly insults at him. Pairing up with the two men on patrol, Will Collis and Luic, the four of us headed off up the dune. The dune was massive and it took us a good forty minutes to climb it. It was so dark by this point that you could only tell you had reached the top of the dune by feeling your feet angling over either side of the top edge. Eventually we arrived at what the two recruits thought was a good vantage point and the two of them lay down side by side to keep watch. As time ticked on, it became harder and harder for the recruits, who were already suffering from sleep deprivation, to stay awake. They needed to take turns in kipping, relying on the other man to fight to stay awake and alert. They knew that at any point during the night 'Good Shit Glenn' could pounce on them, as he would be trying to catch them out.

Shirley and I stayed with them for twenty minutes or so, until there was little point in shooting any more footage of two men lying in the desert in deathly silence. We turned on a sixpence on the very top of the dark mountainous dune and tried to follow our footsteps back toward base. When you spend some time in a dark place, with a little ambient light, it is amazing how your eyes adjust and within ten minutes or so you can develop pretty good night vision. Soldiers realise the value of this night vision and desperately try to keep it by using red-lens torches and shielding their eyes from any white light, such as car headlights, etc. It is possible to keep one eye shut and retain night vision in that eye, but sometimes that is just not practical. As I had been shooting with the infra-red camera, the bright monitor had completely disrupted my night vision, which meant that when the light from the camera went off, I was completely blind! I tried for a while to use the camera in infra-red mode to be my eyes as I walked, but it wasn't proving very easy. My only option was to turn the camera off and carefully shuffle along the steep edge of the sand-dune until my night vision returned. Having had no light source to contaminate his sight, Shirley was fine, so he slowly led the way ... his blind friend in tow. A few steps on I lost my footing and fell to the left. It was an odd sensation as I rolled in total darkness, completely disorientated, down the side of the dune. The sand was soft and cold to the touch. As I span over and over I had no idea when or if I would stop. Thankfully the place where I had fallen was a shelf on the top of a great bowl in the sand, and the bowl literally scooped me up. Rushing to help me, Shirley had bounded down into the dark shadows to where I had disappeared. I was fine, though still blind in the darkness. As Shirley arrived to rescue me, he said, 'You alright, mate?' and stretched out his hand for me to grab hold of. Not being able to see a thing I knelt up and two of Shirley's fingers shot straight into my eyes! With a whimper I replied, 'Ah! I was until you arrived!' We both burst into a cackle of laughter, which I'm sure 'Good Shit Glenn' cursed us for, but we were just glad to be heading back to camp for a nice cup of tea.

The Farm went well and the recruits proved their metal. There was one final test remaining before they were to receive their mock Cappe Blanc. The final route march was a punishing twenty-six-miles across some of the most inhospitable terrain on earth. To add to this ultimate test of endurance each recruit would be carrying a heavy rucksack as well as his rifle. En route there were snakes, ticks, spiders, mosquitoes and, of course, the lethal heat of the sun. If they made it to the end of this march they would have survived three brutal weeks of hell.

Led by the mega-fit Chef (who back in France runs mountain marathons for the fun of it), they left the camp at 4.30 a.m. Heading off on a bearing to the West, it would be hours before they would stop to rest. The way we covered this on film was for Richard and Rupert to accompany the recruits walking with them and filming on smaller DV cameras. This was a massive test for these two, as not only did they have to cover the same distance at the same pace on foot, but they also had to try to capture the story of the pain the recruits were suffering and the effort that they were expending.

I lucked out. Duncan, Shirley and I had been given the enviable task of driving to various waypoints marked on our GPS (Global Positioning Satellite) in our air-conditioned four-by-four jeep! We arrived ahead of the pack of soldiers in order to get the big-vista shots that would illustrate just how far they had travelled and how hard it was.

We leapfrogged from position to position and then raced off to set up for the final vista shot which was, in a word, epic! The shot would encapsulate the most phenomenal view of vast sand mountains disappearing into the distance, as the relatively tiny train of recruits snaked its way through the bottom of the shot. Once I was set up with the tripod in position, the correct lens attached and a graduated filter in the Matte Box I could relax. We estimated that it would take about half an hour before the tiny dots came into view, so the three of us started to throw rocks down the steep cliff a few feet in front of us. As the minutes ticked by we moved on to more elaborate games, such as rolling the rocks down the cliff and trying to get the rock to run out of speed and halt by the last rock (a rough-and-ready game of 'Bowls'). Two hours and literally hundreds of rocks later, we were still there with no sign of the recruits. Since we were in radio contact with them, we knew they were on their way, but they had taken a wrong turn, so had ended up taking a longer route than expected.

Duncan manned the radio as Shirley took photographs with his stills camera (only ambient sound was need for such a huge shot – which required his microphone to be lodged between some rocks, aimed in the general direction of the movement). I stood by the camera waiting for the right moment to press 'Record'. Eventually the men became visible in the far distance and I began to shoot various sizes of shots. When they had passed way below us we repositioned to the beach, another five miles away. Driving onto the beach I found the perfect position for the reveal of the recruits seeing the water and arriving at the end of the march. I trained the lens over a sand-dune, so that I would see the triumphant men appear in a perfect silhouette as they ascended the final sand-dune. It worked as planned, and we shared in the elation of the group as they almost collapsed at the sight of the glistening sea. With no encouragement they all stripped down to their underpants and ran into the water. This was the perfect crescendo to the shoot and, after congratulating everyone and taking photos, we all headed back to the fort for a well-deserved drink!

It had been a tough few weeks for all and that night we held a makeshift Wrap Party in a Bedouin tent erected next to the fort, where we all let off some steam over a number of beers.

Looking back I have to force myself to think of the harder times we had while out there. It's all too easy to romanticise about the good times we shared, but I do remember that at the time we all swore we would never do it again. However, if Richard phoned me tomorrow and offered me more weeks in the Sahara, I would be there like a shot!

9

War Torn

Bosnia

It was 6 p.m. and I was heading down the M1 on my way
home from a job in Newcastle when my mobile rang. I
struggled to answer it as I was driving. It was one of my best
friends, Danny, who also worked in TV but as a director/
producer. Without even saying hello, he asked me, 'How
about coming to Bosnia with me?' 'When?' I replied. 'We fly
tomorrow at 3 a.m. from RAF Lyneham. Back in five days. I'll
need to pick you up at midnight tonight.' I didn't need to
think. 'I'll see you at midnight!' I told him and hung up.

When you first meet Danny Fagerson, you immediately
realise that his world is slightly different from all of ours. He is
as enormous in personality as he is in stature. He was born in
Afghanistan, yet holds an American passport and speaks with
a Scottish accent! His hair is as wild as the twinkle in his eye

and his childlike sense of humour echoes something of his wonderfully sensitive soul. He is one of life's great characters and I consider myself honoured to have him as one of my best friends.

When he was younger, Danny attended a private school located in central Scotland. Rannoch School was a humbler version of the famous Gordonstoun School (which the royal princes attended), yet compared with my local secondary school in Tonbridge it was palatial and frightfully posh! In his final year Danny was Head Boy and his father, 'Lad', served as the School Chaplain: no wonder he appeared to be the school favourite!

Even though Rannoch was a very good school, in later years due to competition from rival schools it hit upon hard times. During a particularly tough year, the Headmaster looked into new ways of marketing the school and he came up with the idea of producing a promotional video. Danny's father heard about this and suggested to the Head that Danny, being a professional in the TV industry as well as an ex-student, would be the ideal person to produce the video. The idea was snapped up!

It was on this shoot that Danny and I really got to know one another. During the week we spent at Rannoch filming the school and its pupils, we laughed as hard as we worked. We sang together as we raced up the magnificent Scottish mountains that surrounded the school, striving to stay ahead of the students we were filming. We messed around as though we ourselves were back at school. I remember, during the main interview with the Headmaster, we had to leave the room twice due to fits of stifled giggles, which when outside the room exploded into tears and hysterics! It was a memorable shoot.

With a school of such calibre it is common for the ex-pupils to go on to achieve great things, and this was the theme that Danny adopted for the promotional video. We interviewed Tom Jones, the Scottish International Rugby Prop Forward; a woman who had become a leading veterinary surgeon; and then a boy who was Britain's under-eighteens' clay pigeon champion. In addition, there was one more ex-Rannoch pupil that Danny was desperate to feature: Sarah, a Captain in the Royal Logistical Corps of the British Army. It was a considerable achievement for her as a woman to have attained this rank. Danny traced her whereabouts and she agreed to be involved. The only problem was that she was serving in Bosnia as part of the Stabilization Force.

With typical gall, Danny pushed further, suggesting that he and a cameraman could fly out and visit her in Bosnia. To his surprise, she agreed, and not only that, but she also arranged for the two of us to join a Hercules flight from RAF Lyneham within the next few days.

It was around 1 a.m. as we drove through the gates of the Royal Air Force base in Wiltshire. Once through the inevitable security checks we sat dozing quietly for a few hours in the sparsely furnished room used as the 'departure lounge'. On schedule at around 3 a.m. we were shown to a door that led us out onto the tarmac. As we stepped out, the cold night air hit our faces and the intake of breath froze our weary lungs. In front of us was a huge dark shape sitting in the dark, growling . . . waiting. This wasn't like the usual airline experience, with a queue of tourists in a brightly lit departure gate.

It was quiet and dark, and felt serious and almost secretive. We were led to the aircraft, where we boarded through the troop door and were welcomed by the Load Master. He didn't ask to see our boarding card and he wasn't wearing a hat with a blue ribbon; instead he wore an impressive-looking flight helmet, complete with visor. With few words, he showed us to where we would be sitting within the very belly of the enormous metal bird. There were no seats as such, just para-webbing (cross-hatched strips of orange nylon): it wasn't particularly comfortable, but then again we weren't expecting Business Class treatment. In front of us was a gap of several feet before more webbing seats that ran across the opposite wall. To our left were a dozen palettes bearing various covered loads. Some of the loads were obviously of a mechanical nature, others looked like troop supplies – Bergans (rucksacks), etc. Joining us on the flight were a few regular soldiers. They nodded to say hello as they sat with us along the walls, displaying a distinct curiosity as they looked at us in our civvies. No words were exchanged as the Load Master handed out pairs of foam ear defenders and, with a hand gesture, directed our attention towards a small curtained hide, which was the on-board lavatory – a blue-rinse bucket!

Within a few minutes the noise increased as the Hercules rumbled into life and crawled into the darkness of the night. As the engines roared and the aircraft was propelled up the runway, the noise was unbelievable. It was clear that there wasn't going to be a lot of conversation taking place in economy class! Danny and I looked at each other and wryly smiled like two excited schoolboys.

The flight took around eight hours in total, including a brief stop at a British airbase in Germany. The last few hours had left us tired, numb and completely deaf, so there was a sense of relief and elation as we looked out of the small round windows behind us and saw the breath-taking sapphire-coloured shores of Croatia. We flew into Split, which is situated right on the border of Croatia and Bosnia. Split is the location of the huge British Army base, providing easy access by road into the troubled land of Bosnia. We were there shortly after the war and even though battles were no longer raging, the country was still very unstable and required a considerable military presence to sustain peace.

On the tarmac we met Sarah, who was exactly how I had imagined her: strong in stature, neatly tied-up dark brown hair, with an air of authority about her – a woman finding success in a man's world! She was warm and seemed genuinely glad to have us there. Having already been on tour for a number of months, we were obviously a break in the monotony of an ordered, routine life while serving abroad.

After visiting the security office and being issued our passes, we were given a brief tour of the army base and then shown to our quarters. The base was huge, with hundreds of people dressed in combat fatigues dashing around, as they went about their business. The men we passed addressed Sarah as 'Ma'am'. It was strange suddenly to be in such a hierarchical society, where even older men would address a relatively young woman in this way. We walked towards a block of army-green porta-cabins, stacked one on top of the other. These were to be our sleeping quarters. I was sharing with a young officer, who was most welcoming and again seemed glad to have a fresh face around. He showed me the shower block and then led me to the Mess for some supper.

As guests of the British Army we were treated extremely well. We ate in the designated Officers' Area and, after a hearty meal, we headed to the Officers' Mess for a nightcap before bed. It was good to meet the military personnel, from the cooks and drivers all the way up to majors and captains. We were warmly welcomed.

The next morning we were going to drive into Bosnia with Sarah. We were taken to the outpost where we were met by a Land Rover, driven by a Private. Both he and Sarah went to the armoury to be issued with their firearms. In the car we also had flack jackets and helmets, just in case things went pear-shaped. Danny and I jumped in the back of the Land Rover and we drove off, across the border and into potentially hostile territory. Steve, our driver, kept himself to himself, only speaking when he radioed in our position every thirty minutes or so.

As we drove along the long, winding, deserted road from the border, it was the terrain that took us most by surprise. I guess, having watched the news reports from the war, we were expecting a grey, cold and desolate landscape – and, indeed, this was to come – yet the mountain region we were driving through could have been the foothills of the Swiss Alps! Sarah reminded us that both Croatia and Bosnia boasted ski resorts in their former days of glory. However, what we were seeing on that journey were snow-less ski runs that time had forgotten.

A couple of hours into the journey we passed through our first village. It was cold, dull and eerie. There was no one to be seen and there was no murmur of sound, except the hum of our engine and the crunch of our tyres against the gravel road. It was literally as if everyone had left ... which they probably had. We saw the damage that only war could inflict – the gaping holes in the sides of buildings, the houses, once homes, now rendered derelict. Wall after wall was peppered with bullet holes. Small craters had been left from mortar fire and burnt-out vehicles littered the streets. It wasn't so much the damage that was shocking but the thought of what had actually happened when such destruction took place! You could imagine the artillery fire raining down from the hills, the aggressive 'Brrrrr ... ' of the machine guns and the sporadic 'cracks' from close-quarter gun battles. It was sobering to think that people had died there.

As we drove, I filmed from the window. Although the camera was constantly being jolted, it seemed somehow fitting for the scenes I was capturing. Every now and then we would see wooden crosses on the side of the road – they stood like milestones, a bitter testimony to lives lost. I figured that they were partly erected out of respect for the deceased, but partly also to serve as a poignant reminder and warning of what happened. A few miles further on we passed a field where a burnt-out tank sat abandoned and destroyed. It was a ghostly scene.

Further on into the country, we approached a village that Sarah wanted to show us. As we pulled off the main road and headed toward the nest of buildings, Sarah and Steve became noticeably edgy. She explained that the small remaining population of this particular village were definitely not pro the SFOR (Stabilization Force). Slowly driving into the village, we saw an old man standing behind his broken garden wall. He stopped what he was doing and watched us as we passed by. Sarah was keen that we should not draw too much attention to ourselves and requested that I keep my camera low and out of sight, which I did. A few hundred yards up on the left we saw an older woman, who again stopped and stared at us as we passed. It was as if they hadn't seen anyone in months. Yet, when you considered their recent trauma and the fact that we were driving in a military vehicle, you could understand why they should be both wary and intrigued. At a nondescript junction on the road we drew to a halt. In front of us there stood a pile of grey rubble the size of a small building. Placed at the top of the rubble was a large wooden cross.

Sarah explained to us that in a church on this site half the local community had been gathered when a shell hit, instantly killing everyone inside. In one fell swoop the population of the village had been decimated! She was quick to make it clear that she wasn't showing us this site as some kind of war tourism, but rather to illustrate the immensely important role of the Stabilization Force. Sensing the intensity of the situation and seeing it reflected in Sarah's face, Danny suggested we filmed a quick interview with her standing in front of the ruin. She hesitantly agreed, providing we were quick. We filmed for about five minutes before a few locals seemed to come out of nowhere to see what was going on. This was still an unstable, hostile environment and to be seen filming their heart-breaking memorial was not good for the reputation of the SFOR, not to mention our own safety. Both Steve and Sarah were keen that we withdrew immediately and Danny and I agreed – we had enough footage to make it work, so we boarded the Land Rover and retreated back to the main road.

We drove on for a few more hours, sometimes talking but mostly just thinking. Time was getting on and we had seen enough to give us an adequate picture of Bosnia, so Steve swung the Land Rover around and we headed back towards Split and the Croatian border. Still routinely radioing our position back to base, Steve was informed that a British Army convoy was heading our way. I shall never forget the moment we saw the convoy approach us. We had stopped for a pee break on the brow of a hill and, while standing behind a rock taking care of business, in the distance I could see a increasingly huge cloud of dust. It was late afternoon and, as the low sun was wilting, the light was fading and the colours, even to the naked eye, became sepia (a warm yellow/brown-stained hue). The vehicles, making up the convoy (at least a dozen), were black – cutting out their shapes on the dust-obscured horizon. The headlights of the vehicles twinkled as they pierced through the dark haze of exhaust and dirt. Land Rovers sandwiched each of the troop-carrying trucks, which dwarfed them as they escorted the trucks through the epic, barren landscape. I ran back to our Land Rover for my camera and tripod, found a spot a few feet in front of the vehicle and set them up as quickly as I could. Anxious not to delay the shot, rather than attaching the Matte Box I just held the Coral Filter in front of the lens by hand. To this day it is still one of the best shots that I have ever taken. The scene was powerful, dramatic and yet beautiful. With photography the magic moment often happens right in front of your eyes

without warning. It's a matter of recognising the composition
as it develops and then reacting quickly enough to capture
it on film. This was a beauty and I nailed it! Once it was
edited and set to classical music the scene was extremely
moving.

We spent the next few days filming different aspects of
Sarah's life in the army. We rode on tank carriers whose single
engine is the size of a Mini! We filmed army dogs patrolling
the fuel stores, which were under constant threat of enemy fire
and theft. We brought dozens of cheap CDs from the NAAFI
store, and on the last day we witnessed a Presentation of
Medals to soldiers who had finished their tour of duty and
were on the way home. It was an amazing insight into the
world of the military operating overseas. I was impressed, yet
also sympathetic to the thankless, tough and routine nature of
the majority of their work.

The flight home to the UK was less exciting, as we knew the
hours of discomfort that lay in store. However, this paled into
insignificance when, as we were saying goodbye, Sarah told us
that a rumour had spread around the base that we were SAS
on Special Ops. It was the civvies, the special treatment and
the lack of clarity about who we were and why we were there
that had fuelled the flames. We like to think it was more to do
with our tough looks and oozing professionalism. As you can
imagine, we loved this rumour – and it was priceless to see the
faces of the servicemen who'd joined us on the plane home
when Fagerson and Mungeam were asked to step through a
separate door on arrival at RAF Lyneham. They thought we
were being whisked back to Hereford ... the reality was that
Danny had an American passport!

Rwanda

I am reminded of North Wales as I sit in the open back of a battered old red truck. We twist and turn our way up and down the dry, dusty dirt mountain roads. The warm air rushes past blowing hard against my face and making my eyes water. The valleys below are cavernous and seemingly never ending. The huge hills are covered in thick, lush, green bush. The soil is deep red and rich in minerals. This land is fertile and, unlike many African countries, there is definitely no shortage of food for its people. As the truck rattles and snakes its way across the backs of the giant hills, I stare into the distant valleys as they swirl beneath. I see hundreds of huts and traces of human dwellings peppering the land. In my glazed stare, I imagine the sight of torches of fire moving through the scrub, a fairy-light trail bringing fear and destruction. Homes are burned to the ground and human lives are devastated. Killing squads, wielding machetes, work their way over the mighty hills and through the valleys, hell-bent on their merciless task. Blood-curdling screams pierce the air as the Hutu strike their horrifying revenge on the Tutsi. Tribal warfare, ethnic cleansing, genocide, call it what you will – one million people killed in one hundred days, I categorise that as a human atrocity!

This is my second trip to Rwanda in one month. The first was a personal trip, not so much a holiday as a professional favour for a friend, Debs, who wished to document on film the story of her family, who had dedicated their lives as missionaries to the people of Rwanda. It entailed a two-week tour of Rwanda and Burundi, which was enlightening and entertaining; but it was the second trip that would permanently etch itself into my memory and conscience.

One week after returning from my first trip, I received a phone call from a Canadian director, Michelle, whom I knew from Lonely Planet days. She asked if I fancied a trip to Rwanda? I told her that I had been in Kigali last week, but I was willing to go back. She was surprised as Rwanda is not the most frequented of countries, but she was also relieved – as it meant I would know what to expect and also know my way around. The assignment was to shoot *B Roll* for a National Geographic documentary on the 'wind-up radio'.

For Rwandans the radio is a lifeline. Living in such remote settings, the vast hills and valleys can leave people feeling isolated and unaware of what is going on in their cities. As well as providing music and entertainment for domestic dwellings, radios also serve a far more serious purpose – they bring news. The country's politics could radically change and the whole country could be taken over, but it would take weeks for the news to filter through to the rural population. Radios have proved themselves critical to the lives of citizens of developing countries who can't afford the technologies that we, in the west, take for granted. Each radio set is highly valued and cherished by its owner. The invention of the wind-up clockwork radio is revolutionary for those millions who don't have access to, or couldn't afford, the batteries required to power a radio. Now, with the simple turn of a clicking dial on the rear of the box, the airwaves have become available to all.

The bulk of the documentary was covering the conception and invention of the product. Our job was to illustrate the radio's effectiveness. We had to demonstrate how radically these radios would change the lives of the Rwandan people.

Michelle picked me up from my home in Wandsworth, and we shared a cab to Heathrow. Ten hours later we were in Kigali airport. For me it was like 'Ground Hog Day'. I wondered if Passport Control would be suspicious as to why I had come back again so quickly. Fortunately they couldn't have cared less.

Wheeling our trolleys piled high with kit through the doors of the Customs Hall and spilling into the Arrivals pen, we were welcomed by a large, jovial, white-haired man called Frank. As soon as we arrived at our hotel, we dumped the camera kit in my room and went to the bar with Frank, who brought us each a large Irish whisky. Frank had left his beloved Ireland many years ago, when he embarked on his long service in the Irish Army. With no ties, he had admirably decided to utilise his retirement to 'give back'. Joining an NGO (Non Governmental Organisation) he had moved to Rwanda a few years previously and had made his home in the capital, Kigali. His job was to manage the various projects run by the charitable organisation, including hosting any media liaisons, a role which he had carried out while in the army. I immediately warmed to Frank, as he was a 'man's man', but with a heart of gold.

Over the next few days he took us on a tour of various projects that were embracing the wind-up radio concept. We visited small villages, schools and orphanages as well as remote, isolated homesteads. It was perfect material for our assignment, but also served as an incredible personal education for Michelle and me. As we approached a location, Frank would share with us the history of the place and tell us about the people that we were to meet ... All the stories were sad; some were shocking!

High in the hills, our Land Cruiser pulled into the front drive of a tattered, old, whitewashed building which served as the local school. We were greeted by a large group of children, most of whom burst into smiles on the sight of Frank, who reciprocated with some bearlike hugs. Michelle and I were then introduced to the teachers who graciously let us film a lesson, which was held outside under the shade of an enormous tree. After the lesson we were joined by the rest of the school pupils who were highly excited to see some more white faces and, of course, a large TV camera. Clambering to be in shot, the ever-increasing mass of little faces beaming big white smiles swarmed around my tripod and shouted. I took the opportunity to just stand there, angle the camera down and film a good five minutes of this sea of beautiful faces. It was great fun and the energy was electric, though the reality hit home when Frank pointed out to us one little girl. She must have been about nine years old and stood with a little baby tied to her back, swaddled in a tribal patterned cloth. He called her over and introduced her to us as Anna. The little baby on her back burst into hysterics! She was glancing at us and then screaming her little head off. Frank explained that, other than him, the baby would never have seen white people before. We 'Muzungus', as they called us 'whiteys', were terrifying the little one. Anna joined us in laughing at her little sister's fit, but in order to reduce her ordeal, she shook our hands and walked off to get us out of her sight. As she left, Frank explained that Anna and her siblings were orphaned in the genocide. With both parents killed, it came down to her, as the first-born, to take charge of the family. At nine years of age she was responsible for five other kids younger than her! One of the many terrible repercussions of genocide is the way whole generations are simply wiped out. In Anna's case, there were no aunties, uncles or guardians to take care of her and her brothers and sisters – they were all dead! It is left to the surviving local communities, churches, charities and NGOs to pick up the pieces and try to provide help for such innocent victims as Anna. The charities do a good job in their effort to help, but they are constantly overwhelmed by the need and lack of funding, resources and staff.

En route to the next location, we stopped at a small huddle of huts that Frank wished us to see. This settlement had been supported by his NGO, which among other things had built a concrete shelter for a woman who was slowly dying of Aids. We stopped at the side of the road and walked down through the scrub into the small plot of farmed land. As with all visits, particularly when filming in Africa, there are customs that you are expected to adhere to. You must first pay respect to the senior person in the family or village and present your greetings before whipping out your camera and getting on with business. Frank led the greetings and paid our respects to the elderly man who was present. We were warmly welcomed. The old man then led us to the concrete structure.

As we walked in we could hear groaning. It was dark and stuffy and, as our eyes slowly adjusted to the light, Frank walked ahead and sat on the floor next to a woman who was curled up in the shadows in the far corner. She woke, turned and sleepily breathed her welcome. She smiled as Frank joked with her. This woman was destined to die with full-blown

HIV/Aids, but the likes of Frank weren't about to give up on her. He was committed to see her living her last days in relative comfort and dignity. He was truly bringing light to a dark place.

On the way out I asked the elderly man (through broken sign language) if I could take his photograph. As I pulled out my stills camera, he stood proudly and looked straight down the lens. His face was full of character and made a brilliant portrait, which is now framed and adorns my wall at home. He smiled and was evidently chuffed to be the subject of my interest. As I drew the camera down from my face, Frank passed behind me and whispered that I should offer him a gift for having the photograph taken. I didn't want to give him money, as I didn't know what amount would be acceptable, so I looked into my shirt pocket and saw a new biro pen. I unclipped the pen and offered it to the man. To my delight his face lit up and, looking at the shiny blue pen, he walked off like the cat that got the cream. Simple gestures from us can mean a lot more when in a different context. After staying a while and filming the scene, we said our goodbyes and climbed back into the jeep. As we pulled away we congratulated Frank on his work and dedication, which he bashfully accepted.

As we drove further down the road, Frank said, 'There's somewhere important that I think you should see before you leave Rwanda.' With this he steered off right at a fork in the dirt road and we continued down a pot-holed track. As we turned a corner to the right I saw a fence with a gate that was locked with a chain and behind it a shaggy lawn leading to a derelict, whitewashed church building. We pulled up outside the fence and disembarked from the vehicle. 'Come, Mungo,' Frank said as I pulled out my camera and followed him. We climbed over the fence and stepped towards the old church building. It was late afternoon by this point and, even though the sun was dipping, it was still hot and we were doused in sweat.

Underfoot the grass was thick and dry. I held the camera at my side as we moved closer and closer towards the mysterious building. I noticed that as we got nearer I sensed a change of smell in the air. Africa has a very distinctive smell: it is a cocktail of warm air mixed with wood smoke and diesel. This, however, was different: it was more of a stench, as if there was something rotting. As we approached the building the vile smell grew stronger and stronger. I felt a pang of uneasiness in the pit of my stomach. Arriving at the church, there was no door on this side of the outer wall, but I noticed that there was a large hole about five feet from the ground. I put the camera on the ground and moved towards it. As I did, a waft of wind blew from within the church and hit me like a wet towel. The overwhelming stench turned my stomach and I dry-wretched. What was in there? I thought to myself. I was reluctant to find out, but curiosity got the better of me. I craned my neck through the dark hole and what lay before me struck me dumb. In the darkness of the musty ruin, I could see the vague outlines of the tops of dark wooden pews – there were maybe twenty rows to each side. But lowering my gaze from these wooden shapes I could see what at first appeared to be piles of dull-coloured rags. There were dirty greens, dusty reds and dull blues. My eyes tried to focus closely on the detail of the textile mass and when it did, I wish it hadn't. I could see that the piles of rags were actually clothes that were covering a mass of dark, almost shapeless bodies. To my horror I was looking at a building full of rotting corpses! I jerked and pulled my head out of the hole. Desperately trying to stifle another deep wretch, I sucked in the comparatively fresh air in great gulps. It was astonishing and atrocious. My heart felt heavy and I took a few steps to where Frank was standing. His joviality had waned and his smile had crumpled into blankness. He turned to me and told me the story of the church and its victims.

Civil war had erupted between the Hutu and Tutsi tribes and the radio stations were used to fuel the fighting. The airwaves had cited death to the Tutsi people and, though it beggars belief, the Hutus literally took up arms and went to war. Almost as if hypnotised, insanity took grip of Hutu men who grasped their farming machetes, went next door to neighbouring Tutsi families and slaughtered them. Organised killing squads were sent out to ravage the hills and valleys, ridding them of Tutsis. Their campaign was brutally savage, terrifying and destructive. A deceptive trick of the Hutu rebels was to broadcast a message to the Tutsi people; 'If you go to your church, you will be spared. Go to your church and you will find safety!' It didn't take long for thousands of terrified Tutsis to flee their homes and descend upon the church grounds.

It was in the grounds of one of these churches that I was now standing with Frank and it was here that the Hutu master plan was carried out. Five thousand Tutsi men, women and children were ushered through the cross-wired fence into the safety of the church. As the last few people were led through the gates, to their horror, with a slam the gates were locked behind them and the killing squad revealed themselves. Working on an almost nine-to-five shift the killing squad went to work. Like butchers they slowly hacked their way through the crowd. The Tutsis were like sheep trapped in a slaughterhouse: there was no escape. To prevent the younger, fitter Tutsi men from fighting back the Hutus slashed each man's Achilles' heels to disable them instantly. If the killing squad didn't get to them first, they would be certain to bleed to death during the night.

As Frank finished talking it suddenly sank in that we were standing on ground that had been soaked in Tutsi blood. The foul stench was but a reminder of the evil that had been played out on those dark, dark days. I stood speechless and my camera remained on the ground. I decided not to film any of what I had seen that day, partly as it bared no relevance to our story, but more out of respect to those whose last breaths were gasped beneath my feet. Michelle and Frank returned to the vehicle but I remained standing where I was, motionless. I felt as though I wanted to cry, but I was too numb for any tears. As I stood looking at the church I remember quietly asking God, 'What's all this about?' My mind spun as I searched for some answers. I can't say that I had any revelations, but I had a tangible sense that God was standing next to me, looking at what I saw before me, full of sorrow at what man had done.

It never fails to amaze me what devastation man can inflict in his senseless drive for power. In the west we can watch and say how barbaric these tribal wars are; yet are the wars that we wage any less brutal? We strive for power and riches as much as the next man, but we have the resources to invent super-weapons that keep us from meeting the man we want to kill, somehow easing the guilt. The world is a scary place and these shrines to such atrocities serve as a reminder of just how low we can go.

Sitting on the plane returning to the UK, I was quiet, deep in thought. This trip sticks in my mind, not only because of the sights that I saw at the church that day, but more because it was the day I felt hope leave me. Before that trip to Rwanda I had travelled to over ten countries in Africa. Leaving those countries I had always harboured a degree of hope that a solution could be found for the people. I could see that when the politics are sorted out, then they will know a longer-lasting peace, or when the rains come again, the dry and thirsty earth will again sprout a harvest. Yet, the only solution I could envisage for a country such as Rwanda was to see the hearts of men changed. Who could do this? God? But, then, I had heard that the history of Rwanda was genocide, then Christian revival, then more genocide, and again revival, etc. This evidently wasn't enough. Maybe it is just the cruel cycle of life.

I think that what this world needs are more 'Franks': those rare, selfless individuals who 'give back', as a way of saying thankyou for all they have been given. There lies the challenge!

People often ask me how I cope, experiencing such traumatic sights. I rattle off that I am being paid to be there and I have a job to do. So, I harden my heart and don't dwell on the details. Having said that, I am aware that you cannot let emotion fester in your head or your heart. At some point it will rise to the surface.

A few days after arriving home, I sat at my computer writing an email. Without a definite prompt, I felt an uncontrollable need to grieve for what I had seen and heard of in Rwanda ... I sat and wept.

10

Dark Days in Africa

Jane hummed a happy tune as she walked through the unkempt grounds of the large ex-pats' residence, found in a stunning rural setting ten miles west of Harare, Zimbabwe. The sky was sapphire and there wasn't a breath of wind, as the late afternoon sun beat down in heavy rays upon her bare shoulders. Her tanned, sandaled feet brushed through sun-bleached, brittle long grass, which miraculously existed in the parched dust they called African soil. She was taking time out, alone, as the rest of us sat drinking bitter homemade lemonade on the veranda of the grand old house that could have told a thousand tales.

As she wandered in and out of the low-slung trees, her thoughts were a world away. Day-dreaming she took stock of her truly blessed life, her love and her future. Beautiful, tall and blonde, since birth she had been garlanded with

Hollywood actress looks. Not surprisingly, she had a wealthy boyfriend who worshipped her every move. But, above all, there was Sophie, her adorable six-year-old daughter, who was the jewel in her crown. 'Could life get any better?' she thought, as she reached the far corner of the vast garden.

The corner was enveloped by the shadow of the largest tree on the estate but, despite being dark and somewhat foreboding, it offered shade and a cooler temperature. She sighed with relief as she slipped into the shade that brought the sensation of a cool towel being draped over her glowing shoulders. As her eyes slowly adjusted to the darkness, she noticed that tucked into the corner there was a small, purposefully positioned pile of rocks. Always one to be inquisitive she cautiously stepped forward to take a closer look. When close enough to reach out to touch the rocks, she noticed some wooden trinkets that were hung over individual stones. Then it sank in. Her natural smile faded and her skin grew goose bumps as her blood rapidly ran cold. Her feet stumbled backwards and, with a sharp intake of breath, she thrust herself back into the safety of the bright sunlight. Shocked and without hesitating, she turned her back and ran back to the safety of the big house. The pile of rocks was a Voodoo grave!

I had been recruited into a team of six, as the Cameraman/ Director, to shoot a short film on an orphanage located on the outskirts of Harare. Steve, the catalyst for the trip, had seen me on *Streetmate* and, due to my expressed beliefs, thought that I would be sympathetic to the cause – a private school in the UK twinning itself with an African orphanage. I was sympathetic and thought it a good opportunity to use what I was good at to give back to those who were less fortunate than myself. After a brief, somewhat unorganised meeting in York I had agreed to take on the unpaid ten-day project and before I knew it I was on the plane!

My travelling companions were relatively inexperienced as far as what to expect from Africa was concerned. Steve (45), who was predominantly a businessman with a colourful past – including a spell of hospitality at Her Majesty's pleasure (prison!) – had recently become a Christian and now wanted to put right some things he had taken advantage of in the past. Having visited the struggling orphanage on a previous trip, he had seen that his business skills could be put to good use in its aid. Hence he had pulled together a team of supporters to see first hand and report on what conditions these African kids were living in. Rachel (19) was an innocent and somewhat geeky student who had been recruited from a media course at a local college in York. She had been brought along to lend a helping hand, but was mostly there for the experience. Maureen (39) was a representative from a local supermarket chain, who had been supporting Steve and his project by raising cash donations from their shoppers. Finally Jane (40), accompanied by her daughter, represented the private school where Sophie was a pupil. They had brought with them a shipment of clothing donated by the affluent school. We were a mixed bunch but, entwined by the worthy nature of the trip, we all seemed to get on fine.

On our arrival in Zimbabwe, it appeared that the logistics had been well planned by Steve. We were met by a minibus and driven an hour and a half out of the city to the orphanage. The road out of Harare was typical of an African thoroughfare: although laid with tarmac, the road, due to the vast amount of traffic and the unforgiving climate, was in desperate need of a facelift. As always, for us to drive on such treacherous roads would have been not far from suicide, but our local driver knew no different, so drove with confidence and relative skill. The turning off the main road led us up a mile of deeply pitted, red dirt track, which eventually brought us to the front of the orphanage.

The building was reminiscent of an old school which had been bombed in the war and left as it was! The grey walls were in disrepair and some windows were missing. Up the five steps that led to the front door, there was a long concrete platform that served as a veranda, which reminded me of a small section of the promenade in Brighton. It was here that we first met those that we had come to film, encourage and help – the orphans. It never ceases to amaze me that whenever I meet people in developing countries whom life has dealt a terrible hand to, they still seem to be happy! I figure that they are simply happy to be alive!

There was a mixed group of girls and boys, mixed in age as well as shape and size! As we arrived, they were sitting on the 'Promenade', some hand in hand, others playing games and jokingly pushing each other. As we climbed out of the minibus their faces lit up with huge white smiles, and the more confident members of the group crowded forward to grab our hands and boastfully use their official-sounding English saying, 'Hello, my name is...' or, 'Good afternoon, Sir, my name is...'

Before too long 'Mama', an enormous black lady, waddled out of the front door and greeted us with a subservient handshake and an enormous smile. I watched with interest as she greeted Steve with a huge hug, which was final confirmation for me that we were over here for genuinely good reasons.

For years 'Mama' had taken on the responsibility of running the orphanage. Despite a lack of funds, resources and knowledge (except that of being a surrogate mother to the orphaned kids) she had struggled on. Some of us would be quick to say that what she had achieved was not up to the standard that it should have been, but you can't deny that in her unconditional love and self-sacrifice, she had provided these beautiful kids with a roof over their heads and a place to call 'home'.

With a word Mama called a few of the bigger boys to help us with our bags and to show us to our rooms. The girls on our team would be staying in the main building, in separate rooms, but along with all the orphan girls. Steve and I were taken to the out-buildings found at the rear of the crumbling complex. En route we walked past an empty derelict swimming pool – it had obviously been many years since anyone had splashed around in there! Stepping through the doorway of what looked like an old air-raid shelter, we were led down two long, dark corridors and shown to the room which we would be sharing. Apart from two mats laid on the concrete floor at one end of the room, which was about the size of a garage, it was completely empty. The smooth concrete walls had one tiny window and a single, dim light bulb hanging precariously from the centre of the ceiling. It was basic, in the truest meaning of the word, but it was relatively clean and I had seen worse. I quietly thought to myself that it must have been quite a familiar abode for Steve after his stint 'inside'! Especially seeing that our door was a metal gate, with a padlock on it! Our 'concierge' warned us that even though we were on their side, some of the older boys were not to be trusted. Having started their childhood living on the streets, this to me was completely forgivable. In the poor light I chose the mat on the left and joked around with Steve as we put up our mosquito nets and laid out our silk sleeping bags.

That first night, our meal was chicken and rice, served on well-used plastic plates with cutlery. I knew that all the stops were out to make us feel welcome. It was over this feast that we met one particularly unusual resident of the orphanage. She was the least likely person that I was expecting to see under such circumstances, and not only was she a genuine hero of her generation but for me she would later prove herself to be my only source of sanity!

Avril literally appeared in a cloud of smoke! Her room was situated around the corner from Mama's dining room where we were sitting around the table. As the door to her room opened, it wasn't dissimilar to the scene from *Stars in Their Eyes*, when the guest famously says, 'Tonight, Matthew, I'm going to be ... Elvis!' and then disappears into a fog of smoke, while being silhouetted by a backlight!

Elvis..., I mean Avril, is an elderly, white-haired, little old lady from North Wales. A year previously, while living her sedate lifestyle back in the valleys, she had suffered a heart attack. This left her grateful to be alive, yet also determined to make the most of what life she had left. To her family's dismay, and despite her medical history and her continuing cigarette smoking, she decided that rather than sitting in her lovely little home whiling away the hours, she still had something to offer the world! Many years ago she had been a very capable nurse and although her physical prowess wasn't what it used to be, she still knew how to administer proficient first aid and look after someone. She found out about the orphanage, bought a plane ticket, kissed her family goodbye and moved to Zimbabwe for six months. This brave move not only satisfied her need to do something, but it soon revived her love of life. The orphans loved their 'Grand Mama' and she loved them dearly in return. This remarkable lady fascinated me. Not only had she stepped over the line of what was sensible to discover adventure, but she was helping others in a profound way in the process. She was also armed with a wicked sense of humour, which, having being invited into her room for a cheeky cigarette, we both delighted in!

It was a few days into our trip when things started to go not exactly according to plan. Jane, Sophie, Maureen, Rachel, Steve and I had been on various tours of the local area. Rachel and I had got some good footage of the orphanage and interviews with the kids, etc. We had met some of the families in the surrounding villages, made up of circular mud huts (just what you'd picture Africa to be like in your imagination). In these huts, we talked to numerous relatives who told a disturbingly similar story. Their families, once twelve people strong, now consisted of only two, as the other ten had been ruthlessly wiped out by HIV/Aids! At home, when you hear on the *Six O'Clock News* about the HIV/Aids pandemic, you tend to concentrate on pushing your TV dinner around your plate. Here standing face to face with the survivors, there was nowhere to hide!

Many of the stories we were shooting were very harrowing. Most times death had come so quickly that the surviving relatives would still be in shock and break down in tears at your feet. I had experienced this trauma a few times before in Africa, particularly while filming for Worlds Aids Day in Malawi. Seeing such devastation, sadness and fear in someone's eyes can never fail to disturb you.

We discovered that the reason why there were so many orphans in Zimbabwe was due to their entire family having died of HIV/Aids. Mama and Avril were doing their bit to clear up the mess that the disease left in its trail as it swept the continent. True heroes!

Amidst the sad stories, Steve and I both thought it important to give the team some time off, to enjoy the more pleasant side of Africa. So Steve contacted Barbara whom he had met on his previous trip. Barbara and her father were white Zimbabweans who owned and ran a safari park a few hours' drive from the orphanage. Over the years they had become specialists in black rhino conservation, which included breeding and, when appropriate, relocating them to other safari parks to ensure the survival of the species. By now they had acquired quite a name for themselves in this field, which had increased their need for publicity. Steve struck a deal with Barbara that, in return for a day's safari for the team, I would shoot a short video news release for her own use. Being a shrewd businesswoman and having a shortage of broadcast cameramen passing through, she jumped at the opportunity.

After a few intense days, the day before we were due to go on our safari day, we began our couple of days' relaxation by visiting some ex-pat neighbours of the orphanage. They were again a white Zimbabwean family who owned a vast amount of farmland in the district. We were invited to take afternoon tea with them at their house, which was a forty-five-minute walk through the bush, past a few 'mud hut' villages and onto their land. It was an extraordinary walk that could only be in Africa. It was like walking through the film set of *Zulu*, then into an enormous westernised complex from *Out of Africa*.

The daughters of the family invited us in and introduced us to their eccentric, yet amusing mother. We were then shown into the magnificent main room, where the walls were adorned with mounted gazelle heads and the floor was carpeted with animal hides. The housemaids were sent off to fetch our refreshments, as we revelled in the luxury of a home away from home. We drank homemade lemonade, chatted about our contrasting lives and relaxed in the dappled sunlight on the veranda. Jane went off for a quiet walk to gather her thoughts after an upsetting few days, while we entertained Sophie. It was a happy time and the excitement of the following day's safari had gripped us all. It was late afternoon by the time we thanked our guests and made our way back to the orphanage before it grew dark. Despite our relaxing afternoon we were all tired, so headed for our beds shortly after supper.

The next morning I was first into the bathroom that Steve and I were sharing. I went to the loo and then threw a few ladles of cold water over my head, from the big barrel that was our washing water supply. Every morning this was a shock to the system, but it did the trick and woke me up in an instant! Once dressed I headed over to the main building block, past the empty pool, said 'hello' to a few kids that I met along the way and headed in for breakfast – my favourite meal of the day! As I ate my coveted bowl of porridge Rachel came into the dining room, looking like death warmed up. 'Didn't sleep too well, hey Rach?' I said with my mouth full and in that annoying tone of a 'morning person'. 'We had a nightmare over here,' Rachel replied, and I could tell by the quiver in her voice that something serious had taken place. Quickly swallowing my mouthful of porridge and pushing the plate aside, I took Rachel out to the Promenade, sat her down and asked her what had happened. She then embarked on a story that I could hardly believe I was hearing...

Before they went to bed, Avril and Rachel had been having a smoke in Avril's bedroom. Jane had stuck her head in to say goodnight, as she was passing by from the bathroom to her room, where Sophie was already fast asleep. All seemed fine as they wished each other a peaceful night's sleep. Only that clearly wasn't the case. In the early hours of the morning Avril was woken out of her sleep by Jane standing over her bed with a carving knife thrust above her head, as if to stab Avril lying beneath her! Though terrified, in an instant, Avril calmly said to Jane, 'Jane, dear, what on earth is wrong?' Jane shook, as she stood frozen in the murderous stance, staring at Avril with glazed-over eyes and said nothing! Avril hadn't survived the war, or her heart attack, by being weak, though this was equally as testing. Again, as she lay beneath Jane, she calmly said, 'Jane ... what's wrong?' Still Jane remained frozen, at which point Avril decided to take the risk and move. She slowly sat up, gently took hold of Jane's left elevated arm and with her other hand cautiously took hold of the knife and removed it from Jane's grip. With that action, Jane slumped down, seating herself beside Avril on the bed, and began to weep. After spending some time consoling her, Avril then gently got up and led Jane back to her bed. Obviously, Avril had been through a traumatic experience and, on returning to her bed, locked the door but didn't get a wink of sleep. She later told me that she lay in bed not only thinking about what had happened and why Jane had acted in such a way, but worrying even more about little Sophie's safety.

Having heard Rachel's account of events I went in search of Avril, both to make sure that she was OK and to hear her account of the night's events. I found her in her room, looking surprisingly together. She confirmed, word for word, what had happened and also expressed the opinion that something desperately needed to be done, as she didn't want events to escalate and herself to end up dead! By this stage Steve was in the dining room along with Jane and Sophie, so I asked him to step outside where I told him what had occurred. His face dropped as I told him all that had taken place. Without pausing he voiced his concern, but also that personally he felt too close to Jane to confront her about the matter. It was clear that if Steve, being the team leader, wasn't prepared to act, then I must. I asked him to contact Barbara and postpone the safari until the next day, as people were exhausted due to the lack of sleep and also it would give us time to sort the situation out properly. He did.

I then asked Jane if I could have a word with her and we both went outside. Explaining that I had been told what had gone on last night, I asked her if she was aware of what had happened. Her reaction was strange as, while she seemed to be aware of what she had done and was very apologetic, she seemed to be expecting everyone to just dismiss it and carry on as if nothing had ever happened! She went on to explain to me that the sad, dark environment of the orphanage and the tragic stories that we'd heard were just too much for her to cope with. I thought this certainly could be the cause of some unrest, but it was *no excuse* for holding a carving knife over a little old lady as she slept! I said to Jane that I thought it would be best for her to leave the orphanage, if it was indeed causing such obvious anxiety. I would pay for her and Sophie to stay in a decent hotel in Harare to help her sort her head out and decide whether she would stay. I was hoping that this would result in her buying an air ticket home . . . and in retrospect it should have done!

Jane had an incredible ability to manipulate people. I was convinced that she should leave immediately for her sake as well as ours, but she set about talking to Avril and Steve, persuading them that what had happened was a dreadful mistake, that it wouldn't happen again and that she should definitely stay at least another night. And from that point on she appeared totally normal. This normality was so convincing that, by the end of the day, we pretty much all thought that maybe her actions really were the result of an extremely vivid nightmare. I made a point of consulting Avril, who agreed that she would be happy for Jane to stay at the orphanage and would just lock her door! And so it was . . . To my relief, all seemed to be normal again.

It was a quiet night with no dramas and we all woke up with the happy thought of going on safari. Avril had slept well. Rachel, Maureen and Steve were all putting yesterday behind them and looking forward to the day ahead. Jane was on good form, as was Sophie, who was beside herself at the thought of seeing a real-life elephant. I was just relieved that everything was back to normal again. I packed my camera equipment into the minibus and we all headed off to Barbara's.

The safari park was just how we had hoped it would be. To reach the lodge, you had to drive through a vast grass plain, which was sliced into two halves by the single dirt road. Driving through the gate, you entered a courtyard circled by trees. The lodge itself was majestic, with huge wooden doors, beautiful sash windows and the look of a hunting lodge you would expect to find in the highlands of Scotland. It must have taken years to build, and everything was finished to perfection, obviously without any concern for the expense. As we arrived, Barbara came bouncing out of the main doors. She was a very attractive middle-aged woman, with blonde shoulder-length hair, a sporty gait and a healthy tan. On first impressions I likened her to the actress from *Born Free* and, within a few minutes of getting to know her, I figured that's pretty much who she was like. She told us that her father was one of the great conservationists in Zimbabwe. He had always had a passion for elephant and black rhino. As a child Barbara had grown up living in the lodge where she frequently shared her bedroom with an orphaned baby elephant – they literally had a baby elephant in the same way we would have a dog! She was a wonderfully entertaining hostess and after a few refreshments we set about loading everyone into the Safari jeeps. Between the team we filled two jeeps. They were effectively Subaru utility double-cab vehicles that had been converted, with two-tiered seating benches being added on the open back.

As I was to film Barbara driving one of the jeeps, I joined her in the passenger seat of the cab. While she was driving I interviewed her about the park, her black rhino conservation and various other subjects that came to me. She answered eloquently and intelligently, in between pausing to point out animals to those seated in the back. It was a fantastic morning as we saw gazelle, zebra and a baby black rhino (with a full-time armed bodyguard to protect it from poachers), and we even stopped to watch a family of elephant drinking at a waterhole. Shortly after seeing the elephants we stopped at another idyllic waterhole, where there were more elephants and rhino bathing. Barbara had arranged for her game staff to go ahead and set up a picnic lunch for us in a spot overlooking the magical scene. This was the treatment we all so desperately needed and the events of the night before last seemed as if they had never happened at all.

I'll definitely never forget that lunchtime because, as I sat taking a mammoth bite into my sandwich, I witnessed in front of me a bull elephant mounting a female rhino! I practically spat my sandwich out as I guffawed in laughter and admittedly in some shock! Being the opportunist cameraman, I literally dived for my camera and filmed the event. I remember being particularly amused by the reaction of those around me: some had to turn their backs in embarrassment and others sat silently gob-smacked in disbelief! I sat filming, thinking of the money I could make on the Internet – which I later decided was not really that professional of me.

After lunch (and the circus entertainment!) we climbed back up onto the jeeps and headed back to the Lodge. I decided that, on top of all the other footage I had shot with Barbara, I would need to cement it all together with a more substantial sit-down interview. When we arrived back, as the rest of the team enjoyed sitting in the sun, surrounded by the beautifully landscaped garden, Barbara showed me into her office, where I began to set the camera up on the tripod for the interview. While I was setting up, we were casually chatting about her amazing life. We were just laughing about a particularly funny story when the door burst open and Rachel ran into the room, 'Mungo, quick, Jane's stabbing Steve!' Without a thought I was out of the door and into the garden where Jane was lunging at Steve. 'Jane!' I shouted as I ran towards her. She moved away from Steve and stood panting like a wild animal. Steve grabbed his chest and stumbled away from us. 'Steve, are you OK?' I said, desperately trying to think of how best to deal with this situation. Sophie sat down and began to cry. I knew that I was big enough to physically man-handle Jane, so I stood between them, never taking my eye off Jane. I saw that she was grasping a sharpened pencil (sounds innocent enough, but any sharpened instrument that is capable of puncturing the skin is a good-enough weapon). I firmly told Jane to drop the pencil and come over to me, which she did. Rachel and Barbara were attending to Steve, who had sustained some minor wounds, but the shock had got to him and he was sobbing hysterically. Maureen cuddled Sophie as she led her away from the terrible scene. 'Jane, come on inside with me,' I urged. 'NO!' she screamed and lunged at me with her fists. I grabbed her flailing arms and held them with all my strength, while she hissed and spat at me, as though she was having a seizure (she clearly wasn't). Each time she looked at Steve she went berserk, so I physically yanked at her, pulling her by the arms over the lawn and into the house. Having forcefully dragged her through the doorway, I let her go and shut the door behind us.

Inside the house, she seemed to calm down as she sat weeping and taking very deep breaths. Outside Rachel was trying to comfort Steve who was still crying. Seeing that he was not seriously hurt Barbara joined me inside. While keeping a close eye on Jane, Barbara and I conferred on what to do. I told Barbara about what had happened the previous night and, feeling that she obviously had a mental problem, proposed that we should get her to a doctor as soon as possible. But this was Africa! The nearest hospital was an hour-and-a-half drive away. Here there was no ambulance service we could call on. As we talked, Jane got up and began to walk around the hallway where we were sitting. She was muttering gibberish under her breath and swinging her arms about, as if she was drunk or high! Then she started to sing a strange, off-key song, which sounded like the kind of child's nursery rhyme that you would hear played in a horror film. As she walked and sang she began to get visibly wound up again and then exploded into another rage! I pounced on her again and constrained her arms, and in response she screamed and viciously stared me in the eyes. As she stared me out, I spoke to her in a calm voice, repeatedly saying, 'Calm down, Jane, it's all going to be all right.'

I am six foot two and of a sturdy build; she is five foot six and of a slight build; but I have to admit that at one point when she locked her eyes on mine and gave a deathly deep growl, while on the outside I stayed strong, on the inside I was quite scared! It was as if someone else was staring at me through her body! However, knowing I was the only one able to restrain her, I consciously hid my fear and stood strong.

Whilst screaming obscenities in my face, she then started to shout out that I had raped her and her daughter! I guessed this was meant to shake me. If anything, the reverse happened, as it made me angry and more determined to hold on. Meanwhile, Barbara had dashed off to find some Valium.

By the time she returned with the tablets, Jane had temporarily exhausted herself, so she weakened and sat back down. I let her go. Barbara consoled her and talked to her as you would a five-year-old, saying over and over again that it was all OK, etc. She asked Jane to swallow the tablet. Still somewhat delirious, Jane nodded and agreed. As she took the pill, placed it in her mouth and took a sip of water, the cup being firmly held by Barbara, in the corner of her eye she saw Steve who had come inside. He was leaning around the corner looking at her. That was it. She went ballistic!

'Get out!' I shouted to Steve, as Jane grabbed an enormous glass vase and raised it above her head. As she was about to throw it, Barbara grasped it firmly out of her hands. Jane was literally like a wild animal.

It was now a good hour after the initial attack. The sun had gone down and we were all exhausted but Jane, in particular, was on her last legs. As she screamed again and spun around, I took hold of a blanket that was laid over a chair, stretched it out and, making a dive towards her, wrapped it tightly around her. That was it: I had her and she couldn't move! Barbara saw what I had done and immediately grabbed her car keys. I took hold of Jane, bent down and threw her over my shoulder in a fireman's carry. Barbara opened the door and I marched out of the house into the courtyard. Seeing which car Barbara intended to drive I opened the front door and threw Jane in. Barbara sat in the driver's seat, Jane in the middle and me in the passenger's seat. She was jammed in between us and had nowhere to go. She kept screaming for Sophie to come with her, which made Barbara stop and think. She wondered whether it might have a calming effect if Sophie came with us to the hospital. I went with her instinct and agreed. So Barbara left us in the car and went to fetch Sophie. Meanwhile, I talked to Jane, telling her to calm right down, as she didn't want to do anything to scare her daughter. This worked a treat and had the desired effect. Sophie sat between Jane and me, as Barbara drove us to the hospital. On the seemingly never-ending journey, Jane spoke quietly to Sophie. Barbara and I didn't say a word.

When we arrived at the western-style hospital the nurses took Jane into a room and laid her on the bed. As Barbara briefed the doctor on what had occurred, I played games with Sophie, pretending to be an elephant while she rode on my shoulders and steered me around the reception. The doctors were excellent and took very seriously all that we had told them (I feared that they might think we were the ones who had gone mad!). They agreed that it was best for Jane to stay in the hospital overnight so that they could keep an eye on her. After letting Sophie kiss Jane goodnight, Barbara and I took her into our care and began the long drive back to the Lodge. Within minutes little Sophie was asleep in my arms and, after such a traumatic evening, we all needed to go to bed.

When we pulled back into the Lodge courtyard, Steve was already in bed sound asleep. Rachel and Maureen met us and took Sophie off to bed with them for the night. Barbara showed me a beautiful guest room where I could stay for the night and then offered me a stiff drink. We sat for an hour or so drinking whisky at the Lodge's outside bar, going over what had been a truly bizarre day! Both emotionally and physically exhausted, we eventually crawled into our beds.

The next morning, Barbara phoned the hospital to see what the doctors had decided to do. We felt our prayers had been answered when they said that they thought it best for Jane to return to the UK immediately under Doctor's Orders. We phoned her boyfriend who arranged a flight later that day. We dropped Sophie off at the hospital, where they would be arranging the whole chaperoned trip home.

As we said our goodbyes at the hospital, I asked Jane what she thought it was that had sent her over the edge. It was then that she told us of the Voodoo grave that she had stumbled across earlier in the trip. Maybe it was that a Voodoo spirit had possessed her? The doctors said it was likely to be the Larium, the anti-malarial drugs that she had been taking, on top of a slightly unstable mind. Science and spirituality never did agree! I have to say that what I witnessed certainly seemed far more extreme than a reaction to a drug. I guess we shall never know!

The relief among those of us who were remaining was palpable. Steve was still in a nervous state and we could obviously all do with a proper rest. So, Rachel, Maureen and I took off to Victoria Falls for the weekend, where I had the most amazing white-water rafting trip down the Zambezi River ... just what the doctor ordered for me!

The rest of the trip is something of a blur. We carried on, did what we had to do and left. Once back in the UK Steve and I were in contact once or twice, but then we lost contact. I doubt if I'll ever see those people again, but one thing's for sure, I will certainly never forget those dark days in Africa!

11

Wild Life – Ethiopia Diary

By the time my taxi arrives outside my flat on Wandsworth Common, I have already moved all my luggage (fourteen flight cases of all shapes and sizes) down the stairs from my first-floor flat to the pavement. As always, when a taxi driver sees the amount of equipment his one passenger is carrying, he scratches his head and sighs; yet after years of packing this amount of kit into small spaces, I step in to assist this life-size game of 'Tetris'. Before too long the car is packed and we are driving up the road. As we near the end of my road, I run through my compulsory mental checklist to make sure that I have everything I need.

This is my last chance to grab that one item that if left behind could prove to be a disaster. When going to such remote locations, which couriers can't get to, one missing item of kit could very easily jeopardise the entire shoot. I check: tickets –

yes, passport – yes, camera – of course! Yet I still have that instinctive feeling of unrest that tells me something is missing.

Sitting at the traffic lights I desperately scrummidge through the piles of cases checking off each one ... What is it? What is missing? Like a bolt of lightning it hits me ... the long black cylindrical tripod case is missing! 'Thank God I realised now ... ' I tell the taxi driver who turns his wheel to do a U-turn. As we pull up to the spot from which we had just set off, there standing bolt upright on the pavement is the tripod! I am lucky for two reasons: one, that I have remembered it before getting on the flight and, two, that it is still there at all. I once had two luggage straps stolen from that exact spot, having left them on the ground for no more than two minutes – they were worth a couple of pounds each: the tripod is worth close to £4,000! With the relief of finding the missing piece of my complex jigsaw of kit, I recline my passenger seat and try to enjoy the journey to Heathrow Airport.

Arriving at Heathrow is always a mission; when travelling alone with so much kit, however, it can become like a circus act! As we pull up, I leave the kit in the taxi and run over to the dormant snake of luggage trolleys. I hastily calculate how many I think I'll need (three on this occasion?), and aggressively pull them out and drag them over the bus lanes to the mountain of luggage that the taxi driver is slowly building in my brief absence. With the trolleys buckling under the load I shake the taxi driver's hand and then start the convoy rolling. Two trolleys in front and one dragged behind ... seems to work. I feel as though I'm driving a stage coach in a cowboy movie, as I crack my whip and feel the tug of the metal horses. Occasionally I have to let one freewheel in some random direction, while I wrestle to correct the direction of my other wayward steeds! Keeping a keen eye on the pedestrians, representatives of nations from all over the globe, I manage to attack the looming revolving door with the skill of an expert herdsman. The pedestrians appear to lack faith in my ability and, on seeing me approach them at speed, they, quite literally, dive for cover!

When travelling with such expensive equipment to a country outside of the European Union, one has to get a 'carnet' stamped (official Customs' paperwork proving that I am intending to bring home what I take out of the UK – rather than selling it off in some faraway land). This requires me to visit the Customs and Excise desk, found on the ground floor of the airport terminal, before checking in for my flight. This procedure is never too much trouble, apart from the fact that I have to negotiate my wild stage coach through a sea of wandering, jet-lagged travellers. It just adds one more thing to the strain of my journey.

When I eventually reach the check-in desk, I am already tired, often slightly irritable and always covered in a thin layer of sweat – and I haven't even seen a plane yet, let alone started my twenty-four-hour journey! Scoping out the one check-in agent who looks as though they know what they are doing, I pull my metal horses up to their counter. The response I get is varied: some are exasperated at the sight of my luggage; the more experienced just get on with checking me in. Inevitably they warn me that I am likely to occur a financial penalty for excess baggage, but this is normally pre-paid by the production manager from the production company that I am working for. In the case of a not-so-organised production manager, it has been known for me to put the excess baggage on to my credit card until I return from the trip. However, with the amounts totalling up to £5,000, this is understandably never popular with the cameraman.

When I'm checked onto the flight and I see my luggage disappearing down the 'Outsize Luggage' conveyor belt, I can finally relax. Due to its fragility and considerable cost, I tend to carry my camera as hand luggage – it has been known at check-in for the airline staff to put up a fight, saying that the camera is too large to take on to the aircraft, but I'm yet to lose the argument when I say, 'Would you put your fifty-thousand-pound camera in the hold?' No more questions asked.

Unlike some of my colleagues, I have never been one for buying loads of duty free before a flight … most probably because I've already run out of hands and shoulders to carry it with. With my camera on one shoulder and my Day Sack (small rucksack) on the other, I head straight to the newsagent's where I buy a magazine, a bottle of water and then on to Starbucks. I try to save some appetite for the meal on the plane, so my favourite snack is the tuna melt panini and a café latte.

My flight is direct to Addis Ababa, where I will then transfer to a light aircraft for the last leg of the journey to Gondar. Despite being tired, I feel full of anticipation. To be shooting a wildlife documentary for National Geographic is exciting enough, let alone for it to be in Ethiopia – a new country for me to experience.

I include now some extracts from the diary I kept over the three weeks of the shoot, to try and give a feel of my day-to-day life as a cameraman on location.

Sunday 10 October – Day 1

Flight to Addis, then Gondar. Drive from Gondar to Dembark (2.5 hrs), then to camp (1 hr). I had finally arrived in the Simien Mountains of Northern Ethiopia.

Emily Barnett (Producer) met me at Gondar airport, which is a small, nondescript rural airport, the like of which had become very familiar from previous adventures. As I was waiting by the single, rickety, old luggage conveyor belt set behind a huge glass window I could see Emily and the driver (Abi) standing by the jeep outside. The luggage conveyor belt seemed to be a formality to make the airport feel more 'international'; in reality it would have taken the baggage handler three more steps to deliver it to our feet! This quirkiness was, however, easily forgivable as it reminded you of just where you were. I caught Emily's attention, smiled and waved. She was pleased to see me and also relieved that I had made it on schedule.

In this airport there may have been a luggage conveyor belt but there were no trolleys, so, while I wrestled with all the boxes, Emily tried to enter through the glass door to give me a hand. She hadn't taken two steps inside before getting stopped by a security guard. I continued to drag the cases over as she tried to argue her way in, but the stony-faced guard was not giving an inch – this was definitely Africa!

There was a stormy sky above as Abi, our driver, loaded all the kit onto the roof rack of the four-wheel-drive. On leaving the airport it started to rain. The short drive to Gondar took us along endless long, flat roads through grasslands: to me it seemed more like Kathmandu or some other hilly city than the Africa I had up till now experienced. Due to the storm, Abi advised Emily that it would be safer for us to spend the night in a hotel in Gondar, since the majority of the route to Dembark was by dirt road, which in the rain would become unstable and unsafe. I was happy with this as I'd been travelling for twenty-four hours and all I wanted was a bath and a bed. Emily was ecstatic as she had been camping up in the mountains for the last three weeks and hadn't had a bath or slept in a proper bed for all that time! Abi beamed his toothless smile at us when he saw our reaction to his suggestion and drove us to the best hotel in Gondar.

By African standards the hotel was quite swanky. Built on a hill overlooking the small, rural city of Gondar, it had the look of a game lodge; the interior was made of dark wood and was adorned with animal skins. After unloading the kit and finding our rooms, we gave each other half an hour to get ourselves bathed and dressed before meeting in the bar where we ordered two Chivas Regal whiskys, which is what we always drank when we met at our local at home in London. It was dusk, so, taking our drinks with us, we went for a walk through the overgrown garden to a look-out point on a cliff, from where we could see the twinkling city lights. It was a magical sight, with the yellow and orange lights standing out brightly against the dark, brooding, and stormy sky above. The air was still and it was eerily quiet with only the odd distant car horn echoing in the busy world below us.

On first impressions, compared to my previous visits to African countries, Gondar had a far more relaxed feel to it. Elsewhere you would usually sense some strains of tension or uneasiness, often leaving you feeling somewhat alien and unwelcome. This city (probably due to its remote geographical position – North-East Ethiopia) seemed peaceful and at ease with itself and its neighbours. We returned to the restaurant to have a meal and a few more whiskys before retiring to bed.

It was dark when we went to bed and it was dark when we got up. We had arranged to meet Abi at 5.30 in the morning to start our ascent into the mountains. I carried the kit from my room to the driveway, as Abi loaded it onto the roof rack. It was dark, damp and miserable, setting the pattern for our early morning start every day for the next three weeks!

The journey to Dembark was long, bumpy and hectic. Two and a half hours felt like four, though I could not deny that I was very excited about being there. We trundled through numerous little villages, each with three or four mud-and-stick huts. We must have passed hundreds of kids scattered along the road; occasionally one of them would spot our white faces and wave. I have always felt uneasy, almost embarrassed, about being a 'tourist' and have shied away from the tourist routes wherever possible. The depth of the adventure and experience seems so much more authentic when you travel through towns and meet people groups that are not familiar with visitors. In many countries I have been to, the locals roll their eyes at a new white face; here they were genuinely warm and welcoming.

As we passed by the last few houses on the outskirts of Dembark, it was clear that we had left civilisation behind. The road was beginning to wind sharply upwards onto the foothills of the Simien Mountains, turning the air cold and clean. Watching the altitude rise on my Suunto watch, which has a built-in digital altimeter, I could see we were now rapidly notching up the metres. Out of the half-opened car window, to our left unfolded some of the most breathtaking views I have ever seen! It was like a scene from *The Lord of the Rings*, with densely covered, jagged, green mountains leading off into the distance, as far as the eye could see. I joked with Emily that we had left 'Gondor' (Gondar) and were entering 'Middle Earth'! She laughed ... I think out of sympathy!

The road seemed never-ending, but I was quite happy simply sitting and watching the unbelievable view. As we drew closer to the area where we were camping, we started to look out for the Gelada baboons – no sign of them!

Before too long, having traversed up and down numerous mountain escarpments, we reached an altitude of 14,000 feet. Soon after we finally arrived at the small grassy plateau that was our camp. After four hours of solid driving the time was still only 9.30 a.m.

Just as our battered Toyota Landcruiser pulled into the camp, Paul Williams (Director/Cameraman) appeared from some bushes, camera in hand, having just chased a small group of baboons that had randomly wandered through the camp. Matt (Sound Recordist) and Chadden Hunter (Scientist/ Presenter) had just arrived back from fieldwork – spending time with the Gelada baboons and on this occasion recording their many weird sounds. All greeted me with huge smiles and enthusiastic handshakes ... To see a new face after three hard weeks was like seeing a ship six months after being ship-wrecked on a deserted island!

Before unloading the car, in the great British tradition we had a cup of tea! This was the first time that I had met Chadden and Matt, so we immediately sat and chewed the fat. As a cameraman meeting a perfect stranger for the first time and then spending some intensive time together is an almost everyday occurrence – it's something you grow used to. Your ability to fit in to new teams can be a deciding factor as to whether you work again. On this occasion, as a team we immediately got on famously. We soon found out that we all shared the same dry, sarcastic sense of humour, and it was a matter of minutes before we started taking the mickey out of each other. They were excited to have some new entertainment and I was glad to be there.

The camp was basic, but it had everything we needed: individual tents for each of us to sleep in and two larger communal tents – one to house the camera equipment, which we named the 'Kit Tent', and the other for use as general eating and living area, which we aptly named the 'Food Tent'. On the edge of the camp was the 'long drop toilet' – a hut made of corrugated iron walls and roof, with a floor of criss-crossed tree branches, suspended above a twelve-foot hole dug into the ground. In the centre of the branch floor was a hole that measured about seven inches square. Need I explain more? I will anyway. You held on to one of the upright poles in front of you, placed your feet on either side of the hole, squatted and then sang for the Queen! In order not to paint too pretty a picture of this daily necessity, I should mention that the hole beneath was *originally* twelve foot deep but was now closer to five foot! I'll leave the rest to your imagination.

On top of a small hill to the south of the camp, our local helpers had erected a makeshift canvas shower beneath a tree. It was ingeniously made up of a plastic barrel, hung between two branches, with a tap and screwed-on showerhead inserted in the bottom of it. When one of us wanted to shower, they would boil up a large pot of water, lower the barrel, fill it, re-suspend it and call you over. It was like a scene from a *Carry On* film. You would enter the canvas curtains, turn on the tap and have a two-minute hot shower! Fantastic! After a few failed attempts you learnt to get a move on once you'd turned the tap on. There was a limited amount of water and, if you hadn't managed to soap up and rinse off in time, you would be left stranded – naked, standing on top of a mountain covered in bubbles! One of the best parts of having a shower under the tree was that you would stand naked overlooking the most spectacular mountain views. It's not every day you can do that.

The rest of the day we had off. I busied myself making my tent as homely as possible: rigging my Ipod in the tent's inner pocket and dangling a small speaker from the flysheet roof, etc. Then everyone hung out together, having a laugh as I quickly acclimatised to the new location. At such an altitude it is common to develop 'altitude sickness', the symptoms being light-headiness, nausea and shortness of breath. In more extreme cases this sickness can prove to be very serious, and if it's not treated immediately or the sufferer taken to a lower altitude, it can even be fatal! My reaction to the altitude change was quite mild: just some panting and feeling out of breath when walking anywhere.

Night 1

Phenomenal storm! The sky was dramatically lit up with flash after flash of lightning and the ground was almost literally shaking from the unnerving claps of thunder. It must have been 2 a.m. and all, though lying quietly in their tents, were wide awake. I lay on my back, staring at the roof of my tent, listening to nature's fearsome display of power. Then I felt a drip of cold water on my face. I felt to my left for my head-torch. When I twisted the lamp on, I got a sinking feeling in my stomach ... it was raining inside my tent! The rain outside was so hard that it was literally punching its way through my tent's outer and inner sheet. I then investigated further to see just how wet the groundsheet was and whether I should call for a Lifeboat! In the corners there were puddles, so I managed to drag all my kit into the centre of the tent with me, and that seemed to create a dry island surrounded by a sea. Other than everything I had getting damp, it was not too bad.

Despite the early morning entertainment, I still managed to sleep for eight hours. I thought to myself, 'These mountains will have to do better than that to keep me from sleeping!' I was not born with the ability to sleep absolutely anywhere, but over the years of travelling I have definitely mastered the art: planes, trains, boats, buses, jeeps, in the back of trucks, jungle hammocks, desert sand, Buddhist monastery floors, etc. You name it ... no problem!

Monday 11 October – Day 2

My watch alarm beeped its rude, unwelcome awakening. It was 5.30 a.m. and time to peel myself out of my warm sleeping bag. I didn't allow myself time to think of a lie-in – that was not an option. I'd slept in my thermal underwear, both top and bottoms, and I'd also worn a beanie (woollen hat) to save losing too much heat from my head. In one movement I reached for my mountain bib (similar to ski salopettes), swung them over and pulled them over my legs. I then put on my two fleeces and shuffled on my bum over to the door. I pulled the

zip in its semi-circle shape and the fresh morning air hit me. It
was dark and the weather was bitterly cold. I stuck my legs
outside the tent with my bum inside and pulled on my boots.
Getting up and walking to the bushes for a pee, I yawned and
reminded myself of where I was and what I was doing.

Once we had all made tea in our flasks, we loaded the
cameras, tripods and batteries into the two jeeps. I travelled
with Emily as we're covering the Animal Behaviour and might
well have to film in a separate location to Paul and Chadden,
who were in the other jeep. Matt was sick this morning, so
Paul suggested that he stayed in bed and got some good rest.
It was still dark as we drove out of camp.

Since the others had watched the Geladas disappear over a
certain spot along the escarpment the previous evening, they
had a good idea where they might well rise at dawn. After
twenty minutes we pulled up on the track by the Onion Fields.
This was my first chance to meet the Geladas, and I was very
excited by the prospect. As we left the jeeps and walked
towards the cliff edge, Chad told me where to stand and what
noises to make to reassure the monkeys that we were friends.
By the time the light slowly started to lift we were set. Cameras
on tripods, Paul and co. at one end of the cliff edge and Em
and I at the other. Before too long, up they came. They
appeared in small groups, families together and bachelors
together. They literally hauled themselves over the lip of the
cliff, had a quick look around and then sat, upright, on their
bums and began to graze.

As with all shoots, when you start on the first day, the
subject is so new and fascinating that you tend to overshoot.
In a few days I'll be very selective about what's worth filming.

I love watching them … just be monkeys! There are no scripts, no make-up artists, no tantrums or arguments about their contracts. They just live life as usual and we simply film them doing so.

I was amazed at how accepting of us they are, and how close we are able to get to them – at times we were only one or two feet away. Paul got on and shot pieces-to-camera with Chad, while Emily and I concentrated on the baboons' behaviour.

As the bachelors come of age, one of their strongest behaviours is to 'display' to the group and particularly the females. They do this to show how strong and virile they are! By this stage in their life they are pretty close to fully grown so are relatively large in stature (when seated, about three feet tall) and very powerful. The 'display' consists of a sudden burst of energy, running towards another group of bachelors and picking a fight, by making direct eye contact or flipping their top lip back over their nose (all signs of aggression). The displaying male's plan then is not to fight, but rather to run and have the others chase him! How many other males take up the chase is the deciding factor in how impressive he is to the ladies. The chase inevitably ends up with the instigator charging up a tree and, with deafeningly loud 'whoops', shaking a large branch. Written down, this all sounds like fun, but when you are standing within a few feet of the action it is really rather impressive, and at times even unnerving.

Today I managed to shoot two or three good 'display' sequences. It will take me a while to get used to the J33x lens, which I hired for this shoot to be able to film the baboons close up from a fairly long distance away, to get a feel for both its large features and its unbelievable range. All in all it was a very good, confident start.

By about 10.00, the Geladas were settled and steadily grazing, and the sun was beginning to get to a height at which the light was too harsh to shoot in. So we all headed back to the camp for lunch. I have always loved my food, and on location lunch is one of my favourite meals of the day: by the time you come back to camp you have been out in the field for five hours and your appetite is raging. I had heard from the other crew members that Mingi (our cook) makes the most incredible 'special omelettes' from red peppers, meat, herbs and his 'special' ingredient of fresh chillies. I sat down to my first taste of one of these masterpieces and I was not disappointed! His omelettes could become one of the highlights of my days up the mountain!

Life in the mountains is often a world of extremes. Between 8 p.m. and 9 a.m., the temperature falls to $-5°C$, freezing us in our tents. Yet, by 10 a.m. it shoots up to over $30°C$. Between the morning shoot and the early evening shoot we had a long siesta, during which we kicked about camp, talking, reading, fixing our kit and sleeping. We also took the opportunity to dry out our tents in the warm sunshine, before the onslaught of another sodden, cold night.

At about 4 p.m., we loaded up into the jeeps again and headed out for another two- or three-hour session with the Gelada. We found them in the same vicinity as we'd left them, but apparently quite often they move a considerable distance, which means searching long and hard to find them. The shooting was much the same, picking off various shots of their behaviour, only this time they went back down the cliff to sleep for the night.

As with many animals, it is at dawn and dusk that the Gelada baboons come alive with activity. This suited us fine, as it is far better to shoot at these times because of the low position of the sun. The setting sun, turning pink and then red, creates a beautiful, rich, golden light. In the photographic world we refer to this time as the 'Golden Hour'. We all stood silently watching the Gelada slowly head over the cliff, bathed in this stunning light, with a stillness in the air and hardly any noise … just the odd 'whoop' and 'chatter' from the group. It's at times like this that the world seems to know no wrong and sighs in peace as another day comes to a close. A magical time in a magical place!

Night 2
Dry, but cold. Emily is now coming down with a fever, as is Matt. I hope we don't all go down with sickness as camping up a cold, damp mountain when feeling like death is a miserable existence!

Tuesday 12 October – Day 3
5.30 a.m. call. It was the usual drive out to the Geladas. They were still in the Onion Fields, so to vary my shots I decided to climb down the edge of the cliff and get some footage from the side of them huddling together clinging to the cliff face. The spot I slowly worked my way down to was very close to the edge. Below me there was a 500-metre drop down to the dark-green tree canopy in the Low Land. With no ropes on such a steep vertical angle, I had to tread very

carefully on the wet long grass. In retrospect it was pretty risky, but well worth it for the breathtaking scenery and a magnificent shot!

10.30 a.m. Back to camp for three helpings of Mingi's omelette – awesome! Sun was shining, so hung everything out to dry.

Soon after lunch (1 p.m.) the sky clouded over and it began to rain. Paul quickly left the food tent to set up for the 'rain' piece-to-camera with Chad in camp. Having only recently dried all our kit, we followed begrudgingly! Ten minutes into filming the heavens opened! In the torrential rain, we huddled under golfing umbrellas, giving priority to keeping the camera dry – within seconds we were all drenched from head to toe! We figured that since we were already wet, we might as well continue. A few moments later there was a riotous explosion as the air seemed to get sucked up and spat out again in an enormous clap of thunder! Our plateau shook and there was a strobe effect in the sky as the devastating thunder and lightning continued. Our camp was partially flooded, along with our tents! Yet still we 'British' stood resolute until we had finished filming the very last shot.

With soaking wet clothes and dampened spirits we retreated to our tents to change and get some kip before leaving for the afternoon shoot.

4.30 p.m. left camp. The Gelada were only around for a short while due to the terrible weather conditions. So we hung around while Chadden shot a time-lapsed sunset and we took a few crew photos. Having a laugh together at the end of a hectic day sent our spirits high as we watched the sublime sunset.

Night 3

Mostly dry except for one huge downpour around midnight. Matt's feeling better, but Emily's not well. Paul doesn't feel 100 per cent but is soldiering on. Chadden and I are on fine form.

Wednesday 13 October – Day 4

5.30 call. Cloudy again!

After a quick mug of tea and a bowl of porridge, we drove out to the cliffs. Matt's back on top form and Emily's health is slowly improving. Paul is struggling with a lack of energy. When you bear in mind that he's got twenty years of age on any of us, he is amazing! Typically ... he plods on, regardless.

The sun showed its face for a few hours, which made filming more acceptable. We waited with one Gelada group for close to four hours, but they were somewhat subdued (probably due to the weather). Not much point in shooting for the sake of it. So we headed back early to camp for brunch – more omelettes!

During brunch, a stray band of Gelada wandered into our camp. Not further than ten metres from where we sat in the food tent stood a group of ten Gelada. It was almost as if the roles had been reversed and they had come to watch us eat, and do what we do! The butter still on his knife, Paul crept out of the tent to get his camera and I picked up the fake leopard (a prop we had made for a later experiment). As Paul filmed, I cautiously approached the group while dangling 'Brian', the leopard, in front of me. We were coaxing the Gelada to react, and react they did ... spectacularly! They screamed, jumped and ran wild in a frenzy of panic! We didn't want to abuse their trust in us, so we only did it the once. What we caught on film was a great example of how they react to the threat of a predator. A bit of fun in the morning with the sun out was a treat. The crew's spirits are on an all-time high.

Later, Paul started to feel rough again, so he's gone to bed for a nap. Chad is in his tent 'working on the scripts' (sleeping!) and so Emily, Matt and I watched the first half of *The Green Mile* on DVD. We played it through Paul's laptop, but halfway through the battery ran out and starting the generator would have woken Paul, so we left it to watch another time ... and time we had!

By the time we left camp for the evening shoot, it had clouded over. Filming would have been pointless, but we went to see where the Gelada were sleeping for the night, for the following morning.

Night 4

Very cold but dry. Before we went to bed, there was a spectacular electrical storm. It really was extraordinary as the camp was directly beneath a clear window of black, starry sky. Around this round window there was a full circle of huge cumulonimbus clouds. No matter where you looked, intense lightning was flashing every few seconds. It was so intense that there was constantly a lightning fork somewhere in vision. It was like nothing I have ever seen before. The lightning was more on than off! We knew we had the scenery from *The Lord of the Rings*, but now we had the theatrical skies as well! By the time we went to bed the clouds had their victory in the battle and the whole camp was enveloped in a white-out. Slept well.

Thursday 14 October – Day 5

Woke at 5.15 a.m. Usual routine: dragged on my cold weather gear and unzipped the tent: what greeted me today, however, was a sight for sleepy eyes. The entire sky was crystal clear with the electric blue you only find at that time in the morning: all our spirits soared! I likened it to my experiences of getting up for an early surf, when we knew the swell was up! A fever of anticipation swept through our blood.

When the sun came up, we were not disappointed: it was golden and the Gelada shared our excitement at its arrival. Filming for four and a half hours seemed like one hour, as there was so much baboon activity going on. We got so much in the bag that for the first time we felt our breakfast break and omelettes were well earned!

The sun continued to blaze for most of the day allowing us to hang out in the afternoon wearing only shorts, t-shirts and flip-flops.

Saturday 16 October – Day 7

Another stunning morning … this seems to be becoming a trend. All the crew were up and out this morning, all feeling much better. First thing we played with the jib (a counter-balanced boom device for moving the camera around) and the sweeping shots we got were very impressive. We even managed to include some Gelada who were playing to their script!

Due to the amazing weather we decided to crack on, and after a quick breakfast we set off to shoot some more pieces to camera making the most of the jib. The location we went to was down a steep grassy hill, at a beautiful spring that looked as though it should have been in the foothills of Austria or Switzerland. We shot there for about three more hours. Everyone seemed glad to finally get a full day's filming in. Just as lunch was being served back at camp, a tawny eagle settled in the top of one of the trees, so Paul took the opportunity to get it on film – beautiful.

In the afternoon we planned to put some offal from a slaughtered sheep out on the cliff edge to coax some vultures and other birds of prey into shot. We spent a while waiting with little result, so we postponed the set-up.

Sunday 17 October – Day 8

One week today since I arrived. Even though at times it has seemed as though time was passing slowly (mostly in the cold and wet early hours of the night), generally time has flown. It's amazing how in this line of work you acquire the ability to adapt to any situation in a day or two. Before too long you adopt a routine to live by.

In the morning I get dressed, carry my camera to the kit tent and then wash my hands. Returning to my tent I put my contact lenses in before securing my tent and heading over to the food tent where I devour a bowl of porridge and warm up with a cup of 'builder's' tea. Now fully awake, I head back over to the kit tent, pick up my camera, tripod and rucksack, take them to the jeep and hit the road.

At the end of the morning we come back ravenous. The first thing I do is order my omelette and make more tea. We then rest in the sun until lunchtime. After lunch we make a few adjustments to the kit, put the batteries on charge, etc., and then retire to our tents for an hour's siesta.

On the dot of 4.30 we load up the cars and drive out to the Gelada again for the evening session.

Returning for the night at around 7.00, we rush to our tents to pull on our thermals and woolly hats as by this time the temperature has plummeted to well below zero! When dressed, we crowd into the eating tent to get stuck into a supper of a variety of slightly westernised Ethiopian dishes.

Soon after dinner we disperse back to our tents for the last time that day. I take my camera to my tent, wrap it in my big puffer jacket (to minimise the exposure to the moisture), then go to the tap and wash my face and hands. I take my contact lenses out, brush my teeth, pull off my boots and undress. My favourite time of the day is climbing into my four seasons sleeping bag where I rapidly slip into a coma!

Today was slightly different: as a Sunday treat we agreed to get up half an hour later. It doesn't sound like much of a lie-in, but when it means waking up in daylight, you can't under-estimate the pleasure it brings! The morning was spent filming the Gelada as usual, and we tried setting out some meat for the birds again. One of the Simien Mountains' greatest treasures is the Lammergeier vulture. This time we weren't disappointed. At least three of the enormous, magnificent birds of prey came and gorged on our generous offering. It was amazing seeing these huge birds swoop over our heads and land fifty feet in front of us. It was also a welcome break to be filming something other than a 'furry rugby ball' (Gelada). Birds are not always the easiest creatures to film, and I was very pleased with the shots that I managed to get.

As it was Sunday we were keen to allow ourselves the concept of a weekend, so after breakfast Emily, Paul, Chadden and I headed down to Debark, the closest town to our camp. Matt had reached that point of the shoot where one desperately needs some time to oneself, so he stayed in camp and enjoyed the sunshine and the space. In Debark we made our base the local hotel (a very basic building with some rooms to rent – more like one of our Youth Hostels), where we consumed numerous 'Macchiato', the local speciality – a very sweet café latte. We also made phone calls home, as the small telecom building is considerably cheaper than the satellite phone we were using up in the camp. After an early dinner we jumped back into the jeeps and drove back up the mountain, while listening to Peter Gabriel through my Ipod. We had only spent four or five hours off the mountain, but we were euphoric with the stark change of scenery and the mental relief that it gave.

Back at camp we instinctively fell into our routines and within the hour we were all tucked up in our sleeping bags, drifting into the comfort of oblivion!

With our minds rested from work after our weekend treat, we all slept soundly.

Tuesday 19 October – Day 10

5.30 a.m. start. Filmed the Gelada in the Onion Fields. As an experiment this morning we used a mirror to show the baboons an image of themselves to see what their reaction would be. The experiment proved to be very amusing, with a few of the young males really acting up to the image of themselves. There was a great deal of threatening 'lip flicking' at the stranger mimicking them in the glass, and one courageous little guy even threw a punch at the mirror image of himself. Brilliant!

Set up the vulture feeding session again, but no show from the mighty birds. The minute we packed the camera kits back into the jeeps, some buzzards showed up and scavenged all the meat that we had laid out – typical! Still, I guess that's all part of wildlife filming – it rarely goes to plan!

Afternoon: siesta in the sun. Wrote diary (obviously!).

Early evening shoot: Gelada in the Onion Fields. Filmed some nice sunset shots with them silhouetted in the foreground.

Wednesday 20 October – Day 11

Bitterly cold this morning, with a frost on the ground (really doesn't feel like Africa!), though as long as it remains dry I'm happy. Leaving at the usual time, in the usual routine, we reluctantly headed back to the Onion Fields. The 'Onion Fields' were not so named because there are onions growing there, but because there are thousands of plants spread over the grass that have the appearance of onion plants (whatever they look like!). In the course of his research for his PhD Chadden has spent close to five years studying Gelada baboons here in the Simien Mountains, during which time he has named many of the grassy fields at the top of the vast mountainous escarpments. The names were purely for his own use, in order to remember a particular location, and in this process Chadden's humour ran riot! Within an approximate ten-mile range, as well as the Onion Fields you can visit: Sunset Boulevard, CGI Background, Dog's Knob and Bachelor's Bowl, to name but a few. Our Sound Recordist, Matt, was privileged to have one named after him: 'Heaving Meadows', as early one morning he was feeling decidedly ill and heaved, though he wasn't actually sick!

On arrival the wind was up and brutal! We stood for almost an hour, without the Gelada appearing from the shelter of the cliffs, though who can blame them? I guess if we humans want to film such animals, then at times we have to pay for it ... This was one of those times!

This evening I used the satellite phone to phone home. Got the answering machine – typical! Still, I took it that no news was good news.

Thursday 21 October – Day 12

Usual drill. Very successful filming today. The sun was hot all day and because of the great conditions we seemed to get a huge amount done. Finally nailed the 'Vulture' sequence. Emily and I were surrounded by seven or eight huge birds of prey within five minutes of laying the cow bones and offal out. I was very pleased with my shots. I'm confident that they'll make the programme, which is a reward for all the hanging around.

Spent the afternoon in camp grooming myself: a shower, shave/beard trim and cutting of finger and toe nails ... After three or four days of not washing, the feeling of comfort and elation cannot be underestimated!

In the late afternoon/sunset shoot we pulled off some great jib shots. All in all a great day and everyone's spirits are high. Due to the good results of the day, Paul has decided that we can give the Onion Fields, etc., a miss tomorrow and instead we'll head up to Chanek. A change of scenery will be awesome!

Friday 22 October – Day 13

Up at 4.30 a.m. in order to get some porridge down our necks before leaving camp at 5 a.m. Incredibly early start, but due to the 'day out' feel to our trip we are all up and raring to go!

Chanek is about a forty-five-minute drive from camp. It's another 500 feet higher and boasts some stunning cliffs and escarpments, with views to die for. We arrived after a bumpy ride in the dark and walked straight out to a ledge positioned in the centre of a vast valley. My brief was to shoot a time lapse of the sun rising; over the space of only forty minutes it illuminated the huge cliffs to my left, transforming them from a big, black, featureless shadow into a glorious golden mountain. The time lapse wasn't exactly a difficult task, as once the camera was set up I could sit and enjoy the panoramic view for the following forty-five minutes or so. This proved to be one of those precious moments where I had to force myself to stop and just take in what was before me. It was breathtaking.

We stayed in Chanek until midday, by which time we had shot some amazing jib shots and sequences. Another great morning, but the 4.30 a.m. start caught up with us and on arriving back at camp at around 2 p.m. we were all absolutely exhausted!

We went out again in the evening. I shot the Gelada as they retreated to the cliffs for the night while the rest of the crew shot a night sequence with Chad. I enjoyed being with the Gelada by myself as by now we had formed some sort of friendship. They definitely recognise me. The fact that the babies play with my bootlaces and the alpha male comes and sits only a few feet from me, has to be a sign of trust and acceptance. Or maybe it is the beard that I have grown that fools them into thinking I am one of them?

Exciting news: I received a call on the satellite phone from Julia back at the office in the UK – my dad has left a message with her to pass on to me: the purchase of my flat back in Wandsworth completes on Wednesday the 27th, before I return from this trip. That means that I can go and pick up the keys to my first home ... AWESOME!

Monday 25 October – Day 16

Woke at normal time again, 5.15 a.m. Gelada were in the Onion Fields – spit! They were dull ... nothing more to say on the subject. After brunch we walked down to the Heather Forest and shot two more sequences, which went really well ... plus we had a real laugh!

Four and a half days to go before we go home – all of us are gagging to get home now. Me particularly for my new flat!

Siesta.

During the afternoon shoot we carried out the 'leopard experiment' – revealing a fake leopard (as mentioned earlier) to see how the Gelada reacted to a predator in such close contact. The experiment went really well – they went mental! The sound was deafening as all two or three hundred of them screamed the 'Predator Warning' and ran like the wind. It was fascinating to observe how the large males actually stood up on their hind legs and confronted the fake leopard, risking their own safety to protect the group. Chad had told us to look out for how the male Gelada would stand almost exactly as far away as the predator could leap. They proved this fact and did just as he said. Although we freaked them out, it was an amazing sight and a valuable demonstration for the documentary.

Tuesday 26 October – Day 17

5.15 a.m. up, 6 a.m. leave. Gelada dull . . . though caught a few good behavioural acts for the programme. That's the nature of filming wildlife – you can sit for hours with absolutely nothing of interest happening, then suddenly without warning it can all kick off! You've just got to make sure that at that crucial moment you're not daydreaming or going for a toilet break. Some of it is using your knowledge and developed initiative but most of it is down to luck!

During the afternoon siesta time three South African guys, whom we briefly met at the hotel in Debark, arrived at the camp. They are driving their Landrover from London to Durban over six months. Having been on the road for the last three months they have a rich library of stories and stayed to chat over a few beers for an entertaining few hours. Once again it's been great to have some new faces around the camp. It turns out that one of them lives in Earlsfield, which is literally five minutes from both my flat and Emily's . . . a small world!

Went to bed early and slightly tipsy – slept like a log!

Wednesday 27 October – Day 18

As I took my camera to my tent last night I managed to pull a muscle in the top left side of my back. It's the same injury as when I was filming in Abu Dhabi last year. It's not debilitating, just very uncomfortable. Still got up at the normal time and went to work, but after climbing a very steep cliff for this morning's shoot I got back to camp, took some painkillers and went to bed. I slept for an hour or so and woke up with it still there. When I pulled the muscle in Abu Dhabi, the following day I was due to be filming from a Huey Helicopter (as seen in the Vietnam war films). I was paranoid that I would be unable to hold the camera in the difficult positions required for 'chopper shots'. I was in acute pain for twenty-four hours but, having taken two Ibuprofen tablets and got a good night sleep, I woke up and the pain had completely disappeared! That day I shot from the chopper without even a twinge! I'm hoping the same will happen this time.

Gelada were very quiet and dull this morning ... hard to keep interest up, though we have one and a half day's shooting left, so it's not the end of the world!

My flat should 'complete' today. I have so much to look forward to when I return, it can't come quick enough!

✤ ✤ ✤

Filming wildlife is a fantastic experience and to be living in such a magnificent environment is often a once-in-a-lifetime trip. Yet, I am definitely not one who could spend a year staring at animals, no matter how extrovert they are ... I would simply get bored. I admire people like Chadden who has spent a total of five years with the Gelada baboons and I have to admit that I cherish my relatively short time with them.

We celebrated the end of the shoot by staying in a magnificent five-star hotel in Addis Ababa for our last night in Ethiopia – and the change of environment was extremely overwhelming. Once in my seemingly palatial room I took my time shaving my bushy mountain beard off and took delight in sitting on a loo seat for the first time in many weeks. The tiny little luxuries in life had become the close focus of our attention. That evening we enjoyed our last time together as a team by sipping cocktails beside the salubrious swimming pool and then ate in magnificent style. Although I have to say that in the morning even the five-star hotel chefs couldn't match the wonder of Mingi's special omelette!

Back on UK soil it never fails to amaze me just how quickly you adjust back into the way of life. Within literally two days of being 14,000 feet up a mountain with baboons in Ethiopia, I was collecting the keys to my new flat from the estate agent in Wandsworth. No matter how small the world becomes due to advances in travel, our individual worlds will always be oceans apart!

12

It's a Mad, Mad World!

I write the final chapter of this book sitting on a veranda in the Cook Islands – a tiny cluster of islands set in the middle of the South Pacific Ocean. The view over my laptop screen would make the perfect picture for a postcard: aqua seas, palm trees and cloudless skies – I am in paradise!

Accompanying me on this two-month shoot in paradise is my faithful sound recordist, Shirley. Over the years Shirls and I have become a memorable duo ... As you can imagine, people never forget a crew with the nicknames 'Mungo' and 'Shirley'!

During our forty-hour journey to get here, Shirley commented that the day before our flight left he had seen a TV commercial for an airline that boasted of its ability to take its customers to the world's greatest destinations, all of which, they stated, 'You must see before you die.' He commented that as he watched this commercial, it dawned on him that we would be able to tick off one hundred per cent of the dream locations featured. We laughed and counted up our blessings.

So, once again, I find myself in an extraordinary work situation and in this idyllic place I have time and space to reflect on my years of exposure to the sublime and the ridiculous!

As a member of a film crew you get to places that most people would never dream of visiting. In such locations, because we are making a TV programme, we often gain access to sites where the general public would never be allowed, which makes our experience of that place quite unique. I think, for instance, of the opportunity to be part of the first crew ever to film the dark, damp caves of Laos, from which the communists directed the Vietnam War and of the opportunity to film ancient tombs deep within Egyptian pyramids, which hadn't been opened for hundreds of years. I have visited regions of countries that only the most intrepid traveller would even know about. I have stood in the wings of prestigious theatres and walked onto the hallowed turf of famous sporting arenas. I have been into the homes of royalty and sat on the dirt floor of mud huts with the poorest of the poor.

It is not just the places that stick in your mind, however, but also the remarkable people that you meet along the way. I have laughed with Hollywood film stars and sung along with the idols of the music world. I have talked to the traumatised survivors of unspeakable events and played football with groups of indigenous kids (using a few scraps of plastic rolled up into a sphere and secured with broken elastic bands as a ball). I have dined with politicians and consoled the starving and dying. I have had to learn how to relate to all people, often in extreme situations and at both ends of the scale.

On my travels I have been carried on all forms of transport known to man: large planes, small planes, military planes and parachutes; trucks (with engines the size of small cars), rickshaws, moto-taxis, Rolls Royces, stretched limousines, top-of-the-range sports cars and army tanks; helicopters and hovercraft, big ships and boats; sunseekers (luxury cruisers) and wooden canoes, jet skis and surfboards; horses, camels, donkeys and elephants! It amuses me that human beings have developed so many ways to get around.

What also interests me is the way human beings communicate. Here in the west we have witnessed the explosion of computer science and Information Technology; we communicate through sophisticated mobile means, often wire-less and hand-held. Yet still, in an almost parallel world, other countries communicate in the same way they have done for centuries. In the Amazon jungle, for example, the tribes still beat trees to communicate in a Morse-code-like system, the sound booming over the canopy of the trees. In the mountain regions of South-East Asia, people simply shout over the vast valleys, their voices echoing the repeated messages to their distant neighbours. I can hardly imagine how we existed without mobile phones or laptop computers – although I do sometimes wonder if they are always an advantage!

Languages have never been my strong point. In fact, to this day I proudly state that I am bilingual ... as I am fluent in Australian! I believe that like music, sport or art, you have to be born with the correct faculties to learn languages easily. Yes, you can work hard to learn or improve in all these disciplines, yet to some it comes very easily and naturally. In my travels, being English and speaking English has hindered my attempts to learn languages, as no matter where in the world you go, there always seems to be someone who speaks my mother tongue. This makes you very lazy. I have often heard people say that to learn a language effectively, you need to go and live in the country. Maybe the fact that I make such transient trips adds to my inability, or is this is just a poor excuse?

I remember one occasion when, while filming a Lonely Planet Guide in the remote mountains of North-East Cambodia, one evening my sound recordist Richard and I walked into a tiny village of wooden huts to get some dinner. We had no idea where to go or what to say as our fixer/translator was still at the traditional wedding celebration we had been filming earlier that evening. We had literally to follow our noses and when we smelt some food, we tracked the scent and wandered into the small, dark hut from which it was emanating. The hut had a dirt floor and the odd tatty poster and out-of-date calendar on its walls. The small room was scattered with colourful plastic tables and chairs just like those you would find in a roadside café. To our delight we had stumbled across the only restaurant in town. The only problem was that nobody spoke a word of English and we didn't speak a word of Cambodian. Following an impromptu game of charades, trying to act out the words 'chicken' and 'noodles', I resorted to taking hold of the waitress's pad and pen and drawing a cartoon rooster chicken and some swiggly noodles. My four years of Fine Art training must have paid off as she took one look at my artwork, smiled, giggled and then headed off behind a dilapidated wooden screen. Ten minutes later, Richard and I breathed a sigh of relief when we were presented with a magnificent plate of fried chicken and noodles. We smiled at each other as we tucked in, to the delight of our hostess who had obviously not seen western tourists in her village for a while, if ever!

Some people react with disdain when I say that there are negatives to my job, as they will often only see the glamour and the advantages. Yet, consider for a moment what it's like to mix with the world's elite as well as the world's most disadvantaged – it raises mental and moral issues that one has to endeavour to come to terms with.

On my first trip to Africa I remember being quite naive. There was one shoot when I found myself questioning how good it was that I was there at all. I had brought a new pair of basketball boots for the trip and as I stood in front of a group of African children they stared at my boots, then looked at their bare feet. You could see them questioning why it was that they didn't have a pair of these flash boots. Or any shoes at all for that matter! I thought that if I had never gone, they would never have known what they lacked.

I have learnt that people accept they live in a completely different world from us, and because of this they have different values in life. In the west, we tend to be career driven and to be constantly thinking and planning for the future. In poorer countries they live a day-to-day existence, and their plans for the future rest on whether they will see the sun rise tomorrow. Although for us this seems a tough way to live, I think there is a real beauty and liberty to be found in this simplicity.

A few trips later, while driving through South-East Asia, I found myself cringing when, in incredibly poor villages, the local children would cheer and wave as we swept past them in our luxury, air-conditioned jeep. While these were, of course, fun and innocent greetings, I would experience a twang of conscience (possibly over-exercised), knowing that behind those smiles and waves the people were fighting to exist.

These days I am aware that my heart has grown a lot harder towards such issues. Is this because of the further exposure I have had to it, I wonder, or because I have grown up?

I desperately don't want to come across as being too 'worthy', but I can't help expressing the way that my eyes have been opened to situations and issues that we see in our world today. It's a fact that around 95 per cent of the world's wealth is held by 5 per cent of the world's population. If you have a roof over your head and any small change in your pocket, then you are part of the wealthy 5 per cent. It's sobering to think that a person's wealth and quality of life are pretty much decided by which country he or she is born into. I agree with the fact that having money, houses and health certainly doesn't guarantee our happiness – in some ways I think having many material possessions jeopardises it – but, ultimately, it cannot be denied that in the west our lifespan is likely to be longer due to our better health care and nutrition. I realise now how lucky I am to be born British: to be born into a country that is relatively very stable, safe and wealthy; to be educated and have money in my pocket and a roof over my head; to have employment, health and people who love and care for me; but, most of all, to have my freedom.

Once you get started on this subject it is hard to stop. I regularly find myself soul-searching at the most unlikely moments. While making a cup of tea I find myself thinking about the badly-paid people who picked the leaves in the little white teabag. When I run the tap in my kitchen, I struggle to let it run, remembering those who have no fresh water to hand – I have learnt how precious water is. Watching the news on television, often people glaze over when they see more scenes of famine, more countries ravaged by war; yet my exposure to such environments won't allow me to turn a blind eye.

My life's education has been acquired not by reading books, but rather by going to other countries, experiencing a variety of different cultures and situations, and meeting people face to face. It is this education that I count as one of my greatest privileges.

Yet, all good things come with a degree of sacrifice. I am now thirty-six years of age and I am single. While most of my colleagues have managed to find the fine balance between holding down relationships and continuing their work, I am less fortunate. Some of the girlfriends I have had along the way found it hard to accept the demands of my work schedule. When I arrive home from a long shoot, for example, I hit the ground running and within a short space of time take off again to another faraway destination. They get the impression that when I go away on these trips, I am really going away on a sort of holiday. This is because, on my return, they tend only to hear about the good, positive times and amazing experiences we had. Maybe if they understood what hard work it is the majority of the time, they would be more forgiving. We cameramen are expensive, so in order to get their money's worth, the production companies often have us working from the minute we touch down in a country to the minute we take off again! As a younger man I used my singleness to its fullest advantage – by living the ultimate maverick lifestyle. Now, however, when returning from such trips, my colleagues are welcomed back at the airport by loved ones while I am still met by a suited sign-holding taxi driver. More than ever I now realise that there is a price that I have paid for refusing to settle down. Having said that, I am also aware that I am only just thirty-six and there is plenty of time for the right girl to come along; but I can tell you now she will have to possess the patience of a saint!

Time away from home can be tough for anyone. Being away from family and friends can take its toll. Relationships become complicated through absence and regrettable friction can arise. Living in numerous hotels and strange places can develop loneliness and a sense of being disjointed from the normal way of life back home. I have found that the only way to survive in the face of such disruption is to surround yourself with friends who work and travel with you. Then you find a sense of normality in the familiar faces. Also, as bizarre as it seems, there is a sense of routine and normality that comes from working with the same equipment and kit.

No matter how amazing the shoot, at some point you hit a wall – bringing with it pangs of wanting to be home, living a normal life and being a consistent presence in the lives of your loved ones. As a young man I found this maverick lifestyle easy, due to my lack of commitment and distinctly less responsibility, yet as I grow older I count the cost far more. Nevertheless, after so many years on the road I feel totally conditioned to a transient life and soon develop itchy feet, which makes me unable to fully commit to certain aspects of normal life.

We all want to be loved and if we can find that love and acceptance, we are the luckiest people in the world. I witness many who strive for love and acceptance ... for example, seeking it in fame, a subject I touched on earlier in the book. It is ironic that being worshipped by millions can often lead to a sense of isolation and loneliness. This point is best illustrated by the infamous words of Janice Joplin, who after playing at the Woodstock music festival, said, 'Tonight I made love to ten thousand people, yet I go home alone!'

We must learn to appreciate all that we have been given.

No matter what job you do, work is work! We all get times when we feel the monotony and routine of our vocation. Yet, work is such an important aspect of life. By its nature and timescale, it is all encompassing and also completely necessary to our survival, both financially and, I believe, mentally. When I was younger, I had a stint of being unemployed and know from experience that it is demotivating, confidence shaking and, quite frankly, miserable. Work helps us to find equilibrium. It gives us a sense of worth and provides stability. Many hundreds of thousands of people in this world would give their right arm for a good honest job. It is one's attitude to work that counts. Do you live to work or work to live? My suggestion is to strive for the latter.

Sometimes I feel as though my working life as a cameraman is like a continuous Fancy Dress Party. Every other week brings a new theme – desert, jungle, beach, mountain ... – each requiring its own specific clothing/costume and specialist equipment for the environment.

Due to the rapid advancement of air travel, the world has become a very small place. At times airports serve as my office and travelling on a plane is now second nature. There have been times when I have found myself in Central Africa one day and then literally days later found myself on the ski slopes of the French Alps. In one day I have found myself dining at a table with a street urchin begging for my food in one country and then literally hours later shopping in a state-of-the-art towering shopping centre in another country. I have touched the bellies of the malnourished in a distant land and then, a few days later, rubbed shoulders with the rich and famous in the Formula One paddock. I remember flying over Tahiti looking at the islands far below – most of which are the tips of submerged volcanoes – and I as stared out of the window comparing them to the volcano we had climbed in Guatemala three weeks previously! One minute you can be standing on the summit of Mount Sinai, then in a matter of hours you are in a taxi driving through the traffic in Wandsworth, London.

I have found my own methods of dealing with these radical changes of environment, and have developed my own routines for settling back home into London life. One of my methods of settling back in is to visit Starbucks on the Northcote Road. The minute I have been there, I feel I can relax: I know I am home. It is a strange routine, but one that grounds me in the familiar.

I have learnt that this world of ours is a wonderful place; it is rich in beauty, colour, sights, sounds, tastes and fragrances. No matter how much you are able to see of it in your lifetime, you will only scratch the surface of all it has to offer. In your lifetime, make the most of it, appreciate it and care for it.

With such privilege comes a weighty responsibility. How should I react to the need in the world when, compared to the majority of people, I have so much? It's a dilemma that I face almost every day of my life. It is not easy to find a balance in this mad, mad world. In fact, I would go as far as to say that I think it is impossible. You have to try to do your best with what you have been given and treat others how you would want to be treated.

A member of the Press once asked Mother Teresa, 'Mother, there is no denying that what you have accomplished in your lifetime is great. However, don't you see that it is just a drop in the ocean?' Mother Teresa quietly replied, 'Ah yes, but the ocean is made up of many drops!' Her life's work was but a drop in the ocean, yet she had made her personal contribution count.

There lies the challenge to us all!

If you are a songwriter, write your songs and make them count.

Bankers, be generous and calculate ways to help the needy.

If you are a builder, use your skill to build for those who don't have shelter.

Students, don't squander your gift of being educated: make the most of it. Live and lead positively in the future. Find *your* own way of giving back for all you have been given in this life.

I am eternally grateful for the opportunity of making my living as a cameraman. I have never taken it for granted. Through television, millions of viewers have seen my work and I sincerely hope that some of those lives have been touched. Yet, I can safely say – hand on heart – that no life has been more changed than my own.

www.mungothecameraman.com

As well as filming and writing his book
Mungo, along with Richard Farish,
has set up a website company
called Expedition Media –
the ultimate database for crews,
production and specialist organisations
in adventure TV.

Log on for more information:
www.expeditionmedia.co.uk

EXPEDITIONMEDIA
www.expeditionmedia.co.uk